365 TV-FREE ACTIVITIES
YOU CAN DO WITH YOUR CHILD

Plus 50 All-New Bonus Activities!

Steve & Ruth Bennett

Adams Media Corporation
Avon, Massachusetts

Dedication

To our children, Noah and Audrey,
who have inspired our lives and who inspired this book

Published by Adams Media Corporation
57 Littlefield Street, Avon, MA 02322 USA

ISBN: 1-58062-755-2

Printed in Canada.

J I H G F E D C B A

Library of Congress Cataloging-in-Publication Data
Bennett, Steven J.
    365 TV-free activities you can do with your child / Steve & Ruth
Bennett.—3rd ed.
        p.   cm.
    Includes index.
    ISBN 1-58062-755-2 (pbk.)
    1. Family recreation. 2. Games. 3. Play. I. Bennett, Ruth (Ruth
Loetterle) II. Title.
GV182.8.B45   1996
790.1'91—dc20   96-994
                                                          CIP

This book is available at quantity discounts for bulk purchases. For information, call 1-800-872-5627.

Visit our home page at *www.adamsmedia.com*

Safety Reminders

Use these symbols to select safe play environments and to monitor potentially tricky materials.

Supervise
Closely

Small Parts

Stove

Great Outdoors

Plastic Wrap

Balloon

Sharp Object

CONTENTS

Atlas Adventures 13

Babble Dictionary 14

Backwards Spelling Bee 15

Balancing Act 16

Balloon Volleyball 17

Bas-relief Pancakes 18

Bean Bag Basics 19

Bean Bag Olympics 20

Bedtime For Animals 21

Big Kids' Bingo 22

The Biggest and the Smallest 23

Biodegrading Lab 24

Blindfold Guide 25

Body Trace 26

Box Car 27

Brainstorming, Part One 28

Brainstorming, Part Two 29

Breaking Out of the Box 30

Bubble Basketball 31

Bug Motel 32

Business Card Bonanza 33

Cable Cars 34

Capital Bingo 35

Captions 36

Careers 37

Carrot Top 38

Celery Leaves 39

Cereal Box City 40

Chain Drawing 41

Chain Laughter 42

Chain Story 43

Checker Calculator 44

Chicago Busmobile 45

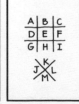

Chicken Scratch 46

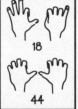

Chisanbop 47

Cleanup Games 48

Clock Time 49

Cloud Watching 50

Coin Collection 51

Coin Toss 52

Color Blots 53

Color Esp 54

Color Mixing 55

Columbus 56

Compass Explorer 57

Concentration 58

Construction Paper Greetings 59

Cookies You Can Read 60

Crayon Copier 61

Crayon Games 62

Crayon Rubbings 63

Crazy Nines 64

Crazy Olympics 65

Creature Deck 66

Cryptograms 67

Currency Game 68

Custom T-Shirt 69

The Day I Was Born 70

A Day In The Life Of... 71

Describe It 72

Designer Memo Pad 73

Dictionary Fakeout 74

Dino Bone Hunt 75

Dinosaurs On Parade 76

Dioramas 77

Do It Yourself Letters 78

Doctor's Office 79

Dollar Quiz 80

Doorknob Hangers 81

Dots, Dots, Dots 82

Draw A Meal 83

Easy Bird Feeder 84

Easy Flannel Board 85

Easy House of Cards 86

Easy Trail Mix 87

Eat Right 88

Egg Quiz 89

Eightfold Path 90

Elephant Dance 91

The Enormous Radio 92

Family Book Of Records 93

Family Calendar 94

Family Coat Of Arms 95

Family Flag 96

Family Gazette 97

Family Historian 98

Family Tree 99

Fancy Footwork 100

Fantastic Creatures 101

Fantasy Baseball 102

Fantasy Baseball (advanced) 103

Fast Talkers 104

Feed The Birds 105

Finger Puppets 106

Fingerprints 107

Flashlight Color Lab 108

Flip Book 109

Flower Press 110

Follow the Arrows 111

Food Face 112

Forest Crowns And Bracelets 113

Fox and Goose 114

Geography Rorschach 115

Giant Blocks 116

Giant Dice 117

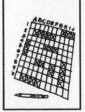

Giant Theme Books 118

Gotcha! 119

Grandmother's Button Box 120

Grass Whistle 121

Grasshopper Anatomy 122

Green Hair 123

Grid Game 124

Grocery Cart Rembrandt 125

Grown Up Stuff 126

Guess The Object 127

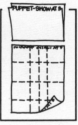

Half and Half 128

Hand Shadows 129

Hat Trick 130

Have It Your Way 131

Heart Song 132

Heavy Stuff 133

Hello 134

Hide It 135

Hollow Eggs 136

**Home
Planetarium 137**

**Homemade
Dashboards 138**

Homonyms 139

**House
Detective 140**

House Of Cards 141

House of Cups 142

**Household
Factory 143**

**Household Gallup
Poll 144**

Ibble Dibble 145

Ice Cream Vendor 146

Improbable Cuisine 147

Improvised Card Games 148

In the Bag 149

Indoor Safari 150

Indy 500 Balloon Race 151

Initial Game 152

Instant Orchestra 153

Instruction Manual 154

International Capitals 155

International News 156

Invent-an-
animal 157

I've Got a List 158

Jet Races and
Others 159

Judy's Clay 160

Juice Bar
Delight 161

Junior Robot 162

Just In Time 163

Keeper of the
Cans 164

Kiddie Bank 165

Kids'
Celebrations 166

Kids' Circus 167

Kitchen
Camping 168

Kitchen Finery 169

Kitchen Trace 170

Knuckleheads 171

Leaf Pressing 172

Lean 'em! 173

Lemonade Stand 174

Letter Exchange 175

Letter Number Addup 176

Library Fun 177

Lip Reading 178

Little Kids' Bingo 179

Living Room Sandbox 180

Macaroni Cards 181

Magnet Fishing 182

Magnet Sculpture 183

Mail Call 184

Make A Bird 185

Make A Book 186

Make Your Own Record 187

Map Puzzle 188

Maple Seedling Olympics 189

Mapping The World 190

Marble Raceway 191

Masks And Helmets 192

Matching Game 193

Milk Jug Catch 194

Mirror, Mirror 195

Mnemonics 196

Mom And Dad On The Job 197

Monster Bubbles 198

Morse Code 199

Musical Chairs 200

My Best Friend 201

My Own Place Mat 202

Mystery Clues 203

Name Game 204

Name Poster And Book 205

Nature Display 206

Neighborhood Historian 207

Neighborhood Travel Guide 208

Number Alphabet 209

Number Hunt 210

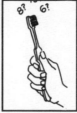

Obstacle Course (indoor) 211

Obstcle Course (outdoor) 212

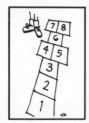

Old-fashioned Hopscotch 213

Old-fashioned Papermaking 214

Old-fashioned Quill Writing 215

One-sided Paper 216

Oobleck 217

Organic Mobile 218

Orienteering 219

Our Favorite Mud Pies 220

Palindromes 221

Paper Airplanes 222

Paper Baskets 223

Paper Chains 224

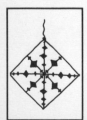

Paper Cutting 225

Paper Hats 226

Paper Helicopters 227

Paper Plate Masks 228

Paper, Scissors, Rock 229

Papier-mache 230

Parachutes 231

Parental ESP 232

Pen Pals 233

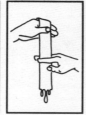

Philately Fun 234

Phone Words 235

Photographic Memory 236

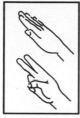

Photography Studio 237

Piggy Bank 238

Ping-pong Ball Game 239

Pinwheel 240

Pipe Cleaner Fishing 241

Pitching Ace 242

Pizza Delivery 243

Place Mat Magic 244

Planet Mobile 245

Plant Map 246

Play Modeling Clay (basic) 247

Play Modeling Clay (advanced) 248

Play Office 249

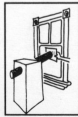

Playroom Observatory 250

Pop Stick Architecture 251

Portrait Painter 252

Post Office 253

Potato Heads 254

Potato Print Shop 255

Potato Sack Race 256

Pots And Pans 257

Pretzel Mania 258

Quarter Journeys 259

Rainbow Art 260

Read me a Story 261

Record-a-letter 262

Restaurateur 263

Reverse Tic-tac-toe 264

Reverse Writing 265

Rhyming Game 266

Rice Maracas 267

Roman Numerals 268

The Root Stuff 269

Rub-a-leaf 270

Rubber Band Jump Rope 271

Rule for the Day 272

Safe Darts And Board 273

Sand Paintings 274

Sardine Hide & Seek 275

Scavenger Hunt 276

Scramble! 277

Searchlight! 278

Secret Handshake 279

Secret Word 280

Self-Portrait 281

Sense Diary 282

A Sentence A Day 283

Sewing Card 284

Shoe Box Greenhouse 285

Shoe Box Guitar 286

Shuffle Story 287

Silent Game 288

Silhouettes 289

Simple Code Language 290

Small Ships 291

Smell The Roses 292

Snow Angels 293

Snow Scene 294

Sock It To Me 295

Sock Puppets 296

Space Suit 297

Speed Boat 298

Spoon Fun 299

Spoon Hanging 300

Spray Bottle Painting 301

Spring Patrol 302

Sprouting 303

Square Five 304

Static Electricity 305

Statue Games 306

Straw Sculptures 307

Strawberry Baskets Forever 308

Streamers 309

Styrofoam Stencils 310

Sun Shadow 311

Super Bubble Bath 312

Super Memory 313

Tabletop Hockey for Two 314

Tambourine a la Bottlecap 315

Telephone 316

Tell Me What's Missing 317

Ten Hints 318

Ten-tube Bowling 319

This Is Your Pilot Speaking 320

Three-legged People 321

Thumb Wrestling 322

Tiger Suit 323

Time Zone 324

Tongs For The Memories 325

SLIPSHOD SHOES HERE

Tongue Twisters 326

Toothpick Architecture 327

Tortoise And Hare Race 328

Touch A Leaf 329

BEWARE

Toy Animal Zoo 330

Toy House 331

Toy Maker 332

Trash Brigade 333

Travel Times 334

Treasure Map 335

Tribal Lore 336

Twenty Questions 337

The Uncrackable Egg 338

Undersea World 339

Utensil Puppets 340

Velcro Catch 341

Verbs and All That 342

Veterinary Clinic 343

Vials and Glasses 344

Walking Paper Puppets 345

Wally's Toss Game 346

Waterscape 347

Weather Ace 348

Weekly Hand Print 349

Weird Words 350

Well-dressed Animals 351

What Am I Drawing? 352

What Else Happened that Day? 353

What If . . .? 354

What's Different About Me? 355

What's That Sound? 356

Where I Live 357

Which Row Has More? 358

Wildlife Notebook 359

Wind Chimes 360

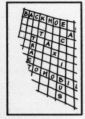

Wordgrams 361

World Animal Map 362

Write the President 363

Your Favorite Martian 364

Zany Television 365

50 Bonus Activities

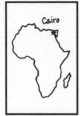

All About People 1

A Matter of Place 2

Animal Gifts 3

Animal Restaurants 4

Bank on It 5

City Guide 6

Combo Inventions 7

Dictionary Name Games 8

Do-It-Yourself "Ologies" 9

Every Number Counts 10

Fancy Duds of the Future 11

Fifteen Minutes 12

Fill in the Blanks 13

Go West, Young Kids 14

The Gravity of the Situation 15

Great Entertaining 16

Hole Story 17

Household Road Signs 18

If Pickles Could Talk 19

Instant Lecture Series 20

Inventions We'd Rather Not See 21

Keeper of the Zoo 22

Kitchen Shapes 23

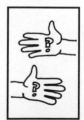

Left-and-Right Switcheroo 24

Link That Stuff 25

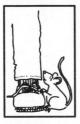

Make a Sentence 26

Marvelous Menus 27

Math Codes 28

Mouse-Eye View 29

Oral History Book 30

Pay by the Word 31

Perfectly Silly 32

Pop Goes the Quiz 33

Presidential Mixer 34

Read My Lips 35

Science Fair 36

Preface

Five years ago, if anyone had told us that when we became forty-somethings we'd spend our time finding new ways to write about fun with cardboard tubes, recycled aluminum foil, and paper bags, we'd have told them they were crazy. But that's just what happened.

The success of *365 TV-Free Activities You Can Do with Your Child* is particularly gratifying, because it validates our belief that:

1. It *is* possible to triumph over the tube by teaching your kids how to entertain themselves through their limitless creativity.
2. Quaint as it may sound, your kids want to play with the person who can leap tall buildings and set the world right—you!
3. Grownups can relearn how to play and enjoy the great benefits of becoming a child again.
4. It's really the *quality*, not the quantity, of time you spend with your child that counts. Ten great minutes here, twenty great minutes there, can go a long way.

For our household, too, this new edition marks a special milestone. We wrote the original to see if we could devise enough zany and challenging activities so that we wouldn't need to devise a TV-watching policy. Five years later, we still don't have a policy, and our household remains pretty much TV-free. Our small set still lives in the closet 98 percent of the time and our children are living full and creative lives, learning about the world through their own senses, through books and school, and through good talk with friends and family. Best of all, "I'm bored" is rarely heard around our house.

By popular request, we've added 50 new activities designed for middle-school and older kids. These activities will help you become a better at-home educator and challenge your kids to strut their knowledge of history, geography, and other subjects; exercise their reading skills; and use their creative problem-solving abilities.

Again, we invite you to send us your suggestions for improving the book. We all share a strong interest in helping our children curb their TV-watching habits. And we can learn from each other as we try to make childhood the meaningful stage in life that it was meant to be.

Now, let's see, if we just connect that paper tube to this scrap of felt . . .

—Steve and Ruth Bennett

Acknowledgments

We're often asked how we came up with so many activity ideas that kids and parents could enjoy instead of watching television. Truth be told, we got lots of help from family and friends. First and foremost, we'd like to thank our kids, Noah and Audrey Bennett, for serving as chief consultants on the fine art of play, especially for this revised edition.

Stacey Miller earned the title of "Official 365 Funmeister," first as our publicist and later as an editorial consultant and prolific member of our activity team. Thanks for your help and inspiration, you big kid. Our editor on the first edition, Brandon Toropov, was also a major source of ideas. (Brandon, we're still sorry about the pizza that almost put a premature end to your career.) Brandon's successor, Ed Walters, joined us on the second round and shepherded the book through production. Bob Adams was instrumental in making this book a success. Thanks also to all the people at Adams Media who kept copies of this book rolling out the door, and helped focus national attention on the importance of curbing TV watching.

Other people played important roles in the project, too. Mike Snell—a fountain of great activities for kids and families—offered lots of zany and clever suggestions. Hats off to you, Mike. Arch Loetterle, Susan (Loetterle) Lozinyak, and Lynn Loetterle also contributed all sorts of ideas and corrections (not to mention invaluable child care).

Thanks also go to Vicky Benedict for revealing the secret formulas for oobleck and other concoctions, to Mary Ehlers and Susan Ferguson for sharing their mnemonics, to Daniel Charrette for explaining how to make a bug motel, to Judith Burros for showing us how to make baker's clay, and to Marion Wingfield for teaching us how to transform a paper bag into a lifelike elephant costume.

Others who reviewed activities, helped us refine our work, or cheered us across the finish line include: Peter Kinder, David and Emily Hawkinds, Glenn Smith, Anne James, Gail Norcross, Jan Litwin, Caroline Chauncey, Richard Thal, Lynn Gervens, Richard Freierman, and Kerri Collins.

Finally, we'd like to thank everyone who patiently waited for us to rejoin the civilized world while we experimented with toilet paper tube bowling, turned our kitchen into a mad scientist's chemistry lab, and found the best way to turn our sofa into a magic bus.

INTRODUCTION:
Of Quality Time and
Quality Play

If you're like many parents today, you probably
think that your children should watch less television. You'd probably like to replace some of your
kid's TV viewing time with quality family time, too.

This book can help you achieve both goals by
showing you games and activities that require little
or no preparation, yet provide hours of entertainment and play that might otherwise be spent in front
of the tube. With a year's worth of TV-free activities
in hand, you can confidently offer your kids exciting
alternatives to programming of questionable value
and an endless stream of advertising.

While we've tried to include a variety of indoor
and outdoor activities, and some that tie in with the
changing seasons, most can be done right in your
living room or kitchen with minimal planning. (It
was our son Noah who taught us just how easy and
fun it can be to whip up TV-free activities from
couch pillows and pots and pans; even our infant
daughter Audrey taught us how much fun a cardboard box can be.)

The activities fall into the following categories:
Arts and Crafts, Creativity, Fantasy Play, Food Stuff,
Group Play, Indoor Play, Math and Numbers,
Memory, Older Kids' Play, Outdoor Play,
Recycled/Reused Household Materials, Science,
"Tire 'em Out," Toymaking, Words and Language,

and "Your Time Only." Use the index at the back of the book to pinpoint activities that appeal to you and your child.

We placed the most emphasis on activities that are easy to do and require minimal energy on your part. Many of these can be real life savers when you're just too beat to think, yet you want to give your kids quality time rather than turning to the "electronic baby sitter." You might want to keep a list of your favorite TV-free activities right by your emergency phone numbers!

For those activities that do require materials, we've selected items that can generally be found right under your nose in the kitchen or pantry. Which brings us to the next section—what to gather for use in play.

The TV-Free Activity Supply Center

Just about any kind of container, lid, or cardboard tube can be turned into a nifty toy or used in a TV-free activity. Many people will find this ecological aspect of the book especially satisfying. (See the "Recycled/Reused Household Materials" category in the Index.) In fact, TV-free activities are a great way to press materials back into service that can't be recycled through conventional means. Here's a list of the kinds of things you should be saving:

- *Boxes*—cardboard, shipping, cereal, food, etc. Use them to make everything from dashboards to toy factories.
- *Toilet paper tubes*—One of the most underrated and valuable items in your TV-free tool kit. You'll find numerous calls for them in the pages ahead, such as "Ten Tube Bowling,"

which tests everyone's skill and dexterity on the living room bowling lanes.

- *Paper towel tubes*—also a squandered precious resource. A paper towel tube can be used for everything from a telescope to the main piece of a wind chime.
- *Cardboard milk cartons*—Cleaned and dried, these can be used to make giant dice and even entire cities.
- *Plastic containers and tops*—You can use yogurt, cottage cheese, and other tubs to hold paint, as papier-mache molds, and for many other noble purposes. The lids also make great dials and meters for play dashboards. Plastic milk jugs make great piggy banks and catcher's mitts.
- *Caps from soda and water bottles*—These make the perfect knobs for spacecraft control centers, time machines, and other everyday vehicles.
- *Paper bags*—Like toilet paper tubes, these under-rated items have a wide range of uses, from masks and space helmets to magnetic fish tanks.
- *Cotton from vitamin bottles*—This is very important for making hair for puppets, smoke for volcanoes, and other purposes.
- *Used gift wrap, used aluminum foil, and tubes*—Many of the activities in this book provide the opportunity to decorate homemade toys and game items. Used gift wrap and foil are ideal for this purpose.
- *Egg cartons, Styrofoam takeout cartons, Styrofoam cups*—These gems can be used for seed starters, as paper molds, and in many TV-free activities.
- *Scrap paper*—The backs of these sheets of writing and computer paper can be put to good use. (Your kids won't reveal the intimate

details of your taxes.) Also, contact local newspapers to see about purchasing the ends of their newspaper rolls, which they don't use in the printing process. You can often pick up large quantities of very wide paper for a song.

- *Junk mail and catalogs*—the scourge of your mail slot? Sure. But also a great source of pictures and props for various games. And best of all, they're free.
- *Magazines*—Every magazine contains pictures that can be used in a TV-free activity, as a background scene, a playing card, or decoration.

Once you've incorporated TV-free activities into your everyday life, you'll start seeing "trash" in a new light—you'll come to see just about all packaging that you would normally discard as a toymaker's and game inventor's treasure.

Finally, some of the activities call for flashlights. We urge you to use rechargeable batteries because of disposal problems. Each battery you toss out is a little toxic waste capsule waiting to burst and leak chemicals into your landfill. Do the planet (and your wallet) a favor and buy rechargeables.

Safety Issues

None of the TV-free activities require dangerous materials or unusually dangerous tools, although several do require the use of scissors or a knife to cut cardboard. A few involve cooking or baking ingredients. We expect that adults using the book will exercise appropriate common sense and handle all cooking tasks.

(Activities that involve small parts, balloons, scissors, or the stove are labeled with a "Safety

Reminder" emblem, just to remind you to be even more careful than usual.) Here are some safety issues to think about before you dive in.

- When asked to provide common decorating materials, choose water-based markers. These are safer for you and kinder to the environment when they're thrown out.
- A number of nontoxic glues can be purchased from stationery and toy stores. Always use these when glue is called for in one of the activities. Under no circumstances should you use rubber cement—it's too dangerous for children (and adults should treat it with respect, too).
- When empty cans are called for, make sure the edges are smooth. The same goes for coat hanger wires—bend back exposed ends so they can't poke or injure anyone.
- When engrossed in a project, watch little ones who might be eyeing the knife/scissors or small items. Also, a few of the activities require plastic wrap—watch inquisitive children who'd love to get their hands on it. Likewise, be careful around balloons—when bitten, they can burst in a child's mouth and become choking hazards.

Above all, simply exercise common sense as you do the various activities. The play should be relaxed and fun for both you and your child.

Doing TV-Free Activities with Your Child
With a few of the activities, you can make a toy or start your child on a game, then trot off to cook,

clean, unwind, or tend to your business. Almost all the activities in this book, however, anticipate your interactive involvement with your child. Here are some suggestions that will enhance the quality of the play and provide you with a framework for doing TV-free activities with groups of children.

- Gauge the action for your child's age and abilities. If an activity or level of play is too hard, you'll frustrate your child. Start easy, congratulate your child on his or her skills and accomplishments, and then suggest making the activity more difficult.
- Go with the flow. Hackneyed, but true. TV-free activity rules are merely to get a game going. Be flexible and let your child run the show. In fact, you should encourage your child to invent his or her own version. This will foster creativity and self-confidence.
- Don't force competitive, winning-oriented play. Young children often play games very cooperatively. Enjoy and foster that spirit as long as you can. For example, if several kids are playing a game, make the object to beat the clock, not each other. Or make the prize for winning the right to select the rules for the next game, or to think of a silly thing for everyone else to do.

Weaning Off the Tube

Should you donate your TV to science before proceeding with this book? Not necessarily. The issue is one of control rather than eradication. Determine what and how much television your children should watch, then enforce your decision vigorously. Some parents we know have a basic rule—their children must ask permission before turning on the TV set. Others simply keep the tube under wraps, except for special occasions.

If your children have already habituated to a certain dose of television each day, it's not fair to simply pull the plug—you'll be punishing them for reasons beyond their comprehension. With the exception of quitting smoking, few things in life are best done "cold turkey." The best approach is to gradually cut back on the amount of television your kids watch until you've achieved the desired viewing level.

If four hours of Saturday morning television is the norm in your household, then try for three-and-a-half at first, then three, and so on. Put the change in a positive context—more fun and play, rather than less television. And use this book as a bridge to achieve your goal. Flip through the pages with your child and see which illustrations capture his or her fancy. Then talk about the activities you'll do today, tomorrow, and next week. You'll probably find your kids becoming less and less resistant to change, and more eager to invent games and activities of their own. Eventually, the knobs on your TV set or the buttons on your remote control might actually begin to collect dust.

While we cannot cite long-term scientific studies proving that reducing television to a minimum makes happier and better adjusted kids, it's a safe bet that the more quality time you spend with your children, the happier everyone in your family will be.

And it just makes sense that the family that plays together, stays together.

Steve Bennett
Ruth Loetterle Bennett

Adopt a Tree

The next time you take a walk, encourage your children to "adopt" a tree in a park or other public place. This makes for a personal connection between your child and his or her environment, and also builds a sense of local knowledge. Explain that no one can really own a tree, but that a person *can* take on the role of the tree's special friend and caretaker.

What are the responsibilities of tree-keepers? First and foremost, they must get to know the tree—do bark rubbings with crayons and paper in the winter, collect and press leaves in the fall (see #172), look for flowers and fruits in the spring, and do leaf rubbings in the summer (see #270).

On walks, your child should bring along a drink of water for the tree. Older kids might also keep a little "log book" (sorry), noting the tree's characteristics: height, leaf color, flowering time, fragrance, and so on. In addition, you might show your child how to use a tape measure—and note the tree's girth on a chart.

Finally, be sure to take pictures of your child standing next to the adopted tree once or twice a year. As your child gets older, the tree will serve as a reminder of the patterns of growth common to all the residents of your community—human and otherwise.

Required:
• A tree

Optional:
• Crayons
• Paper
• Notebook
• Tape measure
• Camera

Alphabet Hands

Y ou might think of the sign language alphabet below as being of most interest to older kids, but we've seen kids as young as four take to it. It's great fun to be able to spell your name with your hands—and to know how to converse with others who know the alphabet!

Required:

• Your time only

Alphabet Zoo

You don't have to go to the zoo to watch the animals—you can create a zoo right in your living room.

Cut up cardboard into small squares and have your child write individual alphabet letters on each one. Now shuffle the pile of letters and have your child select one. Your child should then list animals whose name begins with the letter selected. Write down the animals on a sheet of paper, then have your child choose another letter, until you've run through the whole alphabet. (You can skip "X".)

A variation: pick a letter and then have your child draw (or find) pictures of animals whose name begins with the letter in question. You can provide magazines, books, encyclopedias, dictionaries, and similar volumes as source material.

Make the cardboard squares big enough, and you can make your own animal flash cards with drawings or photographs. If you run out of animals, you might want to browse through a book or two at the library. Then you can add critters like the Aye-Aye (a rare primate found in Madagascar), the Cuscus (a relative of the kangaroo), and the Wagtail (a bird of North America) to your list.

Required:

- Cardboard
- Crayons or markers
- Safety scissors

Alphamixup

Can you write with a cemoprut? Do you know how to ride a bcceily? Did you ever eat in a aaenrrsttu?

These mixed-up words aren't nonsense—they're Alphamixups. To make one, you take an ordinary word and put the letters it contains in alphabetical order. In this way, apple becomes aelpp, doggie becomes deggio, and so on.

Required:
• Pencils
• Paper

If your children have some spelling ability, they'll probably get a kick out of constructing Alphamixups. But the real fun is in the game you play *after* you've made them up. Two players take as much time as they need to come up with ten good mixups; then they exchange lists and, under a predetermined time limit, try to guess the words. (You can gauge the time limit to your children's abilities, and offer written or verbal hints if appropriate.)

Now then: you knew that cemoprut was computer, bcceily was bicycle, and aaenrrsttu was restaurant, didn't you?

Ambidextry (Or, Two Hands Are Better Than One)

When we say someone is "ambidextrous," we're using two old Latin words that suggest that the person has "two right hands." To be fair, they really should come up with another word; lefties would probably rather think of themselves as having two *left* hands.

In this activity, have your child draw or write with the hand that he or she does not favor. This is a fascinating exercise, one that clearly shows how much "automatic pilot" work the brain does for us most of the time. By using the non-favored hand, your child actually has to think of each step as he or she draws or writes—and after a few minutes, this can be very tiring.

Feeling brave? Take the activity on yourself, and show your child what your non-favored artistry looks like—or demonstrate how to eat Cheerios with a spoon in your non-favored hand!

Required:

- Pen or pencil
- Paper

Anagrams

An anagram is a mixed-up version of a word or phrase; the phrase "pen, card, white tuna tubs" is an anagram of "peanut butter sandwich." All the letters of the first phrase appear in the second.

Have your older child make an anagram of his or her name; it's great fun for kids with some spelling ability. "Brian" might become "brain"; "Michael" could be "he claim"; "Elizabeth" could translate to "I, the blaze." For shorter names, try making anagrams of both the first and middle names. Once your child gets good at this, he or she can move on to anagrams involving first, middle, *and* last names!

The neat thing about anagrams is that you can make so many of them. "Helen Ann Russo" might be "Share N, sole nun." Or it might be "Unsnore Al's hen." Or any number of other quizzical expressions that sound like they might mean something at the end of a long day.

(See also: Alphamixup, #4; Initial Game, #152; Letter/Number Addup, #176.)

Required:

• Your time only

I, the blaze?

Here

I, the blaze

Animal Footprints

You can easily make their own mystery tracks in snow or dirt—and then lead an expedition to track the elusive critter.

You can create footprint makers out of all sorts of scrap materials. Sheets of Styrofoam or pieces of plywood work quite well. Draw a pattern on paper; consider webbed feet, feet with exaggerated toes or claws, feet with pads, or just your own customized silly clodhoppers. If you want to get real fancy, go to the library and consult a nature guide. Cut out the footprint (remembering that cutting is a grownup activity), then fashion two straps made out of leather, string, or some elastic material. The straps are used to hold the footprint maker to your child's shoes or boots. Don't make the footprints too big, or your child won't be able to walk in them safely. (Of course, you should be sure to keep your child away from stairwells and other hazards.)

Next step: hitting the great outdoors. For groups of kids, one child can play the track maker, and the rest can be the trackers.

By the way, we have a policy about capturing imaginary animals—they can only be snagged by non-violent means, and they must be released to the wild as soon as they're caught.

Required:

- Scrap wood or Styrofoam
- Strap material
- Cutting implements (for adult use only)

Animal Groups

Most people know that you call a group of fish a school and a group of sheep a flock. But how about cats, rabbits, and other common animals? Here's an entertaining activity that will teach your older child some animal family names.

Required:

• Magazine pictures of animals or flash cards

• Index cards

On index cards, write the following words: brace; clowder, drove, flock, gaggle, herd, kennel, knot, pace, rafter, swarm, warren, and wedge. Next, draw or cut out magazine pictures of the following animals: bee, cat, chicken, cow, dog, donkey, duck, frog, goose, pig, rabbit, swan, and turkey. (If you have flash cards with pictures of the animals, all the better.) Each of the words is the name given to a group of one of the animals. Place the word cards and pictures face up, then show your child how to match them.

By the way, the correct answers are: bee (swarm); cat (clowder); chicken (flock); cow (herd); dog (kennel); donkey (pace); duck (brace); frog (knot); goose (gaggle); pig (drove); rabbit (warren); swan (wedge); and turkey (rafter).

CLOWDER

Animal Kingdom

Your child can certainly tell the difference between an elephant and a snake. But does he or she know what really separates the mice from the frogs? Here are some facts to amaze your child.

Mammals: They have live births—with the exception of the platypus and the spiny anteater, which lay eggs. They're warmblooded (so their bodies stay at the same temperature no matter how cold it is). They produce milk for babies. And most are partially or wholly covered with hair.

Required:
• Your time only

Reptiles: They're coldblooded (meaning their body temperature is close to that of the outside temperature). They're dry skinned and usually scaly. Most live on land (except crocodiles) and lay eggs on land.

Amphibians: Like reptiles, they're coldblooded. But they begin life in the water, then become land-based (or partly air-breathing water-based) adults. Their skin is moist and their eggs are laid in water without shells.

Rattle off a list of animals and see if your child can classify them as mammals, reptiles, and amphibians. Quick—is a salamander a reptile or an amphibian?

Animal Puppet Stage

With this activity, you can create a jungle scene complete with moving animals.

Take a large piece of stiff paper and fold the ends forward so it can stand unsupported. Decide on an "ecosystem" and have your child draw the plants, soil, and sky—all aspects except the animals. Next, draw or tape pictures of animals on the same paper stock and cut them out.

Required:

- Stiff pieces of paper 2 feet by 1 foot
- Drawings or pictures of animals

Now cut out stiff paper tabs—about four inches long by one inch wide. Attach these to the back of the animal. Have your child decide where you want the animal to be in the ecosystem and cut a slit below.

If the animal is going to just move a little, cut a short slit; if you want the possibility of more movement, make the slit longer. (See the illustration.)

Place the stage at the end of a table so the tabs hang down below. Your child can then tell a story and move the animals as appropriate. But don't let your kid hog all the action—switch places so you can tell an animal tale, too.

Ant Farm

This activity shows you how to make an ant farm with a few common household items.

All you need is a clear, large, wide-mouth plastic container and a smaller plastic container or drinking glass that fits inside, leaving a space about one-half to three-quarters of an inch wide. Careful—if the space is too wide, you won't be able to see the tunnels.

Fill up the area between the two containers with dirt, tamping gently. Add ants from your garden or back yard, and place a screen over the top for air. (If you can dig up a queen ant—she's larger—you'll extend the life of the ant farm.) Every few days drop in a bit of candy, jam, or fruit-sweetened cereal. In a week or so, you should have a top-notch tunneling operation.

When your child has finished observing the ant farm, have him or her release the inhabitants back into the yard—their natural habitat. This is a good way to foster respect for *all* the critters on the planet.

(See also: Bug Motel, #32.)

Required:

- Two jars
- Soil
- Ants
- Jam, cereal, or candy for ants

Any Other Name

How many feminine first names can you think of that begin with the letter "T"? That's the type of puzzler you'll face when playing this game for two.

First, decide whether or not you want to use masculine or feminine names; then start with the letter A. Designate one of the players as the keeper of the tally; have him or her write down the letters of the alphabet and make a tic mark for each name called out. The first person might call out "Andrea," the second "Allison," the first "Angelique," and so on.

The game continues until one of the players is stumped—you can institute a thirty-second time limit if you want. When the last name for the letter is called out, count up the tics. Save your tally sheet for the next game so you can applaud all the new records—and have a goal to work toward for each letter.

It sounds easy, but you'd be surprised how challenging it can be to come up with the names one after another. Besides, after Xanthippa, what do you do for X?

Required:
• Your time only

Atlas Adventures

While you probably wouldn't rely on a ten-year old map or atlas for your next cross-country trip, you can have a lot of good TV-free fun with either.

Select two points on the map—say, two large cities. Then tell your child to take a crayon or marker and trace the red roads that connect them, without lifting the marker from the map. Be sure to explain the names of the cities and the states being connected. Ask older kids to find: the longest (or shortest) route; or a route that doesn't cross water; or the route that only uses small roadways (which may mean explaining the color scheme of your map); or perhaps even the route that passes through the most towns. Try using your home town as the starting point, and then use a city where friends or relatives live as the second point. You can also include cities you have visited or passed through during family vacations.

Explain to your child that you're donating the old atlas or map to the cause of navigation, and that only special books are for writing in. How else could you get from Columbus to Atlanta for the price of a dog-eared highway map?

Required:
- Old atlas or map
- Crayons or markers

Babble Dictionary

Does your child invent words? Our son once defined a "bo-box" in this way: "It's a very special box and it has no sides or back, and it's used to catch a special animal, a flouse, and a flouse is as big as a house but it doesn't have arms or legs."

Every time you hear something akin to a "bo-box," jot it down on an index card. (You can even make up nonsense words for your child to define.) When possible, have your child draw a picture connected to the word. You and your child can make a card file box, or purchase one from a stationery store. Make or purchase dividers, too. Another approach is to purchase a small ring binder and write entries on separate pages in alphabetical order. As the dictionary file grows, leaf through the definitions and ask your child to make up a story or skit based on the words. Sometimes your child might have an update—an alternative definition or a new use.

Keep your ear attuned for new words that creep into your child's language—you might just find out the true meaning of "flapmunk" (noun) or "snortleplink" (verb)—as in "My cat was snortleplinked at the vet's."

Required:

- Index cards and small cardboard box or small notebook and paper
- Crayons

Backwards Spelling Bee

Maybe your child can spell forwards—but how about in reverse?

In this game for kids with some spelling ability, the object is to figure out what a strange-sounding backwards word really means . . . before anyone else does.

Have your kid look around the room, select an object, and then, without telling anyone what has been chosen, work out the backwards spelling of the word. You can help here if necessary, offering assistance in both reversing the spelling and in backwards pronunciation. Use a pad and pencil if you have to, but don't show any other players what you've written. Now other players gather around and take turns trying to guess, by sound alone, what the player selected.

It's tough—and fun! Each player has one minute to guess the object; you can keep time with your watch or, if you want to add to the drama of the game, a small egg timer or other timepiece. Once a player guesses an object, he or she gets to select the next one.

So . . . give this activity a yrt the next time you're looking for a fascinating new emag!

Required:
• Your time

Optional:
• Paper
• Pencil

16 Balancing Act

Can your child balance a ruler vertically in the palm of his or her hand?

It's fun to try; demonstrate for your child how you can catch up with the ruler's center of gravity by carefully shifting hand position. The object is to keep your adjustments smooth and minimal—too much reaction to a shift, and you'll find yourself running around the room to catch up with the ruler.

Which, come to think of it, isn't that bad an idea. When it's your child's turn, clear away a safe space and let him or her move as the spirit dictates. After the ruler test, you can try more challenging objects—but be sure to monitor all balancing activities closely.

This activity is a great exercise in hand-eye coordination. Perhaps you'll be laying the groundwork for a career in juggling.

(See also: Vials and Glasses, #344; Which Row Has More, #358.)

Required:
• Ruler

If Pickles Could Talk

What would the inanimate objects in your household say if they could talk? Ask your child to choose an everyday item and tell you what that object has to say.

For example, if pickles could talk, they might say, "Hey, I've been cooped up in this jar for way too long. No! Don't spear me with that fork! Use your fingers. Wait a minute. You're not planning to take a bite out of me, are you? Ouch!"

Or the table might say, "It's almost time to get me ready for dinner. I really enjoy wearing the silk cloth, but I suppose I can settle for the plastic one today. How many place settings will I get to hold? Oh, four. Good. I like it when everyone's around for mealtime."

You can take on the role of an inanimate object, too, and have a conversation with your child, who is also in character. If pickles could talk . . . what do you suppose they would say to one another?

Required:

• Your time only

Instant Lecture Series

How would you like to turn your living room into a lecture hall and host some of the greatest thinkers—within your family, that is—at the drop of a hat?

You can easily transform your child, and other family members, into experts on topics of their choice or subjects that you select (for example, the Declaration of Independence, state capitals, multiplying fractions, prehistoric animals, parts of speech, and the like) by letting each participant study related information in encyclopedias, textbooks, atlases, and whatever other reference books you have available for a predetermined length of time (say, fifteen minutes). Speakers might want to also prepare visual materials (charts, drawings, and so on) to enhance their talks.

When your family members are ready, let the lectures begin. You or another participant can act as moderator, introducing each guest speaker and his or her topic. Lecturers might also conduct question-and-answer sessions after their speeches and further research any particularly interesting areas.

So, how will your child's theory that tyrannosaurus rex really evolved from the ancient cockroach go over in your family's distinguished lecture hall?

Required:
- Reference books
- Drawing supplies

Inventions We'd Rather Not See

The world of science and engineering brings us all kinds of great and useless things. But what about the *truly* useless or silly things that haven't been invented yet? Here are some ideas to get your kid's creative juices flowing.

"Complexity Is Beautiful." Simple might be elegant, but complex can be fun. Have everyone imagine, and then diagram or verbally explain, the most complicated device they can think of for turning on a light switch. Or opening a door. (Maybe the device begins with a cage that opens and frees a mouse, who scares an elephant with a rope tied to its tail that . . . you get the idea). You can make a game of it, too, by awarding points for each step in the complexity process or bonuses for exceeding a certain level (say, 25 steps).

"Machines in Search of a Need." What if you had an appliance that could simultaneously skin a potato, wash behind the dog's ears, wax your car, and (wait, there's more!) inflate the tires on your neighbor's bicycle! Ask everyone to come up with devices that do the greatest number of unrelated tasks; for an additional mind-boggler, have them come up with names for the new product.

Hurry—our car really needs waxing. And the dog needs his ears cleaned!

Required:
- Your time only

Keeper of the Zoo

If your child can't visit the zoo often enough to suit him or her, why not bring the zoo to your living room? And best of all, your child can be the zookeeper.

The zookeeper is responsible, first of all, for gathering the animals (use plastic or stuffed animals, if available, or cut pictures from magazines). Once the animals are in place, the zookeeper gathers information about them from encyclopedias and whatever other reference materials you have handy. Kids with reading skills can serve as reference "librarians" for their younger siblings.

Using his or her knowledge of the animals' habits, preferences, lifestyles, and the like, your child creates habitats for them (perhaps by drawing a scenic poster or strategically scattering appropriate props and pictures). When the animals are comfortable in their new homes, your child creates a placard for each, including such details as the animals' native countries, what they like to eat, how to care for them, and so on.

When the preliminary work is finished, the zookeeper can point out the zoo's highlights to "tourists." Whoever said that if you've seen one zoo, you've seen 'em all?

Required:

- Reference books
- Stuffed or toy animals
- Magazines

Kitchen Shapes

Are your kitchen cupboards and drawers filled with all sorts of foods and dishes? Look again—everything you see has been reduced to its simplest shape, and just in time for a game of kitchen geometry.

Call out a shape, such as circles, and see how many items of that shape your child can find in your kitchen. For example, your child might spy plates, cookies, jar lids, yogurt tops, and the like. Or, as a variation, you and your child can take turns calling our kitchen objects that fit the bill, and see who can add the most items to the list.

For an even greater challenge, your child can look for kitchen objects that contain two or more of whatever shape you call out. For instance, if you say "squares," your child can choose a kitchen tile only if each tile is divided into two or more squares (of course, your child can say "the whole floor" if it's made up of squares).

Finally, how about seeing whether you can get your whole kitchen into tip-top shape!

Required:
• Your time only

Left-and-Right Switcharoo

Required:

• Your time only

Because most people are right-handed, we live in a world where items—scissors, keyboards, and so on—are for the benefit of right-handed people. Ask your child how things would change if the reverse were true. What items might your child have a hard time using? How might your child compensate for the inconvenience? What would be the benefits of accommodating a world that suddenly favored left-handed people? Ask your child what inventions might help him or her function in the new, reversed world.

Once your child has explored the possibilities of a left-and-right switcharoo, ask what would happen if most items were manufactured for giants. Then ask what would happen if items were built for small people. Come up with as many switcharoo possibilities as you can.

For the supreme challenge, ask your child to explain what would happen if the whole world were upside down. Hmmmm. Perhaps antigravity boots might help level the playing field!

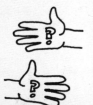

Link That Stuff

One way or another, you can find links between even the most seemingly unrelated objects. Here's how to turn those links into great fun.

Place several objects in front of your child and ask him or her to describe how they might be connected. For example, the objects might be a green marker, a set of chopsticks, and a toy dinosaur. How do they relate? Well, green is the color of plants, chopsticks are made of wood (typically), which comes from plants, and many dinosaurs were herbivores (and those that weren't ate their plant-eating buddies).

You can vary the difficulty by changing the number of items involved or by setting a time limit for making the connections. Another alternative is to award points for each link made and subtract points for items that can't be folded into the explanation. To reduce competition, kids can compete against their own best scores, rather than against each other. Or they can work together to boost the family's score. In yet a third variation, players walk around the house, randomly pointing to objects that must be linked together.

Ready? What's the connection between this book, your socks, and your toothbrush?

Required:
• Common household items

Make a Sentence

How good are you and your kids at creating stories on the fly? Find out with this activity.

First, get five sets of blank index cards, with ten cards in each set. (You can also make your own from thin cardboard or paper.) Write numbers on one set of cards, one per card. On another set, draw various shapes. On another, put colors (again, one per card). And on yet another, write the name of animals. You can put the names of anything else you like on the remaining set.

Required:

- Index cards or paper, writing/ drawing supplies

Each participant in the activity takes one card from each set. They must then create a sentence using all of the elements on the cards. You can increase the challenge by adding more card sets with more difficult items to incorporate in a coherent sentence. Or you can have other players draw cards that will be incorporated into more sentences to create an amazing tale.

All right! So five red monkeys ate 50 pounds of pizza last week. After that, they were green!

Marvelous Menus

We have some good news—your child has just been hired as a chef at a world-famous restaurant. Now the bad news—the patrons are tired of the outdated menu and are demanding that your child overhaul it from top to bottom.

Your child's task is to create a menu that incorporates his or her knowledge of good nutrition. Also, he or she must include a variety of foods sure to please everybody's palate. Review the food pyramid with your child, and be sure he or she offers balanced meals featuring plenty of fruits and vegetables, ample grains, enough protein, and so on.

Once your chef has a variety of breakfast, lunch, dinner, and snack ideas, he or she can create a menu. Younger children can draw pictures; older kids can write out names and descriptions of the meals.

Ask your child to compare his or her masterpiece with the menus found at various restaurants the family frequents. What could the local eating establishments learn from your child's nutrition sense and good taste?

Required:

- Drawing supplies
- Food pyramid diagram

Math Codes

Required:
- Writing supplies

Kids love to make and break codes. (See activity number 290, Simple Code Language, for a list of other code activities.) Here's a variation that adds a new level of fun and reinforces basic math skills at the same time. You can easily adjust the level of challenge for your child's math and reading level.

First, think of a secret message that you want to deliver to your child. Assign a number substitution for each letter in the message (the letter E might be represented by the number 8). At the top of a sheet of paper, draw a blank space for each letter in your message. Underneath each blank, write the number that corresponds to that letter.

On the rest of the paper, create age-appropriate math equations, such as 4 + 4 = E. By solving the equation, your child learns that the answer 8 corresponds to E in the code. When the remaining equations are solved, your secret message will be decoded.

<u>H a v e f u n</u>!

Mouse-Eye View

Yikes! You've been transformed into a mouse. But that's okay. Now you can see the world from a mouse-eye view.

Tell your child to imagine what life would be like as a mouse. Then, in character as a mouse, have your child describe the world. What does the room look like? How do people look different? And what about those favorite mousy spaces, like under the sofa and in the air vents, where humans almost never go?

Your child can describe a day in the life of a mouse. What did your child, the mouse, have for breakfast? How was school? How did other members of the family react to seeing a mouse?

Once your child has explored the nuances of mousehood, choose another critter—say a squirrel or a bird—for your child to playact. You might even take on a creature character of your own and interact with your child's new role. Two can play at this game.

Required:

• Your time only

Oral History Book

Shazam! Your family has been transformed into a living history book, and the title is *The History of the World*.

Assign a historical event or era (such as the Ice Age, the Middle Ages, the rise and fall of the Roman Empire, and so on) to each family member. Each participant uses whatever reference books are available (encyclopedias, textbooks, etc.) to acquire the essential historical facts.

When the research is complete, bring your book to life. Family members each give a three-minute speech about his or her piece of history, present pictures or graphs he or she has drawn or copied, and answer questions from the other participants.

As a follow-up, family historians can mix up the order of their presentations and present a jumbled oral history of the world—perhaps beginning with the latest presidential election, continuing with the Agricultural Age, and ending with the Jurassic period. So, which dinosaur do you think stands the best chance of being elected as the next world leader?

Required:
• Reference materials

Pay by the Word

What if conversations were telegrams and every word counted? Your child can learn to speak concisely—or to "pay" the cost!

Challenge your child to describe a movie or book in as few words as possible. Add up how many words your child needed to use before you could name the movie or book. That's the cost of the telegram. See whether your child can lower the transmission cost of the next telegram.

Now it's your turn to send a telegram. Count up the words it takes you to describe a movie or book. Add words until your child knows what you're describing.

So who can send a telegram less expensively—your child or you? If you find yourselves using too many words to communicate, don't worry. That's why e-mail was invented.

Required:
• Your time only

Perfectly Silly

If every day were perfect, what could possibly go wrong? Challenge your child to figure it out!

Ask your child to describe a perfect day. Maybe the sun would shine from early morning until bedtime, every mealtime would consist of pizza, and there would be no school or chores. You can enhance your child's vision of Utopia or create your own.

Required:

• Your time only

Then, together, talk about what would happen if every day were perfect. What if, for instance, it were always sunny out? Where would farmers and gardeners get water for their plants? If we ate pizza three times a day, how would our bodies get the nutrition they need to keep us healthy? And if we didn't study or work, how would we feel productive? Who would do all the chores?

Naturally, even perfection has its drawbacks. However, it's fun to think about all of Utopia's benefits once in awhile!

Pop Goes the Quiz

Does your child aspire to be a teacher? If so, he or she will undoubtedly enjoy practicing one of the most important skills of the trade—administering pop quizzes!

First, your child reviews a topic he or she has recently studied in school. He or she might want to reread related textbooks, homework assignments, and so on. Then, the young instructor-to-be lectures the recruited "students" (family members or friends) on the subject, making sure to include all the points that will be covered on the quiz. Jotting down important facts, figures, and dates on index cards will make your child's task easier.

The junior teacher answers any questions the students may have (and looks up the answers, when appropriate), and then administers a pop quiz. Your child might choose true/false, multiple-choice, or fill-in-the-blank exams. When all the quizzes are in, your child can grade them and offer test-takers the correct answers.

So, how will your family fare when the newest teacher on the block decides to get *really* tough and set a time limit for taking the quiz?

Required:
• Pen and paper

Presidential Mixer

Have you met anyone interesting at a party recently? Well, this is your chance to mix with some of the most prestigious party guests of all—U.S. presidents, past and present.

Choose a time when you and your kids can throw a presidential mixer (you might want to invite other family members and friends, too). A week or so in advance, your children can choose their favorite presidents (or first ladies) and research the person they've selected (using encyclopedias, history books, and the like). Then your kids dress up in period costumes and attend the party as their chosen characters, answering questions about their lives, decisions they made, their most important accomplishments, and so on as they mingle with other guests.

Alternatively, you might throw a masquerade presidential mixer. All of the guests attend incognito, so nobody knows for sure which president (or first lady) is which. Guests ask each other questions to try to identify each other's characters. At the end of the party, everyone guesses which distinguished guests he or she has met, and who was play-acting whom. So, did George and Martha Washington really mix here?

Required:
- Reference materials
- Costumes for guests

Read My Lips

Can you create memorable sound bites worthy of a politician?

Give your child examples of famous sound bites and talk about the events they help memorialize. Read newspaper headlines together, and see which of them are pithy and flashy enough to qualify as sound bites. Then see whether your child can improve upon the headlines to create unforgettable slogans or catch phrases.

Required:
• Newspapers

Alternatively, cut a dozen or so articles from an old newspaper. Discard the headlines. Have your child create sound bites for each article on an index card to replace the headline. Your challenge is to match the sound bite to the article. Then turn the tables. See whether your child can match your sound bite suggestions to the same articles.

Who knows? Maybe well-crafted sound bites will turn all the stories that enter your home into good news.

Science Fair

Is your child eager to demonstrate his or her scientific knowledge? Why not organize an at-home science fair and invite everyone in the family to participate?

Each person can select a topic he or she is interested in, or you can offer suggestions (such as electricity, magnetism, nutrition, and so on). Participants research the subjects (using encyclopedias, science books, etc.) and accumulate as many facts as possible. Family members then prepare a presentation, demonstrating his or her knowledge of the topic and including homemade charts, graphs and illustrations, working models, and the like.

When everyone is ready, family members take turns sitting in a "booth" (a designated work table and chair in the living room, perhaps) and revealing their scientific expertise to fellow science fairgoers. Each presentation can be followed by a question-and-answer session. And don't forget the best part—all participants should receive blue ribbons for their great scientific achievements!

Required:
- Research materials
- Drawing supplies

Secret Mathematical Formulas

Here's a game where your child knows all the answers. But does he or she know the questions?

Think of a mathematical formula that reflects the type of problems your child is studying in school (for a younger child, you might choose a simple addition or subtraction problem; older kids might be challenged by using other arithmetic computations). Give your child the answer (say, "5"), then see whether he or she knows how you arrived at it.

Younger children might guess that your formula is "4 + 1," "5 + 0," or "8 – 3." Encourage older kids to use division or multiplication, or even percentages to come up with potential candidates.

Once your child guesses the correct formula, turn the tables—your child gives you the answer, and you try to figure out how he or she arrived at it. You'll undoubtedly want to keep plenty of scrap paper hand when it's your turn to guess!

Required:

• Pen and paper

Shopping Math

It's true that everyone loves a bargain. But do you and your child know how to spot one?

On your next food shopping spree, ask your child to use his or her math know-how to find the best bargains in the store. Your young helper can bring along a notepad and pencil to calculate the actual costs of items per unit (for example, the price of a single orange when a dozen costs two dollars). Using his or her figures, your child can advise you about such issues as which brands are the best buys, whether to buy bigger or smaller packages, and the like.

Encourage your child to keep a running list of all the bargains he or she finds as you shop, whether or not you need to buy the items on this trip. Who knows—maybe on your next run to the supermarket, you'll want to take advantage of the super-saver special they're offering on 144 rolls of paper towels!

Required:
• Your time only

Show-'Em-How Manuals

Sometimes, the only way to really explain something is to draw a how-to picture, or even a series of pictures. And there's no better person to draw them than your child, the budding junior technical illustrator!

Required:
• Drawing supplies

Discuss with your child which household appliances (the toaster, microwave oven, etc.) could use a set of clear, simple instructions, and select one with which your child is especially familiar.

You and your child first review together how to use the appliance effectively and safely. Then your young illustrator draws a series of pictures designed to introduce novices to the item. He or she can then paste the illustrations, in order, onto sheets of paper to create a technical manual. Beside each picture, your child can write step-by-step, easy-to-follow instructions for using the household appliance.

Your child and a friend, or a sibling, can also work together to create technical manuals. Younger kids can work on the illustrations while older children can write the text. Who knows—someday your kids might even create a manual that will teach you how to program your VCR!

THE TOASTER

Spin the Globe

Looking for a great vacation spot for your family? Then spin the globe (or flip through an atlas or scan a map) while you're unwinding, and you and your child can plan the perfect trip.

Choose a destination at random, and discuss the place with your child. See what he or she knows about the language, customs, government, lifestyle, and so on (your child might also check an encyclopedia or another reference book for additional information).

If you and your child agree that it might be a nice place to visit, ask your co-traveler to help you plan an agenda. How would you get there, and how long would it take? What clothes would you pack? What words and phrases would you need to learn? What tourist attractions should you be sure to see while you're there? What noteworthy local people might you run into, and what questions or other messages might you have for them if you did?

If you and your child plan a trip to Great Britain, do stop at Buckingham Palace and give the Queen our best!

Required:

• Atlas or globe

• Reference materials

Spinners

Safety Reminder
Small Parts

Some things are best left to fate . . . and other things are best left to fortune-tellers. Here's an easy way for your child to make a fortune-telling device that's guaranteed to be somewhat accurate, some of the time.

Attach a spinner to the center of a paper plate using a brad, making sure that the spinner can spin freely. (The spinner, which you can cut out of thin cardboard, should measure about 4 inches by ½ an inch and end in a point.)

Divide the plate into various answer zones. Each zone should have a label (Never, Sometimes, Tomorrow, In 5 minutes, Twenty years from now, and so on). Then ask a time-related question. Your child can close his or her eyes, spin the spinner, and read the future. Now let your child ask a question and you can take on the fortune-telling role.

So when will you get a pet dinosaur? Twenty years from now? We'll have to see a picture of that!

Required:
• Paper plate, thin cardboard, brad, scissors, markers

Stealthy Thieves

How slippery are your kids? Here's a fun game to test their ability to be exceptionally *quiet*!

In this game, one person sits in a chair with a key chain full of keys or another clangy item placed on the floor underneath. The "keeper of the keys" then closes his or her eyes and listens carefully for the sound of an approaching "thief." When the keeper hears a suspicious sound, he or she tries to thwart the attempted act by pointing in the direction of the sound. If the pointing is accurate, the thief is eliminated from the game. If, however, the thief can remove the keys without getting pointed at, the mission is a success, and a new keeper takes the chair.

Maybe you can have too many cooks in the kitchen, but you can't have too many thieves in this activity, especially thieves who can work together to distract the keeper of the keys!

Required:

• Keys or other common household objects

Sum of Their Parts

Here's a nuts-and-bolts activity that you and your child are sure to enjoy. It's also a great way of finding out what your child knows about nuts, bolts, and a host of other common "building blocks."

With your child, select an item in your household (such as the telephone, a train set, or a radio) that's especially intriguing. Your child examines the object closely (and, with your supervision, safely), paying particular attention to the nitty-gritty details.

After five minutes or so, see whether your child can list all of the parts that go into the item (you and your child can look up any parts you don't know the names of in an encyclopedia or another reference book). Your child then tells how the items works (again, refer to reference books if you get stuck) and finally, explains how to fix the object if it breaks. Say, where do you think we might find a replacement button for our touch-tone telephone—it's had a broken "9" for weeks, and we really ought to repair it!

Required:

• Your time only

Three, Two, One...

Does your child have a favorite number? Now's the time to turn that number into a story.

Ask your child to create a tale about a number. The story can be serious or silly, possible or improbable. It should feature the number in each sentence. Challenge your child to keep the story going as long as possible.

Required:

• Your time only

Alternatively, your child can start with one number and, with each sentence, increase the value by one. For example, your child might say, "Once upon a time there were three little pigs. Then four nasty wolves came to visit. This happened for five days in a row. Finally, on the sixth day . . ."

Or your child can begin the story with a larger number and decrease the value until the story ends. If your child decides to make Goldilocks visit the home of a hundred bears, the story might take quite a while to unfold.

Toy Tales

Do you know what your child's toys are up to when you're not around? There's one way to find out . . . ask your child to divulge their secret lives!

Ask your child to tell you what a favorite stuffed animal, for example, does at night when the family is asleep. Perhaps the stuffed animals get together and play music that only stuffed animals can hear, cook food that only stuffed animals can smell, or call other stuffed animal friends up on the telephone.

Required:
• Your time only

Your child might also reveal what board games do after they've been put away, what arcade games do once the computer has been powered down, what arts-and-crafts kits do in between work sessions, and so on. You might be especially intrigued to learn that cards don't simply sit around and wait for you to shuffle them. On the contrary—they'd rather play 52-pickup all by themselves than wait around for humans to get a hankering for a round of Crazy 8s!

Two Truths and a Fib

Two rights might not make a wrong, but two truths and a fib can make for a lot of fun!

With this group activity, each player takes turns offering up descriptions of two events that actually happened (like, "I went to school on Thursday and had a science test," and "We had nine homework questions in history"). They also have to create one, shall we say, less-than-accurate statement ("During recess my right shoelace came undone.") It's up to the other players to separate the facts from fiction and identify the "untruth" by asking good sleuthing questions. When everyone has had a turn and the fibs are uncovered, change the challenge to find the truth from two or more fibs.

If players are stumped during the questioning process, the inventor of the truth/fib set can give subtle body language hints, such has raising one eyebrow or twiddling thumbs during questions relating to a fib.

Aha, so your left ear twitches whenever you make your statements. What does that mean?

Required:
• Your time only

Unofficial Biographer

Does your child have a future in reference book publishing? Here's an entry-level assignment that can serve as a preview.

Your child chooses a person he or she is studying in school—a famous inventor, a U.S. president, or another noteworthy public figure. Then he or she writes an encyclopedia entry for that person, including as many facts (such as date of birth, hometown, notable achievements, and the like) as possible.

When your biographer is finished, open an encyclopedia, and read the "real" article. See how many similarities you can find between the actual entries and the homespun bios. If there are any discrepancies between entries, check other sources for verification—don't assume the encyclopedia is always right.

So, Thomas Edison invented the record player, the light bulb, and the ping-pong ball, did he? Only your young unofficial biographer knows for sure!

Required:

• Reference materials

When They Grow Up

Required:

• Your time only

What if your child could gaze into a crystal ball and tell you what other children in the family, the neighborhood, or at school are going to be doing in 15 years?

True, a crystal ball is hard to come by these days. But your child has all the imagination he or she needs to gaze into the future unaided. Challenge your son or daughter to choose a sibling, cousin, friend, or classmate and create a biography—probable or silly—for that person as a grown-up. You can ask such questions as these. Where will the person live? What will he or she do for a living? Will he or she have children? What will their names be?

Then ask your child to describe what it would be like to spend a day with the person as a grown-up. How will your child's favorite games with the sibling, cousin, or friend, such as hide-and-go-seek, dress-up, or building with Legos translate into grown-up fun? Who knows? Maybe your Lego-builder friend will one day design the greatest buildings on earth!

Wise Animals

Have you ever looked at a cat and just known that it was thinking: "A meow in time saves nine?" Ask your child about the words of wisdom that would roll off the tongues of your pets (or animals in your neighborhood) if they could talk.

Share some everyday proverbs with your child ("A bird in hand is worth two in the bush"; "Look before you leap"; "There's no time like the present"; and the like). Then ask your child how a dog, cat, goldfish, bird, or other critter might translate that into a wise animal saying.

Perhaps each animal would come up with a different version of the proverb. For example, the dog might say, "A bark in time saves a missed school bus" in response to the cat's version of the saying. Isn't it about time that you tapped the wisdom of the furry, finned, or feathered inhabitants of the world?

Required:
• Your time only

World's Fair

If you and your child can't travel to visit the next World's Fair, how about bringing the next World's Fair into your living room?

Assign family members specific countries, and they can act as representatives for their areas in the first Family World's Fair. Each country rep sets up a booth (a table and chair, actually) in your living room. Encourage participants to use reference books as a starting point for preparing posters, collages, essays, and stories illustrating the highlights and histories of their countries.

Required:

- Reference materials
- Drawing supplies

Family members can incorporate clothing, foods, buildings, and inventions indigenous to the countries into their booths. Reps might also want to create special items to "sell" to visitors, including recipe books, T-shirts, postcards, paperweights, commemorative coins, and the like; prepare demonstrations of native cooking; offer lessons in speaking the local languages; and provide sightseeing information for potential tourists.

Once the booths are in order and reps are ready, invite friends to tour the best World's Fair ever and explore to their hearts' content—without even leaving your home!

Index

U se the following categories to choose the activities that most interest you and your child:

Arts and Crafts
Creativity
Fantasy Play
Food Stuff
Group Play
Indoor Play
Math and Numbers
Memory
Older Kids' Play
Outdoor Play
Recycled/Reused Household Materials
Science
Tire 'em Out
Toymaking
Words and Language
Your Time Only (No props required)

Arts and Crafts

Arts and Crafts (continued)

Arts and Crafts (continued)

Creativity

Fantasy Play

Food Stuff

Group Play

Indoor Play

Indoor Play (continued)

Indoor Play (continued)

Indoor Play (continued)

Indoor Play (continued)

Indoor Play (continued)

Indoor Play (continued)

Math and Numbers

Memory

Older Kids' Play

Older Kids' Play (continued)

Outdoor Play

Recycled/Reused Household Materials

Recycled/Reused Household Materials (continued)

Recycled/Reused Household Materials (continued)

Science

Tire 'em Out

Toymaking

Toymaking (continued)

Words and Language

Words and Language (continued)

Your Time Only
(No props required)

Your Time Only (continued)

About the Authors

Steve Bennett has written more than fifty-five books in the fields of parenting, business management, and family computing, including *Kick the TV Habit, Kids' Answers to Life's Big Questions, Cabin Fever, Waiting Games, The Tokyo Chronicles, Team Zebra,* and *Raising Children in the Electronic Age.*

Ruth Loetterle Bennett is a landscape architect. She has designed parks, playgrounds, and other public places in a number of cities in the United States.

Ruth and Steve live with their two children, Audrey and Noah, in their home-based TV-free activity laboratory. Their TV set lives in the closet.

Do you have any great TV-free activities that are favorites in your family? If you'd like to share them with us, please write:

Steve and Ruth Bennett
P.O. Box 382903
Cambridge, MA 02238-2903

If we use your idea(s) in future editions, we'll be sure to give you credit in the book.

(All entries become the sole property of Steve and Ruth Bennett.)

Ten-Tube Bowling

Pity the poor toilet paper tube; it waits patiently to see the light of day, only to be mercilessly tossed into the trash. Here's how you can save ten of these undervalued creatures—and entertain your kids at the same time.

Stand the tubes in a "V" formation, then have your children "bowl" with a rubber ball (about six inches in diameter is the best size). You can create "lanes" with books or boxes. Toddlers will delight in the collisions; older kids can make score cards and invent their own scoring systems.

For more entertainment, decorate the tubes with markers, paint, or scrap foil. The object of your game might be knock over three blue tubes, or to leave a special "wildcard" tube standing. Introduce challenges like blindfolds, and awkward or ridiculous throwing positions, such as using your head to push the ball; let winners invent their own silly rules or tube formations for the next game.

Required:

- 10 toilet paper tubes
- Rubber ball

Optional:

- Markers
- Tempera paints
- Scrap foil or paper

This Is Your Pilot Speaking

Is your child intrigued by the thought of piloting an airplane? Here's an activity that puts your child right in the cockpit.

You'll need a dashboard (see #138), and a few rows of chairs. You might want to place belts or string for passengers to use as seat belts. Trays (the kind you can salvage from forays to fast food restaurants) also come in handy for the in-flight snack. You and your spouse or other children can flip for the aisle and window seats.

Your child can play flight attendant, then pilot; if two or more kids are playing, they can take turns carrying out the roles of the crew members. The flight attendant first gives the take-off announcements using a microphone (made out of a toilet paper tube, scrap foil, and a length of yarn). The pilot then takes off, and announces the altitude and other pertinent information, like the weather at your destination.

When the plane has reached cruising altitude, your child can put on an apron and pass out the snacks. Who's minding the cockpit? Hey, what's autopilot for?

Required:

- Dashboard (#138)
- Chairs
- Snacks and trays
- Toilet paper tube and length of yarn

Three-Legged People

H ere's an all-time favorite that's good for parties or anytime fun.

You and your child can play this one, or you can use it with an even-numbered group of kids. Cut up clean rags into strips several inches wide and about three feet long (You can also use old stockings.) Stand close to your child and face the same direction. Now use the rag strips to tie your right leg to your child's left leg (or vice versa).

First, get used to walking together—it takes a bit of practice. Then try progressively more difficult things, like running, hopping or jumping. You can also play mind games like trying to figure out whether the other person intends to go left, right, forward, backward, or no-where at all. This activity is best done outdoors, but you can practice in a room in which all the furniture has been pushed to the side and stairways are closed off. (Monitor closely for safety.)

For an added challenge, set up an easy outdoor obstacle course—some low benches to skip over, a picnic table to climb under, and so on. An oscillating sprinkler can be another great challenge—can you make it from side to side without getting soaked?

Safety Reminder

Supervise Closely

Required:

- Clean rags or old stockings

Thumb Wrestling

Remember this one? It's still a sure-fire winner that will keep your children entertained on a rainy day or during a long trip.

Two players grip hands as shown in the illustration; they touch thumbs to the opposite sides of the other person's hand three times, then come out wrestling. The object, of course, is to hold the other person's thumb down using only your thumb.

Historically, younger siblings have had a disadvantage in this game; you may want to try to even the odds by having older kids limit themselves to purely defensive maneuvers, with no "attacks," for the first ten seconds. Of course, if you're the one playing with your child, all you have to do is put yourself under a similar time limit.

Thumbs away!

Required:

• Your time

Tiger Suit

Here's an authentic-looking tiger suit design guaranteed to delight your child.

Purchase a pair of yellow or orange longjohns or tights and a long-sleeve top. You'll also need black fabric paint to create stripes (check an arts and crafts store). Spread out the pants and top on a table (put down a newspaper first). Take a ruler and draw pencil lines across the pants or top, two inches apart. Dip a two-inch-by-one-inch-wide piece of sponge into a pool of paint. Show your child how to make stripes by pressing the sponge on the fabric along the pencil lines.

While the stripes are drying, cut out "paws" from orange felt—cut two holes so they can be secured with your child's shoelaces.

Next, make a tail out of a piece of soft foam (you may find some extra in an old air conditioning window seal kit). Wrap it in orange felt or cloth, glue or sew it together, fashion a loop at one end, and pass a belt through.

Use face paint to draw whiskers, and make felt ears (affix them to a headband). Your child is now ready for a jungle prowl.

Required:

- Orange or yellow long underwear
- Fabric paint and sponge
- Piece of orange felt
- Face paint for whiskers
- Headband

Time Zone

To a child, the idea that some people are just getting up while others are turning in for the night is mind-boggling. You can draw on that fascination with these "time zone" games.

First, find a world map, atlas, or large globe. Then have your child list all of the activities in a typical day, like waking up, eating breakfast, going to work or school, eating lunch, going home, having dinner, going to bed, and sleeping. Write each activity on colored pieces of paper, coordinating them by time of day. (For instance, yellow could represent morning activities, green afternoon, and purple nighttime.)

Point to different countries on the map or globe, and tell them what people would be doing at the moment; your child would then affix the piece of colored paper. Using Eastern Time as a reference, London is 6 hours ahead; Honolulu, 6 hours behind; Tokyo, 13 hours ahead; Melbourne, Australia 14 hours ahead; Moscow, 7 hours ahead; and Goba, Ethiopia, 7 hours ahead.

Your child will want to know how this is possible. In a darkened room, hold up a ball and a flashlight and explain that the sun only lights part of the earth at a time. As the earth turns, night and day crawl along the surface.

Required:

- World map or globe
- Index cards
- Flashlight

Tongs for the Memories

Safety Reminder
Small Parts

Did you ever play the arcade game in which you retrieve a toy with a mechanical arm? While such quaint forms of entertainment have given way to "pow" and "splat" video games, you can recreate some of that old arcade fun right in your own home.

Collect a series of small toys or household objects, then hand your child a set of barbecue tongs. Start off by simply letting the child pick up items from the table. You can later increase the challenge by cutting a window in the side of a cardboard box and having your kids reach through with the tongs.

One variation entails placing the prizes into a bag or box, and letting the kids retrieve them blindfolded or with their eyes closed. (You can also use this as a memory game, where kids are shown the objects beforehand and must identify remaining objects.) Another twist involves carrying the prizes across the room and placing them in a another box. For accomplished tongsters, try playing the game under a time limit.

As the ultimate test of skill, have your kids use chopsticks instead of barbecue tongs. Steady there!

Required:
- Barbecue tongs
- Small toys/ household objects

Optional:
- Cardboard box
- Chopsticks

Tongue Twisters

How many times can you say, "She sells sea shells by the seashore?"

Ask your child to give it a whirl—you'll probably get a lot of laughs after the two of you stumble a few times. With groups of kids, the laughter will probably be contagious, making it even harder to say the tongue twister. But in case your kids get bored, here are a few more to test the nimbleness of their tongues:

Little Larry lazes in his little lorry lately.

Busy Barry Bear barely bakes berries.

Surely Sheldon Shipley shleps slipshod shoes.

"Yearly," I yelled, "I'll yodel and whittle—and wheat'll wait while I waddle by the yellow isle."

You and your child can try making tongue twisters of your own. The secret of a good tongue twister is simple: make like-sounding words pile up on top of each other. Perhaps you can even have a family contest—the person who can say the proposed tongue twister the most times without tripping up gets to introduce his or hers.

SLIPSHOD SHOES HERE

Toothpick Architecture

Safety Reminder

Small Parts

Required:

- Toothpicks
- Clay

Optional:

- Paper
- Crayons or markers
- Tape

With a box of toothpicks and a mound of clay, you can create a scale model of the Eiffel Tower. But there's no need for beginners to get so ambitious. A house is a fine start.

All your older child needs is some clay and a pile of toothpicks. (This activity should not be done with small children, as the toothpicks may be too small for them to manage safely.) Roll the clay into small beads about a quarter of an inch in diameter. Use the beads as corner joints for holding the toothpicks in place.

For toothpick houses, simply build a square frame and a sloping "A" frame roof. Your child can draw doors and windows on pieces of scrap paper; you can affix these to the frame with tape. How about a bridge? Make a frame, then lay down sheets of cardboard. Your child can the use the bridge with very light toy cars or small clay creations.

Other possibilities include: docks for toy boats, corrals for horses and other toy animals, zoo and circus cages, fences, and tunnels. Once you're done with all that, you may just be ready for that scale model of the Eiffel . . . .

Tortoise and Hare Race

So who's really faster—the tortoise or the hare? Here's one way to find out. All you need is two kids.

Make a tortoise shell by taking a large, shallow rectangular box. Cut out recesses on the sides for your child's arms, legs, and neck—you'll have to do a little custom work to make it fit on your child's back when he or she gets down in the crawling position. Crayons, markers, and tempera paint can be used to add shell patterns.

As for the hare, take two sheets of paper and fold them so they form two rabbit ears. Fold a pleat in the bottom and tape them. (See illustration.) This will keep the ears standing straight; tape the ears to a hair band or the band on a pair of ear muffs. Provide a white T-shirt or jersey and a white pair of tights or longjohns to complete the ensemble.

Make a start and finish line, instruct the rabbit to hop, and the turtle to crawl. The three of you should be able to settle the age-old question once and for all.

Adult supervision is recommended for this activity.

Required:

- Large box
- Crayons, markers, or tempera paint
- Paper
- Tape
- Hairband or earmuffs
- Longjohn bottoms

Touch a Leaf

Many things in the world around us look alike, yet have subtle differences. Take leaves. To a child (and to many adults), if you've seen one leaf, you've seen them all. This activity will shatter that myth forever.

Plan an expedition to the backyard or your local park, and take along two paper shopping bags. Collect a half dozen or so fresh leaves and place them in the bags. Pick the ones that are the most strikingly different. Try to find some that are soft and downy, some that have lobes or "fingers," some with long stems, some "compound leaves" (made up of many small leaflets), and so on. Make sure you pick two of each type, so that each bag contains an identical set of the same number of leaves. Have your child reach in and feel a leaf in one bag and then reach into the second bag to find the matching leaf.

Discuss the many ways to distinguish between the leaves. How do they differ in shape? Texture? When you finish the game, you and your child might just look at the world around you differently—and find you've turned over a new leaf.

Required:

• Fresh leaves

• Two shopping bags

Toy Animal Zoo

Here's the next best thing to going to the zoo—making your own. All you need are some toy animals (or pictures of animals glued to cardboard).

Your child can arrange animals on shelves, tables, or the floor. While you can use this activity to teach about different animal categories, let your child's sense of order rule the day; perhaps gathering animals by color or tail length will seem like the most appropriate ways to arrange the zoo.

If you want to get fancier, place the toy animals in dioramas (see #77), and then arrange the dioramas around the room. You can also wrap rubber bands around small boxes to create bars on the cages. (Do not let younger children play with rubber bands, however.) Ask your child for information about the animals' care and feeding instructions, likes, dislikes, and any special notes or cautions about getting too close. Write the information down on index cards. Older kids can write out their own cards.

Encourage your child to educate *you* about the animals—perhaps you'll even get up the nerve to stick your finger in the mouth of the ferocious Bengal Jackrabbit.

Required:
- Toy animals
- Index cards

Optional:
- Diorama materials
- Small boxes
- Rubber bands

Toy House

An empty carton is a house waiting to be discovered. Here are some ideas for converting a box into a doll or animal house.

The early steps feature a lot of cutting (a grownup job). First, invert the box, and cut off most of one side—this will become the back. On the opposite side, cut a front door with a flap, then cut windows on the front and sides. You can also create a sloping roof by creasing a sheet of cardboard and taping the edges to the top of the box. Cut out matching triangular pieces and tape them on to the sides.

When the cutting is done, your child can begin the decorations—shutters on the windows, a doorknob, etc. Perhaps a little landscaping is in order; place a sheet of posterboard or paper in front of the house and pass out the green crayons or markers.

Furnish the inside with toy furniture, or make your own. Small boxes are easily converted into sofas, kitchen tables, and chairs.

You and your child can use the same technique to make a barn, a zoo, a school, or any other building you wish. Who knows—you could be launching a brilliant career in architecture.

Required:

- Cardboard box (at least 1 foot square)
- Crayons or markers
- Small cardboard boxes
- Scissors or other cutting tool
- Toy people or animals

Toy Makers

I f you have a preschooler with a younger sibling, this activity is for you—it shows bigger kids how to make toys for little kids. Preschoolers will especially like the idea of making something for their brother or sister.

Easy rattles. Drop a very large button or some other plastic item inside a yogurt container. Place the top on the container, and shake it up. (Don't use parts small enough for young children to swallow should the rattle come apart.)

Pop up toy. Affix a picture from a magazine onto a piece of stiff cardboard. Then cut out the picture (a grownup job). Tape or glue a popsicle stick to the cutout, pointing downward. Then make a slit in a small box (one at least as tall as the protruding part of the popsicle stick). Insert the stick and pop the cardboard picture through the opened end of the box.

Baby book. Look through magazines with your child and cut out pictures of infants and other images of interest. Affix them to index-card sized pieces of paper and decorate. Cover them with contact paper or place them in plastic sleeves. Punch holes in the sides and bind with string loops or ring binders.

These are toys that big brothers or sisters will surely be proud to give.

Required:

- Yogurt container
- Large button
- Magazine pictures of animals
- Double-stick tape or nontoxic glue
- Popsicle stick

Trash Brigade

E very day, all of us pass by dozens of bits of garbage and waste on walkways, in parks, and outside our homes. Often, we think to ourselves, "Somebody ought to take ten minutes and pick all this up; it wouldn't be that tough." In this activity, you and your kids are the somebodies who can make an immediate, positive environmental impact.

Required:
• Trash bags

Bring a couple of bags and whatever else seems appropriate to the task—and join the trash brigade! Your first stop should probably be the environment immediately around your home. For city dwellers, this will mean clearing sidewalks of stray bottles, newspapers, and so on. For those in suburban or rural trash brigades, the emphasis might be on collecting tossed soda cans and fast food containers tossed by motorists. (Of course, you should supervise closely for safety and keep an eye out for traffic.)

Trash brigade goes even better if there's a reward at the end of it. You might decide to make a visit to a favorite playground or pond after sprucing up… or to "clean up" a batch of homemade cookies or other treats from the kitchen!

Travel Times

Required:

• Maps

"Are we there yet?" This is probably the most common refrain uttered by children and dreaded by adults during car trips. This activity will give your child a sense of how long it takes to get from A to B—and provide some entertainment without going further than your playroom.

Take a map of the U.S. and pick two states or two cities with which your child is familiar (at least by name). Then use the scale on the map to determine the distance (or use the distance key on the map if it has one). Now compute the time it would take traveling by: Foot (4 miles per hour); bicycle (12 mph); car (55 mph); train (90 mph); jet plane (550 mph); supersonic plane (1,400 mph); and space shuttle (17,150 mph). For young children, try relating the time in terms of reference points they'll easily understand—like the time between Thanksgiving and their birthday.

Try the same thing with foreign cities—you might amaze your child with facts like how long it takes to walk from Paris to Rome. But then again, no one ever said Rome was walked in a day.

Treasure Map

This activity involves finding the pieces of a hidden map. Draw a map of your house or apartment (or a familiar room). Tailor the level of detail to the age and ability of your kids. Indicate the location of a treasure "chest"— a box or envelope containing a treat or reward.

Cut the map into a number of irregularly shaped pieces. Again, match the difficulty of the puzzle to your kid's abilities. For extra strength, glue the map onto a piece of cardboard, let it dry, and then cut it into pieces.

Next, hide the pieces in a room and offer clues as to their whereabouts. In general, keep it simple for young kids; make older kids stretch their minds. Once younger children have assembled the map-puzzle, you might have to offer help reading it; older kids can be turned loose on their own.

Naturally, it's important for the effort to be worthwhile—perhaps make the treasure a coupon that can be redeemed for a home-baked treat, a family outing of the child's choice, or some other prize befitting of the arduous hunt.

Required:

- Paper
- Drawing materials
- Scissors (adult use only)

Optional:

- Glue
- Cardboard

Tribal Lore

People have passed down stories, myths, and lore to guide the next generation for centuries. This activity will be a fun way for your child to imagine life in other societies.

Required:

• Paper and pen or pencil

First, ask your children to pretend that they are members of a tribe of hunters and gatherers. No telephones; no television; no electricity; no cars; no running water. How would people stay warm? What tasks would various tribe members have to perform? Where would water come from? What foods would people eat? How would they cook it? Where would people live . . . and how could you build a house from, say, sticks, mud, or snow? What animals would live nearby? How would they live in harmony with them? How would the group defend itself? How would they get and receive important messages?

Now have your child come up with a special story that illustrates the answer to *one* of the above questions. (After all, without books, stories are the primary means of passing along important cultural lessons.) If the story is about the importance of keeping the cooking coals burning, have your child describe what happened one time when the great wind put the fire out!

Twenty Questions

Here's a classic game that was wildly popular in the years before television began to monopolize family time; you'll find that it's still an intriguing and captivating test of logic and reasoning for family members of all ages.

One person thinks of an object or person; the only rule in selection is that the item must be either animal, vegetable, or mineral, so abstract or overbroad selections such as "post-modernism" or "the Rose Bowl parade" are out. Play proceeds around the room, with each player asking a single question that can be answered with either "yes" or "no."

There is one exception to the "yes-or-no" rule. Traditionally, the first question is always, "Is it animal, vegetable, or mineral?" This can be answered with the appropriate one of the three options. (You may have to explain the three categories for younger players.) The second question is generally, "Is it bigger than a breadbox?"—the first of the yes-or-no questions.

The person being asked the questions keeps track of the number of questions; the first person to guess correctly on or before the twentieth guess gets to think of the next mystery object or person.

For an interesting variation, see Ten Hints (#318).

Required:

• Your time only

The Uncrackable Egg

We usually think of eggs as being fragile; actually, they're amazingly tough.

Hand your child (or anyone, for that matter) an uncooked egg and ask whether, using only one hand and applying equal pressure from all sides, he or she can crack it. The structurally sound egg will remain intact.

Required:

• Raw egg

Why? Because eggs are built to take pressure. (A hen has to *sit* on the egg, remember.) They are examples of some remarkable natural "engineering" and will withstand virtually any one-handed grasp. Try it yourself and see.

Only one proviso is in order: An egg with small cracks in it already will not hold up under the strain. Hold the egg up to a strong light to check for faults. Otherwise, (drum roll, please) the yoke may be on you.

Undersea World

I f you can't get away to the seashore,
bring the seashore to your house or
yard. Here's how.

Take a large dish pan (you can also
purchase a jumbo tub at a hardware or
restaurant supply store if you're really
into it), and fill it with an inch or two
of water. Have your child add smooth
pebbles, a few smooth rocks, and sea
shells—if you can find any—to create
an ocean bottom. Some plant cuttings
anchored by the rocks will make for
authentic seaweed.

The sea is now ready for both denizens of the deep and commercial vessels.
Cut out fish, whales, squid, and so forth
from sponges. You can also put a pipe
cleaner loop through the sponge fish,
so your child can use the fishing pole
described in #182. You might want to
make a sponge scuba diver, too—just
strap on a medicine vial or 35mm plastic
film canister for an air tank. Finally, add
some homemade toy boats.

Empty the water when your child is
done. (Your child may like passing the
water along to the garden or to house-
plants.)

Required:

- Large dishpan
- Pebbles, shells
- Plant cuttings
- Sponges

Utensil Puppets

For a quick puppet show, just look in your utensil drawer. Serving spoons and similar items make the perfect bases for puppets; they have the right shape, and built in handles, to boot.

To make utensil puppets, you'll need some common household items such as tape, yarn, foil, cotton, and twistems. You might take a large spoon and tape a piece of cotton on the top—instant puppet hair. Fashion a beard the same way. You can also make ears out of cardboard and tape them from the back. How about a twistem for a bow tie? Or bits of clay for facial features?

For added fun, make an edible utensil puppet, using peas and other appropriately shaped morsels to make features on the tines of a fork, and top the whole puppet off with a carrot hat. What a sneaky way to get food into your kid's mouth!

See also: Sock Puppets (#296), Finger Puppets (#106).

Required:

- Spoon or fork
- Cotton
- Clay
- Scrap foil
- Tape

Optional:

- Peas, berries, other fruits/ vegetables

Velcro Catch

This sports activity hasn't made it to the Olympics yet, but it's still a medal-winner for your house.

First, apply velcro patches to a ping-pong ball. (See Safe Darts and Board, #273, for instructions.) Next, make flannel mitts. Cut out a piece of cardboard about eight inches in diameter. Make a strap for the back side. This consists of a piece of one-inch wide piece of cardboard stapled or taped to the back. Leave just enough space so that when you put your hand through, the strap holds it in place (leave less space with your child's strap, of course). Turn the mitt over and cover the staple points with tape or another piece of cardboard. Finally, cover the front side with a piece of flannel, wool, or felt wrapping. Glue or tape the the flannel on the back.

Now let the play begin. One person tosses, and the other tries to "catch" the ball with his or her mitt—if the ball has enough velcro, it will stick. Then the catcher becomes the tosser. You can boost the challenge by increasing the distance or making the mitts smaller.

If you get good enough at it, you and your kid(s) may be ideally positioned for the 2008 games in Athens!

Safety Reminder

Supervise Closely

Required:

- Ping-pong balls
- Self-adhesive velcro
- Cardboard
- Flannel, wool, or felt
- Stapler, tape or glue

Verbs and All That

This activity will help your child learn the differences between the two most important parts of speech—nouns and verbs.

Take a pile of twenty index cards and write one word on each; ten nouns and ten verbs. Explain to your child that a verb is an action word, a word that makes something happen. The best test for a verb is whether you can use the word to complete the sentence, "I want to . . ."

Nouns are simple. They're people, places, or things. So now the question is, can your child tell the difference? Show him or her the cards—does the word in question pass the verb test? (Let's face it: "I want to shoe" just plain sounds funny. Your child will probably catch on quickly.)

By sticking with two simple ideas, you will introduce the whole concept of parts of speech with relatively little fuss—and you might even have some fun in the process.

Required:
- Index cards
- Pen or pencil

Veterinary Clinic

If you're like most adults, you probably assume that stuffed animals require no special care or maintenance; any 4-year-old, however, can set you straight on the health care needs of teddy bears and other companions.

Set up a clinic in your living room or playroom by draping a towel or tablecloth over a coffee or end table. Make that the "examination" table. Even if your child already has toy medical supplies, you'll want to improvise—provide popsicle sticks for tongue depressors, and a flashlight to check cloth ears and throats. You can make a thermometer by drawing a scale on a popsicle stick. Speaking of scales, you might want to donate the bathroom scale to the clinic on an as-needed basis. Finally, you can create bandages from your sewing scraps and stray strips of Velcro.

Kids will invent their own doctoring tools and methods; our son insists that his teddy bear needs to have the blood pressure in his ears checked with a turkey baster. Who can argue with success? We can't even remember the last time the bear complained of an earache.

Required:

- Stuffed animals
- Popsicle sticks
- Flashlight
- Cloth, Velcro strips

344

Vials and Glasses

The psychologist Jean Piaget broke new ground by suggesting that children aren't simply miniature adults—they actually think differently. One way he demonstrated this was through the "conservation" test. You can try it too—and maybe even see the world through your child's eyes.

Take two identical clear drinking glasses (tall and narrow work the best). Fill them with equal levels of water and ask the child if they have the same amount. Then pour the contents of one glass into a wide, shallow clear glass bowl. Ask if the bowl and the glass have the same amount. The "pre-conserving" child will claim that either the glass or the bowl has more water. If your child says they're the same (i.e., grasps the idea of the conservation of quantities), ask why they look different. The child who truly understands the concept will explain that all you have to do is pour the water in the bowl back into the glass to prove that the levels in the two glasses are the same.

Kids generally start to conserve from 5 to 7 years. Don't get too worked up about your child's being "on schedule"—the age estimates we've given are rough benchmarks only, not timetables.

Required:

- Two clear plastic vials or two clear glasses
- One clear bowl
- Water

Walking Paper Puppets
(Or, Let Your Fingers do the Talking)

How do you bring paper puppets to life? With your fingers.

First, have your child trace toy people or animals on thin cardboard, eliminating the legs. The cutout should be about three or four inches tall. Next, have your child decorate the drawings with crayons or markers. That's where you take over; cut two finger holes side by side at the bottom of the pictures, corresponding to the legs. (Remember, cutting is a grownup job.) The fingers go in the holes from in back of the puppet; let your fingers do the walking. For people puppets (or for funny animals) you can make shoes out of peanut shells, thimbles, or pieces of paper.

You and your child can take turns putting on shows for each other—or you can each place a puppet on each hand and then coordinate a four-way demonstration of puppeteering skill.

Required:

- Cardboard
- Crayons or markers
- Peanut shells, thimbles, or paper

Safety Reminder

Supervise Closely

Required:

- Paper plates or plastic rings five inches across
- Candlestick, candles

Optional:

- Unopened long-necked bottle
- Colored paper

Wally's Toss Game

Okay; you might not want horseshoes tossed around on your living room carpet. Here's a good substitute from our friend Wally Powers that your kids will find just as much fun.

Find some heavy-duty paper plates, at least five inches in diameter. Cut out the center to form a one-inch-wide ring. Next, place a candle upright in a candlestick holder (or construct a similar arrangement). Have your child toss the paper plate ring, Frisbee-style, and see if he or she can loop it around the "stake." (A full, unopened wine or oil bottle also makes for a good stake).

The youngest kids will enjoy simply letting fly with the paper plate—you can improve the likelihood of them succeeding by placing numerous stakes on the floor. Older kids may want to compose more complicated rules of their own.

Be nimble; be quick; and get that ring on the candlestick!

(This activity requires adult supervision.)

Waterscape

You can fascinate your child by making a sea of color.

First, find a clear plastic container with a screw-on lid. Now add equal parts of water and oil, then several drops of food coloring.

Start off with one color; let your child shake up the jar and watch what happens as the oil and water separate and the beads swirl and dance. Now try adding another color and watch the two mix and transform the seascape in the jar.

(Blue + yellow = green, red + blue = purple, red + yellow = orange).

As your child experiments with different colors, try shining a flashlight through the side of the jar (explain that the light should never shine in anyone's face). Or place a colored filter on the flashlight.

Whatever you do, the waterscape is sure to capture your child's imagination.

Required:
- Plastic jar with tight lid
- Water
- Cooking oil
- Food coloring

Optional:
- Flashlight

348

Required:

- Wooden dowel
- Cardboard
- Thumb tack
- Tape
- Can or jar
- Outdoor thermometer

Weather Ace

Is your child fascinated by the weather? Set up a junior weather station.

To make a wind gauge, start with a piece of cardboard about 5 inches square. Write the initials for the compass directions, N, S, E, and W, in their proper positions. Cut a hole in the cardboard, just small enough that it fits snugly over a wooden dowel. Now make a cardboard pointer and tape a vertical piece to the tail—this will catch the wind. Cut a hole in the center of the pointer, then affix the pointer to the top of the dowel with a thumbtack through the hole. Make sure it spins freely. Place the dowel in the ground, and orient it toward the north (use a compass if necessary). Now your child can track the wind.

To measure the rain, all you need is a tin can or container with straight sides and a ruler. You might also want to purchase an inexpensive outdoor thermometer, one with a dial rather than a mercury column.

You'll probably have to read the "instruments" for younger kids. Older kids may want to take their own readings and keep a log of findings.

Back to you, Jack.

Weekly Hand Print

Like most of us, you've probably stepped back in wonder, looked at your child, and said to yourself, "I can't believe how fast he/she is growing." This activity won't exactly slow down the hands of time—but it will give you a tangible record of the growth of your very young child's hands!

On a predetermined day of every week, sit your child down and do a handprint. (Tempera paint and large sheets of drawing paper are the materials of choice.) Your child will have fun comparing this week's print to last week's—especially if you change colors each time.

Of course, you should be sure to date the handprint each time. Your child may even want to sign the creation or add appropriate notes about the week just past to add to the "time capsule" flavor of this activity. You can keep the prints in a special envelope or bind them together with supplies from your local stationery store. Whatever you do, guard the prints carefully—and keep them out of your child's supply of scribble materials. These paintings are special; they represent a visual testament to your child's growth.

Required:
- Tempera paint
- Paper

Weird Words

Required:

- Your time only

This amusing activity requires that your child know the sounds of at least some of the consonants in the alphabet.

Start off by selecting an object (say a table), then substituting the first letter with another letter, (perhaps "P"). You would say the resulting "pable," then see if your child can guess the object you have in mind. A right answer means that your child gets to try it next. If he or she can't figure it, select another object and use the same letter substitution, say, "pindow" for window. Keep substituting the letter until your child sees the pattern.

Gauge the activity to your child's language ability; for more advanced kids, you can introduce combination sounds like "sl," "ch," and "qu."

You can also have fun with "X's" and "Z's"; can you tell the difference between a "xup" and a "zup?" (It doesn't really matter; you can drink out of either.)

PINDOW

Well-Dressed Animals

This is an old favorite—paper doll clothes—but with a funny twist. Cut out pictures of people and animals in magazines. Actually, the only thing you're interested in from the people is their clothes and shoes. (Remember that cutting is a grownup activity.) When you have a good stock of clothing, let your child begin dressing the animals. He or she can try placing hats, suits, dresses, shirts, pants, shoes, and coats on the animals. Encourage your child to invent stories about what the animal is about to do: go to work, head out for a drive, go out to dinner, head out the door for an exciting adventure in a foreign land, jog or play soccer, and so on.

You can help your child by trimming the clothes for best fit, then helping affix them to the animals with double-stick tape or glue. Next, try gluing the animals to paper to make a book or story board.

My, that gorilla does look stunning in his Brooks Brothers suit. But those shoes . . . .

Required:

- Magazines
- Scissors
- Double-stick tape or nontoxic glue

What Am I Drawing?

E ven if you're no Rembrandt, you can use your drawing skills to entertain your child. With this activity, you challenge your child to identify a work in progress, then help you finish it.

On a piece of paper, start to draw an object, say a car. (Keep it simple.) Begin with just one component—a circle for the outer edge of the back wheel, for instance—and ask your child what it might be. If your child guesses correctly, then let him or her draw the rest of the car. If not, draw part of the front bumper, then the back door, and so on, allowing your child to guess after each addition.

Required:

• Paper

• Pens, pencils, crayons, or markers

For a greater challenge, draw a scene with multiple items, like a house, tree, and a flower. That will allow you to draw even more disparate lines (part of the door, part of a tree trunk, then the stem of the flower, and so on). Again, have your child try to guess the scene as you add each stroke. Let him or her finish drawing each individual part of the scene that is correctly identified. Your child can also make up a story about each drawing once it's finished. Write down the words so you can compile a small anthology from the pictures you've collaborated on. Creating a picture book has never been so easy!

What Else Happened that Day?

This activity requires a trip to the library, but it's well worth the effort.

Head for the periodicals room and look up the newspaper from the actual day your child was born. Find out things like: Who was president? What was the weather like? What was the most encouraging thing that happened in the world that day? What event seems most in keeping with the child's personality?

Those born on Sunday, of course, get a whole raft of color day-you-were-born comics; the rest of us have to make do with black and white. Older kids will probably get a real charge out of seeing and reading the newspaper; younger ones may need some help getting acquainted with the idea of other things going on in the world. (One child we know asked why his birth was not the lead story on the paper's front page. You should probably have a plausible explanation for such logical queries.)

Required:

• Your time only

What If . . . ?

Required:
• Your time only

This activity will fire up your child's imagination; it stands his or her basic experience of the world on its head. Ask your child to describe what life would be like if . . .

People could fly. Would the school bus driver simply attach a rope to each child's waist and lead the way? Would houses need steps? Would the airways be jammed with people flying to work?

The world turned upside down and we walked on the ceiling. How would you keep your soup from falling out of your bowl? Your peas from falling off the plate? From falling out of bed?

The sun never set. How would we know when it's time to go to sleep? When it's time to get up? Where the moon is?

Keep going with ideas like, "What if dinosaurs still roamed the earth?" ". . . people were the pets and dogs and cats were the owners?" ". . . the clouds dropped food instead of rain and snow?" (If this appeals to you, look for *Cloudy With a Chance of Meatballs* by Judi and Ron Barrett—it's a favorite in our household.)

Then let your child suggest one. What if . . . ?

What's Different About Me?

This game can be played almost anytime and anywhere, and will test your child's power of observation and memory.

Have your child study you for a few moments, then walk out of the room and change something about your appearance. Return and ask your child to guess what's different about you. Keep it obvious for young kids—take off your shoes and socks, put on or take off a hat, put your shirt on backwards, put on or take off a jacket, and so on. You can challenge older kids with more subtle changes.

With a group of kids, try putting a time limit on how long they can see you in either the "before" or "after" states. Make sure that your kids get a chance to be the ones who change, too—who knows what you'll discover as you study them from head to toe with an eye for the unusual!

A variation: try rearranging objects in the room while your child shuts his or her eyes.

Required:

• Your time only

What's That Sound?

This game entails making various sounds, then asking your child to identify them. Start off by announcing the category to which the object belongs—things around the house (alarm clock, radio), things that move (fire truck, police truck, airplane), or animals (cat, dog, tiger). Then switch roles and let your child do the sounding off.

Required:

• Your time only

A variation on the game is to create an imaginary sound from a nonsense animal. For instance, a half-rooster/half-cow might make a sound like "cockadoodlemoo." You can suggest the animals to be combined, or you can simply make the sound and ask your child to guess the identities of the creature.

Groups of kids can play, too. Make a sound; the child who correctly guesses the animals involved gets to keep making up new sounds, until someone else makes a positive ID.

COCKA-DOODLEMOO!

Where I Live

Even very young kids should be able to recite their address from memory.

You can help by turning your address into a memorable rhyme or ditty. You can do it with just about any address—here are a few examples.

I know where to go, and I know what to do;
I live at sixteen Bard Avenue.

The number of the house is two-twenty-five;
The name that's on the sign is Parkdale Drive.

Essex Street is where I live; it's just like heaven.
And the number on the doorway is one-sixty-seven.

Putnam Ave. is the place I like to be,
And the number that I like is fifty-three.

I like Oak Street, it likes me;
My door has a number thirty-three.

(See also the advice on turning your phone number into a memorable phrase in #235.)

Required:
• Your time only

Which Row Has More?

(See also: Vials and Glasses, #344.)

Required:

• 16 Cheerios

Here's an interesting game that measures your child's ability to deal with the concept of quantities. (See also: Vials and Glasses, #344.)

Collect 16 Cheerios or other small items of the same size and shape. Arrange them in two rows, eight items per row. Make sure that the items in the two rows line up with one another.

Can your child conserve the idea of quantity? Ask your child if the two rows have the same number of items. Once you get a "yes," spread out the top row and again ask whether the two rows are the same—or whether one has more. The pre-conserving child will probably think that the spread-out row has more, because it's longer. The conserving child will recognize that the quantity of items remains fixed even though their spatial relationship has changed.

As with the vial exercise, challenge your child to make sure he or she really has the idea. ("But isn't this one is much bigger?") Eventually, your child will demonstrate that the two are the same by counting the items for you.

Wildlife Notebook

M ost of us (even city dwellers) are surrounded by far more in the way of animal life than we imagine. Why not encourage your child to keep track of the squirrels, birds, and other members of animal kingdom near where you live?

Here is a partial extract from the notebook of the child of a friend of ours; it demonstrates that, when it comes to wildlife, there really is more than first meets the eye?

Required:
- Notebook
- Pen or pencil

DAVID'S WILDLIFE OBSERVATIONS
Turtles (one big one and one little one)
Frog
Lots of mosquitoes
Robin
Possum
Seagulls (sighted at the beach during visit with Dad)
Chipmunks (three in one week)
Crickets (heard)
Lizard (on rock outside window)
Lion (sighting unconfirmed; heard just after getting into bed)

Required:

- Paper towel tube
  or dowel
- String
- Clean tin cans

Wind Chimes

If you have a porch or a handy tree limb, you're in luck—music is just a few minutes away.

Take a paper towel tube and punch four holes at least two and a half inches apart through one side. On the opposite side, punch two holes. Now take four empty tin cans, with the bottoms still intact. (Make sure all edges are smooth!) Turn the cans upside down and punch a hole in the bottom of the can. (Your job.) With the assistance of your child, pass a fourteen-inch piece of string through the hole in the can, then tie a knot to prevent it from slipping out. Pass the other end of the string through the first of the four holes in the paper towel tube, feeding the string through the opening at the end of the tube. Again, tie a knot to keep the string from slipping out. Repeat this for the remaining three cans.

When the cans are attached, thread a piece of string (about a foot long) through the two holes on the top of the tube, then tie the ends together. Tie another length of string at the midpoint. You now have a working set of wind chimes. Let your child help you hang it from a tree limb or porch beam. Each time the contraption chimes, the two of you will be reminded of this unorthodox way of making your own wind music.

Wordgrams

Here's a great activity for children with some spelling and writing ability.

Give your child a piece of paper marked off into a ten-by-ten square grid, then have him or her create a "find-a-word puzzle" by placing words that run forwards, backwards, diagonally, or vertically. The words can intersect as long as the letters all work; no "turning corners" by mixing, for instance, horizontal and diagonal formats. Try having your child work within a certain theme (such as "things that have wheels"). To make the puzzle simpler, your child can list the hidden words at the bottom of the puzzle.

After coming up with an appropriate number of words, your child can fill in the blanks with random letters, then circulate the puzzle. Try your luck! The clues will give you some intriguing insights into the way your child's mind works.

Required:
- Paper
- Pencil

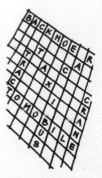

World Animal Map

Even though young children may not understand maps, they know that strange animals exist in faraway places with landscapes very different from their own. Here's a way to help your child begin to think in terms of a global community.

Purchase a large map of the world at a stationery store, or draw one yourself on a large piece of posterboard. Clip pictures of animals from magazines, catalogs, newspapers, or other sources and tape the images to the countries where the animals live. This is a great way to help your kids get a mental picture of the savannas of Africa, the rain forests of South America, and tundra of Alaska.

This activity also represents a good opportunity to teach your child (and yourself) some subtle animal distinctions—like the difference between African and Asian elephants. African elephants are the ones with big ears; both the males and females have tusks. Asian elephants have small ears, and only the males have tusks.

Required:

- Map of the world
- Posterboard/
  atlas
- Pictures of
  animals
- Tape

Write the President

Does your child have something to say to the President? It can be complimentary, critical, quizzical, whatever… the real point of this activity is for your child to participate as an equal (if non-voting) participant in our democratic government. Plus, it's pretty cool to get a letter back from the White House.

Make things easy on the Oval Office: Encourage your child to pose one question or make one comment, then sign off. (Longer letters are less like to be read and responded to.) If necessary, act as secretary, transcribing your child's letter. But make sure he or she signs it personally!

The fun of writing (and the anticipation of receiving a response) is certainly worth a stamp. Give it a try—and let your child sound off. Here's the address:

The White House
1600 Pennsylvania Avenue
Washington, DC 20500

Required:

- Paper
- Pen or pencil
- Envelope
- Stamp

Your Favorite Martian

Many a science fiction story has been written about aliens who visit or eavesdrop on Earth and get the wrong impression. You and your child can pretend you've just landed from the red planet and are quite baffled by some of the goings on here.

First, imagine that you see a man walking dog. Ask your child who's walking who! Next, let your minds' eyes wander to a playground and watch children play. Who's in charge? Are the big people just sitting around because they're not old enough to play? And what about those joggers—who's chasing them?

Continue this line of inquiry with other experiences and aspects of daily life. Then develop with your child a list of questions that will help clarify this confusing world: What do humans eat? What do they do for fun? and so on. At this point, you might enlist the help of a human, perhaps a spouse, friend, or sibling. Or if it's just the two of you, one can be the Martian, the other the human. (Honestly, now, which is more fun?)

Required:

• Your time only

Zany Television

Here's an easy way to get your revenge on the networks in one sitting.

Find a large appliance box, then cut a square hole and a door big enough for you to climb in. Each family member can put on "prime-time" shows for everyone else. Here are a few suggestions for the youngest kids: concerts with musical instruments (like those described in #267 and #315.); drama with toys; or even nature shows in which kids describe the lifestyle and eating habits of their favorite stuffed animals. You can use construction paper and magazine pictures to create backgrounds.

Older TV "stars" can interview you or a sibling—help them develop scripts and ask interesting questions (this may be a good opportunity to deal with touchy issues). Older kids can also play talk show hosts (use a paper towel tube as a microphone) or give editorials about the state of their school, the household, or the cosmos.

Whatever you do, get the whole family involved—that's real children's television.

Required:

- Appliance box
- Scissors (adult use only)

Optional:

- Paper towel tube
- Paper/decorating materials

Create Your Own Activity

Required:

50 Bonus Activities

This section of *365 TV-Free Activities You Can Do with Your Child*—the second addition since the book was originally published—is the result of feedback from readers like you. People told us they'd like to see more activities aimed at kids who have reading and math skills. They also wanted more activities that would help parents become better "at-home educators."

In response to these requests, we developed a set of activities that lets kids use their know-how in a variety of settings. Additionally, we offer projects and games specifically designed to increase children's comfort with using reference materials and expand their knowledge base. The following activities can be adapted for kids at a variety of academic skill levels. Some involve reading, others computation, and some combine fantasy and imagination with a basic knowledge of history, geography, and science.

As with all our other activities in this book, we'd like to stress the ideas of minimizing competition and promoting collaborative play. Also, while the activities can be done "out-of-the-box" with little or no preparation, we urge you to think of them as creative springboards. Think of variations and spinoffs and encourage your children to do the same. And let us know what you come up with (see the last page of this book for our mailing address). We consider our job particularly well done when we help parents unleash their creative energy!

Finally, the activities provide plenty of opportunities for your children to assume the role of teacher and "strut their stuff"—great fun for all, and a good way for your kids to build their self-esteem. You'll also have the chance to become a more experienced at-home educator. And, as the old saying goes: "When you become a teacher, by your pupils you'll be taught."

All About People

Imagine if dogs, cats, hamsters, and other animals could explain the purpose of humans. Why do they act as they do? Here are some categories to think about.

Definitions: How would pets define humans? A cat might define "human" as a being that can use a can opener and serve as a sleeping platform. The dog might describe humans as a being that can spell W-A-L-K. What about some other creatures?

Behaviors: How would a cat, dog, squirrel, or bird explain human laughter or anger? A game of baseball, golf, or checkers?

Physical traits: What purpose would a pet ascribe to ticklishness? To snoring?

Human pastimes: What purpose would an animal give to singing? How about going to a concert? Or . . . watching television?!

Who knows? By considering how our furry or fine-feathered friends regard us, we might learn a thing or two about what makes us tick.

Required:
• Your time only

A Matter of Place

When you hear the words, "Great Britain," what's the first thing that comes to mind? Buckingham Palace, fish and chips, or The Beatles? Perhaps your child can come up with these place associations, as well as a dozen more.

Required:

• Globe, atlas, or map

Pick a city or state (by stopping a spinning globe with your finger or tapping a spot on an atlas or map with your eyes closed), then ask your child to list people, buildings, historical events, or current news stories associated with that place. You can also devise your own special categories of associations, such as foods, languages, styles of clothing, holidays, books, or anything else that especially interests you and your child.

You and your child might take turns offering items that fit into each category, and see who gets stumped first. Or perhaps you can work together as a team, and see whether you can make each category list longer than the last.

Alternatively, you can select a city or state secretly, give your child a list of associations, and see whether he or she can guess the place. You can test your child's knowledge of places by framing your associations as riddles. So, who would ever have guessed that ducklings in transit, hot beverage parties, and a delicious cream pie are all associated with Boston, Massachusetts?

Animal Gifts

Who says your child has to wait until Mother's or Father's Day to create a special gift for you? Make this the day that you receive a special present from your child—the make-believe animal!

Ask your child to role-play an animal. Your child might choose to take on the character of a family pet, a farm animal, or a wild creature. Then ask your child what that animal might choose to give humans as a gift and why.

For example, a cat might want to give humans new furniture to compensate for claw-wrecked chairs and sofas. A squirrel might give humans a jar of peanut butter—as long as the recipients were willing to share.

Once your child, the make-believe animal, has chosen the perfect gift and explained its significance, it's time for the animal to request a gift from humans. What present would an animal want to receive from humans? Why? Your child could probably come up with a hundred reasons for a cat to want a new fish tank.

Required:

• Your time only

Animal Restaurants

Ever heard of the Fresh Fly Café? You would if you were a frog. How about the Hay Loft? It would be your eatery of choice if you were a horse.

The idea behind this activity is to invent zany restaurants from the perspective of various critters. Cats would probably enjoy the Mousecake Emporium, while an anteater would no doubt dress to the nines before going to the Top of the Hill. For each restaurant, suggest that your child include the following in his or her descriptions:

Required:
• Your time only

Optional:
• Writing/
  drawing
  supplies

- The house specialty
- Typical menu items
- Menus for youngsters
- Wall and table decorations
- Price range
- Floor shows, music, and other attractions

For extra fun, consider making actual menus and asking everyone in the family to guess what kind of animal would frequent the restaurant. Hmm, now let's see—who would be likely to enjoy a platter of flambéed spider legs?

Bank on It

Does your child always ask to be the banker when you play board games—and is he or she great in the role? Here's an idea for letting your child practice playing the part.

Set up a table and chair in your "bank" (the living room, perhaps) where your junior teller can work. Then pull a handful of change from your pocket, and place it on the makeshift desk.

You and other family members can play-act the role of customers. Take turns filling out make-believe deposit slips and requesting different amounts of money. See whether your child can give you the cash using the fewest (or the most) coins, the greatest number of nickels, without using quarters, all in pennies, or in whatever configuration of coins you and the other "customers" specify.

You can vary the activity by having your child portray a post office clerk and create novelty stamps in a variety of denominations. So how many yaks, Popsicles, and skateboards does it take to send an oversized envelope first class?

Required:
- Pocket change
- Paper and pen

City Guide

If you'd like to see your city or town like you've never seen it before, ask your child to be your guide.

First, take a trip with your child to the local library. Using the library's resources (old newspapers, history books, and so on), compile background information about your town, such as when it was established, who the first settlers were, and so on. Then switch gears and find out about current buildings and places such as the schools, libraries, parks, etc. Take notes on who built them and when, and any other interesting facts you and your child uncover.

When your child has become an expert, request that he or she take you on a walking tour of your city or town (perhaps other family members will want to accompany you). Your guide can point out important features (such as the oldest school, the first house built in the community, and the like) and offer whatever information and anecdotes his or her research turned up. Perhaps your own home can be turned into an unofficial storehouse for your city or town's rich history!

Required:

• Home or library reference books

• Paper and pen

Combo Inventions

When engineers set out to design something, they typically have a purpose (or function) in mind. What would happen if the process went backwards and the purpose of an invention followed its form?

For this activity, you'll need pictures (from magazines, brochures, junk mail, etc.) of mechanical or electronic things. Next, cut the pictures into smaller pieces: the wheels or headlights of a car, the keyboard from a computer, the keypad from a telephone, and so on. Place the cut out pictures in a bowl and have each of the participants in the activity reach into the bowl, close their eyes, and retrieve a handful. Each person now combines the pieces into a device, appliance, or some other machine, and then explains what the contraption does.

You can vary the activity by setting a time limit for creating a contraption. Or you can play so that others have to guess what the device does. Another alternative is to have everyone finish making his or her machine, then hand out a surprise piece that must be incorporated at the last minute. The possibilities are endless—and so are the goofy gizmos that can result!

Required:

- Magazines, junk mail, and other disposable picture sources

Dictionary Name Games

Required:
- Dictionary
- Pen and paper

What's in a name? A great opportunity for learning new words—with the help of a dictionary.

During breakfast, snack time, or any time you and your child want to expand your vocabularies and have some fun, pull out a dictionary. Then ask your child to select five words or so (adjust the amount according to your child's age and the amount of time you have for the activity) that begin with each letter in his or her name. Our son Noah, for example, might choose "numismatics" (the study of money), "nabob" (an influential person), "neanthropic" (related to modern human beings), "niblick" (a golf club), and "nilgai" (a large antelope), as well as words beginning with an "o," "a," and "h."

Once you've learned what the words mean, see whether your child can use them in sentences and then string the sentences together to tell a story. You can keep the plot moving ahead by looking up new words (simply use the letters in another family member's name) and adding the new vocabulary words to the story.

So, what did the nabob think when he saw a nilgai holding a niblick? Fore!

Do-It-Yourself "Ologies"

Quick! What are the three most important laws of pizzology (the study of pizzas)? Don't worry if you don't know— in fact, it's your job to make them up. That's the whole idea behind this activity: each person invents and describes his or her very own field of science.

First the player invents a new science (dessertology, spaghettiology, toyology, sockology). Next, the new inventor makes up a list of two or three laws or principles. For instance, a law in the science of spaghettiology might be that no two strands of spaghetti can occupy the same sauce at the same time. What tools or measuring instruments do researchers use in the field (maybe something like "the electronic twirling fork")? The inventor must know a little about the history of the science ("Spaghettiology was founded by Dr. J. Pasta Eatmorestarch in 1885"), most important findings to date ("Spaghetti is fun to play with as well as to eat"), the educational requirements for pursuing the discipline ("successful completion of high school, college, pasta school, and proven ability to eat spaghetti without making any slurping sounds"), and highest degrees awarded in the field ("the DSS— Doctor of Spaghetti Science!").

Alternatively, the inventors can describe their science and see if others can guess the name.

Required:
• Your time only

Every Number Counts

Here's a game that answers the age-old question: What do I do with all the phone books I have lying around? Before you recycle them, ask your child to play a math game that requires their use.

Give your child the white pages, or, if you have a gaggle of kids, give them each a phone book. Then, say a number aloud (for instance, 34). See how quickly your child can find a telephone number with digits that add up to that number (for example, 555-6391). If your kids are younger, you might want to choose a lower number and ask them to use only the last four digits (in our example, they'd add up to 19). Or, if your kids are math pros, they might want to work with the phone number and area code.

See how many phone numbers your kids can find adding up to the total in a given time period (say, five minutes), or how long it takes a group of kids to find ten numbers that total the given amount. Or, for the most challenging game imaginable, see whether your children can find phone numbers that, when each of the numbers are multiplied, equals 6432!

Required:

- One or more phone books

Fancy Duds of the Future

W hat will the well-dressed person of the future look like, say, in the year 2300, 2500, or 3000? Fashion trends certainly do change over time. (You and your kids might want to browse through an encyclopedia and remind yourselves what people were wearing 100, 200, 300 years ago or more.)

Perhaps the tie for men as we know it will be out; instead, men will wear *two* ties, one on each shoulder, with tassels or pompoms at the ends. Maybe women will feel in high style wearing knee pads with giant corsages on them. And for children? Why, the multicolored elbow cover will be just the thing to be hip.

Have everyone sketch and share his or her visions of future fashion. Or they can cut out their costumes of the future and paste them on figures from magazines. For the ultimate, try making some of these sartorial inventions and putting on an after-dinner fashion show.

Won't you look lovely with that felt nose cover and matching Popsicle-stick lapels!

Required:
- Drawing supplies

Optional:
- Magazines, junk mail, and other disposable picture sources

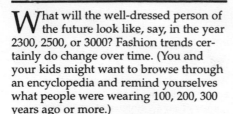

Fifteen Minutes

You've heard that, in the future, everyone will be famous for 15 minutes. Why wait? Ask your child to tell you why he or she is famous—right now!

Pretend that your child has just made the cover of a famous newsmagazine. Ask your child what the article that accompanies the magazine cover is all about. What achievement brought your child to the public's attention?

Alternatively, ask your child to imagine that the newsmagazine features the cover story in ten years. What's the cover story all about then? Did your child accomplish an impressive goal (winning an Olympic gold medal, for example) or a far-fetched one (turning broccoli into ice cream)?

In any case, don't forget to switch places with your child and explain how you earned your 15 minutes of fame. What's it really like to build a better mousetrap—and to be acknowledged as a genius by the whole wide world (except the mice, of course)?

Required:
• Your time only

Fill in the Blanks

Where can you read all about your hometown? In your home reference library—with supplemental materials written by your child, of course.

Your child first finds out whether your set of encyclopedias contains an article about your hometown (or perhaps a place you've visited, or one in which friends or relatives live). If it's not there, he or she writes an entry, using an actual encyclopedia article about a city or town as a model. Younger children can illustrate the piece.

If there already is an entry for the chosen town, your child can embellish it with such "inside" information as what it's really like to live there, which season is the nicest, which ice cream shops and playgrounds are the best, and so on.

Your child might also interview older relatives and friends to get additional information, such as what the city or town was like twenty years ago, which buildings have the most interesting histories, and how the community overcame its biggest challenges to get where it is today.

Before long, your child's reference book will contain all the answers about his or her hometown. So, what do you suppose a kid-improved encyclopedia set ought to be worth these days?

Required:
• Encyclopedia

Lincoln, Nebraska

Go West, Young Kids

14

Do you and your young 'uns have a hankering to travel west? Then we reckon you ought to get a move on and decide which trail to take.

First, your kids study a map of the United States. Then each player tells you which states he or she would pass through to get from the east coast to the west coast. Vary the game by calling out such instructions as "Let's travel through the most states," "How can we take the shortest path?" or "What if we only go through states that begin with the letter "W"?

Required:

• Map of the United States

You can also play the game by asking your kids to name cities, instead of states, that will take you west. Or change the object of the game so that players are traveling from west to east, or north to south.

When your children have beaten a path through the United States, they can travel west through other countries. Or ask them to trace their path west from your hometown—until they've circled the globe!

The Gravity of the Situation

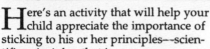

Here's an activity that will help your child appreciate the importance of sticking to his or her principles--scientific principles, that is.

Choose a scientific principle—say, gravity—and help your child demonstrate how it works (by dropping a non-breakable object). You can help your child research the principle using encyclopedias, science books, and so on.

Then, imagine that the scientific principle simply ceased to exist, and ask your child to describe how the world would be different. For example, your child might point out that, without gravity, people wouldn't be able to walk on the ground and favorite toys would fly out of their packages.

Then ask what people might do to cope in this strange new world. For example, in a gravity-free world, we could tie strings to our possessions to hold onto them.

Your child might even have some ideas for great inventions for navigating in a world without gravity, friction, or nighttime.

Required:
• Your time only

Great Entertaining

What's cooking? A meal for very important visiting dignitaries from far away, and you and your child have to plan it!

First, decide where the visitors hale from by spinning a globe and stopping it with your finger (or by flipping the pages of an atlas or map and arbitrarily pointing to a spot). Whichever city or country your finger lands on will be your travelers' homeland.

Required:
- Globe or atlas
- Reference books

Then, use whatever reference books you have available (encyclopedias, atlases, travel guides, and the like) to plan the meal. Ask your child to suggest a menu that includes the dignitaries' native foods. Find out from your junior chef what ingredients you'll need for each course, how long the foods will take to prepare, and so on.

Your child might also do some additional research and tell you what the same travelers would have eaten five hundred years ago. How have common foods in the place you've selected changed over the last few centuries or so? One thing is sure—ancient Romans never microwaved their pizza pies!

Hole Story

How would you like to hear the hole story? All you need for this activity are the stories—your child can provide the holes.

With your child, read aloud a page or two from a storybook. Then call out a part of speech—say, nouns—and ask your child to read the text again, this time without the selected words. You might want to demonstrate by reading a line or two yourself first. For the next round, select another part of speech—for instance, verbs—and have your child eliminate those words (as well as whichever words you chose for the first round) while reading the story again.

As an alternative, you can read the story aloud to your child, omitting words you've secretly selected. Then see whether your child can guess which part of speech you're skipping. Or have your child choose a magazine article you haven't read yet, eliminate a part of speech, and see how much of the story you can figure out before your child fills in the missing words for you.

Thanks again for with us, and again soon.

Required:
• Storybook

Household Road Signs

Required:

• Drawing supplies

No Left Turn. Right Turn Only. One Way. Left Lane Merges Right.

These signs would make perfect sense if you saw them while driving about town in your car. But in your house!? Your kids can have a great time devising directional and other signs that turn your house into a veritable traffic maze. The signs can be made of construction paper, illustrated with markers and paints, and include such exhortations as Do Not Enter or Exit Only.

The signs can be hung from doorknobs, placed on the floor, or affixed to walls with masking tape. The challenge is to control the flow of traffic so that people must creatively get from point A to B. In addition to creating a maze, your kids can have fun by introducing signs such as Hop on Left Foot for Next 20 Feet or Required Singing Zone.

Hey you—don't you know you're in a Touch-Your-Ear Zone? This time we'll let you off with just a warning; the next time you'll have to bake a batch of chocolate chip cookies to pay your debt to society!

Tell Me What's Missing

This game can be appropriate for just about any age group—includin adults. The principle is simple enough: place a group of common objects on a table and give your child a few moments to study the collection. Ask the child to turn around, then remove one of the objects. Ask, "What's missing?"

It's easy to vary the game for kids of different ages and abilities. For the youngest players, use a limited number (three or four) of distinctly dissimilar toys, stuffed animals, or other objects. To make the game more difficult, increase the number of objects, and choose items that are similar in size and shape. For example, your collection might include several blocks that differ only in color. Remove a block and see if your child can point out the missing item.

You can also shorten the time that the child has to view the collection, or the time that he or she has to determine what object you've removed. Another twist is to rearrange the collection in addition to removing an object.

If your kids get *really* good at the game, let them play several rounds at the same time!

Safety Reminder
Small Parts

Required:

- Common household objects or small toys

Ten Hints

T en hints is the opposite of Twenty Questions (#337); the Hinter (probably you) gives a series of clues to the assembled players; whoever wants to can guess at any time. No penalty for wrong answers, and whoever guesses correctly gets to give the next hint.

Required:

• Your time only

Because it takes some preparation, you should take a look at these examples before you get started; before long, you and your kids will be setting up hint sheets on your own! (The second example is easiest; you may want to set up different games for kids of different ages, as the little ones can get frustrated at constantly being beaten to the punch.)

(1) I am a famous American. (2) I lived in the 19th century. (3) I was once a practicing attorney. (3) I was once a congressman. (4) I was known for my skill in debating. (5) I was born in a log cabin. (6) I was famous for having split rails as a young boy. (7) I was elected President of the United States. (8) I signed the Emancipation Proclamation. (9) I am pictured on a five-dollar bill. (10) I am Abraham Lincoln.

(1) I am a famous animal. (2) I have fur. (3) I have whiskers. (4) You hear about me at one special time of year. (5) I love children. (6) I have great big ears. (7) My fur is white. (8) I have a twitchy little nose. (9) I bring baskets full of goodies to all my friends. (10.) I am the Easter Bunny.

Safe Darts and Board

Here's a fun and safe alternative to darts—and it requires just as much skill.

First, place self-adhesive Velcro dots around a ping-pong ball (see illustration). You can get the dots at a good fabric store. Next, make a "dart board." Take a piece of cardboard about 2 feet square. Cover it with a piece of flannel, wool, or felt, and tape or glue the material to the back. (You can also make a traditional round target if you like.) Place the target on the floor, or on an overstuffed chair. You can also affix a gummed picture-hanging eyelet and hang the target on the wall.

Younger kids will enjoy simply tossing the ping-pong balls at the target and watching them stick. For older kids, you might want to use markers, fabric paint, or different colored felt to create zones. Some zones can be worth positive points, others negative. Some might cost a ball, others could offer "bonus" throws. Some might require awkward positions for the next throw.

Make the goal to achieve a certain level, not to beat an opponent—there's plenty of opportunity for competition in life these days.

Required:

- Ping-pong balls
- Self-adhesive Velcro
- Cardboard
- Flannel, wool, or felt
- Glue or tape

Sand Paintings

T he next time your child returns from the sandbox with shoes and cuffs filled with sand, don't break out the vacuum cleaner—save that sand for a painting session.

To make a sand painting, first draw an object or scene onto a sheet of paper with a soft pencil. You can also trace a toy or use your child's drawings of random shapes. Next, pour a small puddle of white glue onto a yogurt container top, and use a cotton swab to apply the glue to the drawing. Keep the layer as smooth and even as possible, and try to stay within the lines of the drawing. Sprinkle an even layer of sand onto the glue. When the glue dries, you can paint the sand with tempera paint.

Finally, you can add other drawings or pictures to the sand painting. For instance, your child might draw trees and sky as the background to a sand painting of a dinosaur, or you can embellish a sand painting of a house with magazine pictures of people and cars. Whatever you do, you're sure to create a work of art worthy of display in the family art show.

Required:

- Sand
- White glue
- Paper
- Tempera paints
- Cotton swab

Optional:

- Toys or pictures to trace

Sardine Hide & Seek

The traditional game of hide-and-seek is still big winner in most households. Here's a variation that a group of kids can enjoy in a large play area.

One player takes off and finds a hiding place—one large enough to house the whole group, like a big closet or the space beneath a king-size bed. After counting to fifty, another child takes off to find the one who's hiding. Upon finding the first child, the second child climbs into the hiding place, too.

Meanwhile, a third child has counted to 45 and joined the hunt. Upon finding his or her fellow players, the third seeker joins the hiders. The fourth player counts only to 40 before beginning the search.

The process continues until only one child remains. His or her task is to find the kids—who are, in general, not that tough to locate. Just keep an ear out for the giggles and guffaws.

Required:

• Your time only

Scavenger Hunt

Did you ever go on a scavenger hunt at a birthday party or at summer camp? If not, you missed out on of the great rambunctious joys of youth. Here's how you can recapture the fun.

Make up a list of objects around the house, your backyard, your neighborhood—as far as you want to extend the hunt. Be very specific. The pre-reading set can enjoy the fun if you give them a picture list; draw simple pictures of the objects they are to find. Keep it easy— a blue sock, a red truck, a book about teddy bears, and so on. Give your child the list and a bag or basket specially decorated for the occasion, and be sure to tag along for the fun.

Have everyone work together on one list, time the hunt, and encourage the team to work even faster the next time. Alternatively, you might have your kids make a list of things for you to find. If you have trouble, just ask a toddler for help—these things are often clearer when you're closer to the ground.

Required:

- Paper
- Crayons or markers
- Household objects

Optional:

- Paper or cloth bag
- Basket

Scramble!

Here's yet another use for the giant dice (#117)—one that will test how limber you are.

Make sure that the faces of the one die all have a color marking (use a crayon or marker if you need to). Take eighteen 8½" x 11" sheets of paper and color them so you have three fully colored sheets to match each face of the die. Next, arrange the sheets randomly on the floor, letting the colors fall where they may. Tape each sheet to the floor securely (this is a good job for your child).

At this point, you're ready to play. Roll the dice and note the color facing up. You must now place some part of your body on one of the sheets corresponding to the color. Roll again and then select another matching square; place any body part there. Alternatively, you can have two players play at the same time, taking turns rolling. Inevitably, they will end up completely entangled. If that happens—or if you fall over laughing—it's someone else's turn.

Feeling really brave? Let your child dictate which body part of yours must be placed on a square of a given color!

Required:

- One color-coded giant die (#117)
- Pieces of paper
- Markers or crayons
- Tape

Safety Reminder

Supervise Closely

Required:

- Toys/common objects to hide
- Flashlight

Searchlight!

With the lights on in the evening, plant various objects around a room—toy animals, toy cars, a shoe, a book, etc. Then turn out the room lights, tell your child what you've hidden, and supply him or her with a flashlight (preferably one using rechargeable batteries). You might also want to provide a special "detective hat" for the occasion (it doesn't have to be Sherlock Holmes style—anything designated as "special" will do).

For groups of kids, you might want to assign each of them different hidden objects. The crisscross of light beams will add to the fun and excitement.

Experience has shown that younger kids will be happy just to run around in the dark with a flashlight. (Adult supervision is recommended.) Older kids will appreciate more of a challenge, so you might want to have them try to beat the clock.

This game may actually be a great way to get your child to eat carrots. What kid wouldn't want to improve his or her night vision after a vigorous flashlight hunt?

Secret Handshake

W hy not sit down with your child and compose your own personal secret handshake? The shake can serve as the password and greeting before classified meetings, deliveries of coded messages, and other clandestine encounters. It's also fun to do just for the heck of it.

Here's one based on a handshake used in our family. Security restrictions prevent us from revealing the actual handshake in its entirety.

Required:

• Your time only

Double pump. (Standard handshake done twice, briskly.)

Index cross. (Still clasping hands, each person extends an index finger diagonally.)

Triple snap. (Each person snaps fingers three times, or does a convincing imitation of it if snapping has not yet entered the repertoire.)

Clap. (Each person claps hands once.)

Forearm bash. (Touch forearms together lightly.)

Single pump. (Standard handshake, done once.)

Secret Word

Remember the old Groucho Marx quiz program, *You Bet Your Life*? Groucho would interview (and usually insult) good-natured contestants—and if one happened to mention a prearranged secret word known only to the audience, a toy duck would descend and the contestant would win a prize.

Required:
• Your time only

We'll go Groucho one better. In this game for three or more, everyone in the family except one person is shown a secret word on a piece of paper (pre-readers can have the word whispered to them). The object is to get the person to say the word *without moving your hands*. Only speech is allowed; take the first turn and demonstrate how to play by engaging in casual, off-the-cuff conversation that leads ever-so-subtly to the topic—and word—you have in mind.

Of course, that's the grownup ideal. The younger the kids, the more likely you are to get clues like, "It's red and round and juicy and you put it on a hamburger and it has seeds and it rhymes with blomato." Hmm. What could that be?

TOMATO?

Self-Portrait

Suggest that your child create a picture of him or herself. The medium chosen—crayons, pencil, watercolor, tempera paint—doesn't matter as much as the atmosphere in which the art is created.

Ask questions. What is the setting? What just happened in the picture? Who or what is your child looking at in the picture? What happened afterwards?

Try to keep the options open—your child's imagination may surprise you. (On the other hand, if your child seems to be drawing a blank, you might help to initiate an idea by saying, "How about a picture of you eating a great big dinner?" Then stand back and see what happens.)

You may want to supply a mirror to assist your child. Another interesting idea is to let the child work from a favorite photograph of himself or herself.

Required:
• Drawing/painting materials

Optional:
• Mirror
• Photograph of child

282

Sense Diary

This activity works equally well for kids of all ages—the only catch is that you may have to help out with the writing for younger children.

Have your child sit quietly for a moment and observe his or her surroundings. Then ask, "What do you see?" The answers (a table, a picture, a bookshelf, or similar responses) all go on paper. "I see a dog in the yard; I see a car parked out in the driveway, a blue car with a white license plate." Then move on to questions about the other senses: "What do you hear?" "What do you smell?" and so on.

The results are often fascinating, even poetic. We find that it is the younger children who can compose the most captivating images in sense diaries—so be willing to act as scribe for prewriters.

You may decide to ask your child to illustrate the result and place the new book in the child's personal library of masterpieces.

Required:

• Pencil

• Paper or notebook

Optional:

• Crayons or markers

A Sentence a Day

This is one of those activities that takes just a moment each day—but adds up to great fun over time.

Keep a special notebook handy for your child; the first page should read, "My Sentence-a-Day Story, by _____ ; begun (date)." Then, each day, preferably at the same time, have your child contribute one sentence—and one sentence only—to a developing story in the notebook. Older kids can make the entries themselves; younger ones may need a little help setting the story down in black and white.

At first, it will probably take some discipline to keep the entries to one sentence only, but as the story unfolds, the game will become more and more fun. Offer suggestions on creating a compelling first sentence. "Once upon a time there was a boy" probably won't inspire much interest the next day. "Once upon a time there was a boy with a bird's nest in his ear" probably will. If your child feels like it, try adding one illustration per day, as well.

Required:
- Notebook
- Pencil

Optional:
- Crayons

Sewing Card

You don't need to be a professional seamstress or tailor to do this activity. In fact, your kids can manage it without even picking up a needle.

On a sheet of thin cardboard, draw or trace a picture of an animal, a house, a car, or whatever else interests your child. At the turning points or angles, punch a hole. For example, where the roof of a house meets the sides, you would punch a hole.

Required:

- Thin cardboard
- Yarn
- Hole punch

Supply your child with a piece of yarn slightly smaller than the holes. Tightly wrap tape around both ends to make a "needle" that looks something like the tip of a shoelace. The object is to feed the yarn through the holes to create the outline that you have drawn with a pen or pencil. Young children will need a hand getting the hang of passing the yarn down through one hole and out the other. Older kids might enjoy using several different colored pieces of yarn to highlight certain parts of the picture. When all the holes have been filled, tie a knot on the back. Then hang the cards in the child's room or the family gallery.

Shoe Box Greenhouse

Egg cartons make terrific seed starter receptacles. As spring approaches, purchase vegetable or flower seeds. Punch drainage holes in the bottom of an egg carton, then fill each compartment with moistened potting soil. Plant several seeds per compartment, at the depth suggested on the seed packet. If you plant different kinds of seeds, be sure to label the compartments.

Next, line the bottom of a shoe box with scrap aluminum foil. Put the egg carton in the box and cover the top tightly with a transparent plastic bag or wrap. (Keep these out of reach of children.) Place the "greenhouse" in a warm, dark place; move it into the sun and remove the wrap or bag when the seedlings sprout.

Your child can water the seedlings to keep the soil moist. Older kids can also keep track of how long it takes different seeds to germinate, recording their findings in a notebook. Transplant the seedlings to larger containers when they outgrow the egg carton, then plant them outside when the weather breaks.

Watching plants grow is great fun for kids and adults. . . and it encourages a healthy respect for all living things!

Required:
- Egg carton
- Shoe box
- Plastic wrap
- Scrap aluminum foil

Optional:
- Calendar
- Notebook
- Materials to decorate box

Safety Reminder

Small Parts

Required:

- A shoe box
- Scissors (for adult use only)
- Rubber bands

Shoe Box Guitar

With the shoe box guitar, your child can learn the fundamentals of the physics of sound. While this guitar is not really tunable, it does produce a fun, boingy sound that is less irritating than, say, a drum set of pots and pans.

You'll have to help with the cutting of the soundhole in the shoe box lid—a grownup activity—and the selection of rubber bands. You'll need 4 to 6 rubber bands of different sizes; use the thick kind that won't snap. (Do not let young children play with rubber bands.)

Before cutting the soundhole in the lid, crush the lid by stepping on its center lightly. The idea is to avoid having the "strings" touch the lid at any point except the ends. Now cut a hole in the lid about 2½" in diameter, as shown. Put the lid back on the box and carefully stretch 4 to 6 rubber bands of various sizes around the box and over the soundhole. Your child is now ready to hit the stage.

Shuffle Story

Break out that stack of magazines, catalogs, and junk mail you've been saving for a rainy day. Or, if you've been faithfully clipping pictures as we've suggested elsewhere in this book, open your files . . . all of them. This activity needs one of everything.

Glue each picture to a piece of cardboard or index card (don't worry if the pictures aren't of uniform size). Then stack them up. Start with the top picture, and ask your child to begin a story. If nothing is forthcoming, make a suggestion. For instance, if the picture is of a house, you might say, "This is Ralph's house, and he's overslept and is late for school..." Then turn to the next picture, and continue the story. Again, you might have to get the ball rolling. Let's say the next picture is one of a spaceship. You might continue, "Ralph overslept because he was dreaming about a spaceship that took him to Mars . . ."

As you can see, the idea is to create a wild, yet seamless, story. Wherever the images go, the story flows. When you're done, shuffle the cards and start over. Be sure to write down or tape record the stories—you might be sitting on the bestseller of the century!

Required:
- Pictures from magazines, junk mail, catalogs
- Cardboard or index cards
- Glue

Optional:
- Tape recorder

Silent Game

This one requires a little cooperation from your child—but it should be forthcoming if *you're* willing to give the game a try.

Here's the question: What is it like to have to go through the day without being able to communicate by speaking to the people around you? The only way to find out is to try silence for a given period—say, ten minutes for starters.

It's tougher than you might think. Writing notes would be cheating, of course—the idea is to try to make yourself understood *without* recourse to a common language. The experiment offers a fascinating look at what many disabled and non-English-speaking people face every day.

Again, this will work best if it is clear to your child that the game is a mutual attempt to learn something about the ways we communicate. Your best bet is to volunteer to go first . . . and see what happens!

(See also: Lip Reading, #178.)

Required:

• Your time only

Silhouettes

A photograph freezes a moment and a likeness, but the old-fashioned silhouette still does something most cameras can't—capture a life-size profile of your child.

Use masking tape to affix a large sheet of paper on a wall, then have your child sit sideways next to the paper. Take the shade off a household lamp, then position the lamp so that the light casts your child's shadow on the paper. The farther the light from the wall, the less distortion you'll get; move the lamp as far away as possible. The farther your child is from the wall, the larger the shadow will be. Adjust the lighting until the shadow size is accurate.

Trace the shadow with a pencil, then remove the paper and cut out the image. Write the date and the child's age on the back. Your child can decorate his or her shadow image . . . and then do a silhouette for each member of the family. When the images are all decorated, be sure to hang them in the family gallery.

Required:

- Lamp
- Sheet of paper
- Pencil
- Crayon

Simple Code Language

Here's a code language designed especially for pre-readers. (See Morse Code (#199), Cryptograms (#67), Chicken Scratch (#46) and Half and Half (#128) for more intricate code activities.)

First, sit down and with your child and agree upon some simple correspondences. For example "milk" might be: "klim" (backwards spelling), or something completely unrelated, like "door," or a number (say, "4") or a nonsense word, like "zoog." In the same way, "drink" might be "knird," cat, 7, or "dweedle."

Required:

• Spiral notebook

Start off with a small pool of words and see which kinds of word correspondences are easiest for your child to master. You can then increase the code vocabulary as he or she gets more proficient. You can also use the code words in different ways. For instance, see if you can have a conversation using the words, or try to use the food-related words during a meal. You might want to keep a code book (hide it well) for future reference and posterity.

Whatever you do, you can't leave the table until you've dweedled all your zoog.

Small Ships

Your kitchen and basement probably contain a veritable shipyard's worth of materials all ready to be put to sea.

Consider those large chunks of polystyrene (Styrofoam) used for packing. You can easily cut them into all manner of miniature maritime craft. Add a stick and paper sail, and the new vessel is ready to sail to the outer reaches of your bathtub. Styrofoam trays from the grocery store make excellent rafts after you've cleaned them. (So can old milk cartons.) And Styrofoam "peanuts," cut lengthwise, make fine dinghies and rafts when outfitted with toothpicks (see below).

You can make neat little boats by cracking walnut shells lengthwise and packing a small amount of clay into each one. You can then hoist a mast by placing a toothpick into the clay and affixing a paper sail to it with tape.

For a more organic approach, try using celery for the hull. In fact, your refrigerator is probably full of fine boat making materials. Remember: If it floats, you can use it to make boats!

Required:
- Floatable scrap materials
- Clay
- Paper
- Toothpicks

Smell the Roses

Can your child navigate through the world with his or her nose? Find out.

Take four or five plastic dishes and add various foods with distinctive aromas. For example, sprinkle cinnamon in one dish, place a dab of peanut butter in another, and put a few crushed cloves in a third.

Required:

- Bowls
- Spices and foods

Let your child get familiar with each dish, then close his or her eyes. Hold up the dishes one by one, and see if your child can figure out which is which.

After a few rounds, you can increase the challenge in a number of ways. First, add some similar spices for your child to distinguish, such as cinnamon and nutmeg. Or combine some foods to make an unusual composite aroma—say, one dab each of chocolate, honey, and maple syrup. See if your child can detect all the ingredients you've added to the mix.

Finally throw in a "ringer"—an empty dish—and ask what's in it. You'll probably get some wild answers!

Snow Angels

Do you remember making snow angels as a child? Here's a refresher course—and a little twist for a new snow creation or two.

Dress your kids warmly, preferably in a snow suit. Have them flop down in some fresh snow, and then wave their arms up and down to make wings. Next, have them move their legs back and forth to create a skirt. Help them up, so that the impressions in the snow remain intact. The resulting snow angels should make a nice addition to your yard.

Now show your child how to make a snow spider. First, have your child make an imprint as before with his or her arms and legs. Then make a second imprint *in between* the first impressions. Repeat the process to make yet another set. (Spiders have eight symmetrical legs, but you can always make just six imprints for a snow beetle.)

If it's warm enough, you can make a whole lawn's worth of angels or bugs. Quite a sight—until the next snowfall!

Required:
- Fresh snow

Safety Reminder

Small Parts

Required:

- Plastic container
- Small plastic toys
- Glitter
- Water
- Spoon

Optional:

- Flashlight

Snow Scene

We're all familiar with those plastic toys that contain artificial snow—you shake them and snow begins to fall over a little Swiss chalet or a sled pulled by reindeer. Your kids can have double fun by making their own snowflake scene with common household items.

Place a few small toys at the bottom of a plastic container. The toys (houses, people, etc.) should be made of plastic, with no metal parts. They also shouldn't float. (If your small plastic toys float, try weighing them down by taping a penny to the bottom.)

Next, fill the container with enough water to cover the toys. Sprinkle silver glitter into the water—enough to make for a snowy scene. When the glitter settles, stir up the water with a spoon, and create another blizzard. Or, if the container has a tight-fitting top, shake it up. You can also mix different colored glitter for unusual effects. For special effects, stir up the glitter, turn off the lights, and shine a flashlight through the glass. The reflections will make for a dazzling light show.

Sock It To Me (Or, the Great Foot Ricochet Game)

I n activity #242, we showed how to use old, unmatched socks to help your child develop a good up-and-in slider—and perhaps take the first steps toward a career as a big-league pitcher. In this activity, you can use the same ball—two rolled-up socks inside a third sock that's fastened shut with a rubber band—for hours of footloose fun.

The goal here is to toss the ball in the air and keep it from touching the ground—by ricocheting it off your feet. After the initial throw, any hand contact with the ball is off limits. How long can your child keep the ball going?

You might want to expand the game by trying it with two kids—it's a real test of skill to pass the ball from one person to another.

Now you have two things to do with those pesky solo socks that keep cropping up after every wash.

Required:

• Socks

• Rubber band

Sock Puppets

I f you're not excited about the prospect of darning worn-out socks, here's a great way to press them back into service. But in this case, hands, rather than feet, do the walking.

Collect a few socks headed for the rag bag, then create faces with markers and common household materials like yarn, felt, cotton, or pipe cleaners. Push in the toe end to create a mouth so your kids can make the puppets talk.

Once you've made the puppets, construct a simple "theater" by draping a sheet or blanket over several chairs. The puppeteer hides behind the blanket and raises his or her hand(s) so the audience can watch the puppets in action. Little kids often like their parents to perform the show. If you encounter stage fright, try using your child's favorite story or a recent outing as your theme. Alternatively, you might choose to use the opportunity to act out a sensitive or difficult issue your child is facing at the moment.

Older kids will probably have their own ideas for scripts. But if you want to get some insights into how they perceive you, try suggesting that they pretend the puppets are parents and kids in your family. You may be surprised at what results!

Required:

- Old socks
- Markers
- Pipe cleaners
- Yarn
- Felt
- Cotton balls

Space Suit

T his activity is good for everyday
fun, costume parties, and, of course,
Halloween.

First, make a paper bag space helmet.
Glue or tape on straws to simulate wires,
tubes, and other important gizmos one
would expect to find on a spacesuit.
(You can also draw them with crayons
or markers.)

The suit itself can consist of long
underwear or PJ's. Before your child
blasts off, make an air tank out of an oatmeal or cereal box. Make shoulder straps
out of yarn or string (watch young children). To make an air hose, tape several
paper towel tubes together (slit the ends
to make it easier to combine them), then
make cuts every inch or two that almost
pass through the tube as if slicing a loaf
of French bread. Tape one end to the air
tank and the other to the helmet.

Start the countdown! Just make sure
your astronaut returns from Alpha Cen-
tauri in time for dessert.

Required:

- Bag
- Crayons or
  markers
- Straws
- Tape
- Cereal or
  oatmeal box

Safety Reminder
Balloon

Speed Boat

A milk or juice carton can make a marvelous hull for a bathtub or wading pool speedboat. Here's what you need to do.

Required:

- Half-gallon milk carton
- Balloon

Optional:

- Cardboard
- Rubber bands

Take a half-gallon carton and slice it lengthwise, as shown in the illustration. Reinforce with glue or tape (from the inside) any seams that have come apart. Next, cut a hole in the back, about three-eighths of an inch in diameter. Place a balloon into the carton, and feed the neck out through the hole. Blow up the balloon for your child, then pass over the boat. Let the child release the balloon—the boat will zoom along the water, jet propelled. (Note: Always supervise balloon play closely.)

For groups of kids, organize boat races. You might choose to add an obstacle course of floating objects (make buoys from scrap pieces of Styrofoam, or make rafts from milk carton bottoms.) You might have a rule that touching an object immediately disqualifies a boat. Or conversely, the boat that touches the most objects wins the Cup.

Finally, think about embellishing the boats by adding a piece of cardboard to make a deck—attach it with rubber bands. You and your child can then make a cabin and other necessary conveniences for the long race.

Spoon Fun

Here's an entertaining and challenging activity you can do with an individual child or a whole gaggle of kids.

The idea is simple enough—hold a ping-pong ball in a spoon and walk about the house. But what if you up the ante? For example, see if your child can get around the house following a certain course without dropping the ball. As your child gets better at it, make up an obstacle course (see #211) or a list of tasks to be done with your child's free hand, like moving a book from one table to another, opening and closing a door or drawer, patting his or her head, and so on.

If your child is older, see if he or she can hop around the course without dropping the ball. To really boost the difficulty, place the ball on an infant or medicine spoon.

Groups of kids can have spoon races or play hide and seek: all of the people who are hiding must balance a ping-pong ball on a spoon as they dash for a hiding spot. If it falls, that's where they have to hide.

Required:
- Spoon
- Ping-pong ball

Spoon Hanging (Or, The Nose Knows)

Required:

- Spoon

Can your kids hang spoons from their noses? Can you?

We'll grant that this might not sound like an addictively hilarious way to spend a half hour, but it is. Take a standard teaspoon and blow on the inside of the bowl gently, so a small fog forms. Wipe the spoon with a cloth or towel until it is shiny, then tip your head upward slightly and apply the hollow of the spoon to the end of your nose.

It will probably take a few tries, but eventually you'll determine the proper combination of tilt, placement, and balance to cause the spoon to hang effortlessly from the tip of your nose. It's quite a sight to see a parent forgo any pretense of dignity in this way; most kids will be unable to resist trying the trick themselves.

Spray Bottle Painting

This one can get a bit messy—but then again, that's the whole point.

Have your child decorate a sheet of finger painting paper (it's extremely smooth and glossy) with washable markers. The decorations might include a target, splashes of color, a drawing of an object, doodles, letters, numbers, patterns, his or her name, or other markings. Next, bring the sheet into the bathroom and tape it to the wall above the bathtub or inside the shower stall.

Get a plant sprayer or any kind of spray or squirt bottle; set it for a fine mist. Have your child stand outside the tub and aim for the picture and—without touching the sheet by hand—try to "erase" the artwork. The water will cause the colors to run down the tub, creating fascinating patterns and shades. The piece will take on an underwater effect. When your child feels the artwork is complete, remove the sheet and let it dry.

There will be a great deal of enjoyment in the novelty of being able to squirt water in the house; your child will also enjoy this new and unique form of artistic expression.

Required:

- Water-based markers
- Smooth paper
- Plant sprayer
- Squirt bottles

Spring Patrol

If you and your kids suffer from cabin fever by the end of each winter, the Spring Patrol might be just the thing to prepare you for the new season.

The Spring Patrol examines each tree or bush in your backyard and/or local park for signs of spring—buds. Before going out, explain to your child that leaves and flowers grow out of buds when it gets warm outside and the days grow longer.

Required:

• Your time only

Older kids might want to play naturalist, keeping a notebook of their findings, and jotting down on a calendar the progress of various types of buds. A local tree/plant identification book will be useful—and can save you from some embarrassment, too. You might also want to take along a magnifying glass to show your kid(s) the fine features of the miniature leaves and buds.

In our family, the Spring Patrol has become an annual ritual, one we believe to be essential to warding off any further snowfalls for the year.

Sprouting

E ven if you don't serve up sprouts for meals, your child will enjoy growing his or her own sprouts. It's easy and requires less patience than you might think.

First, purchase alfalfa seeds or dried beans, such as lentils or soybeans. Rinse the seeds or beans in a strainer (use a colander for large beans). Pick out damaged shells, then put the beans in a plastic container. Fill this with slightly warm water to about four times the height of the beans. Now place a piece of screen or cheesecloth over the mouth and affix it with a rubber band. Let the seeds sit eight to twelve hours, then drain the water.

Prop up the jar at an angle, screen side down, in a dark place. To promote drainage, rinse the beans two to four times every day with cold water. When the sprouts reach a desirable length (it will take a couple of days), remove them and serve 'em up—or just watch them grow.

Required:

- Alfalfa seeds or dried beans
- Plastic container
- Cheese cloth or screen
- Rubber band

Square Five

Here's a real confidence-booster for kids who have mastered the times tables and are moving on to squares in math.

You can teach your child to square any two-digit number ending in five in a matter of minutes. There are only two steps.

One: Multiply the first digit by that same digit, plus one. Let's say you picked 75; you'd multiply 7 x 8, since 7 + 1 = 8. The result, of course, would be 56.

Two. Stick the number 25 on the end of your answer, and there you have it! 75 x 75 = 5625.

It always works. Have your child try it with three or four numbers, then verify the results with a calculator. Who said math was tough?

Required:
• Calculator

Optional:
• Pen
• Paper

Static Electricity (Or, A *Real* Charge)

Safety Reminder

Balloon

Required:
- Balloon
- Mirror

Here's a safe, simple activity that demonstrates the principles of static electricity in an entertaining way.

Blow up a medium-sized balloon for your child, then ask him or her to go to a mirror and rub the balloon vigorously across the top or side of the head. Now hold the balloon slightly away from your child's hair.

To your child's amazement, his or her hair will stand on end!

You can explain that static electricity builds up on an object rubbed against another object, and that this is the reason people are sometimes given a mild "zap" when they touch a doorknob after rubbing the soles of their shoes against a rug.

A hair-raising experience!

(This game is intended for older children only. Younger children should not play with balloons because of the possibility of suffocation.)

Statue Games

These two games for three or more are ideal activities for large groups of kids.

Freeze frame. One person is designated as "it." The others begin hopping, walking, or crawling around the yard or room. "It" then says "freeze." Everyone must then hold their position like a statue, no matter how awkward. The first one to break his or her statue position becomes "it" for the next round.

Flying statues. (Best played outside). One player is the "sculptor" and the others are the "statues." The sculptor holds one of the statues-to-be by the hands and gently swings him or her around once or twice (under adult supervision), calling out an animal or object. When the sculptor lets go the statue must come to rest in a position that impersonates the animal or object and stay still. Once all of the statues have been "spun off," the sculptor gets to pick a favorite. The favorite statue then becomes the sculptor for the next round. Now then—how long can you assume the toothbrush pose?

Required:

• Your time only

Straw Sculptures

The drinking straws from your last restaurant visit are not only reusable for beverages—they make great materials for making sculpture pieces, too.

Before you start making straw sculptures, create a supply of smaller pieces. You'll want to cut up an assortment of straws; your final arsenal should have pieces ranging from one inch to full length. If you have any straws with the ribbed elbows, cut off a few of the joints—these will be invaluable later on.

You should also make a stock of tube connectors. One type of connector, good for angle joints, consists of a paper clip that has been bent open so you have two "U" shaped wires connected by an "S" shaped length of wire. Insert the "U's" into two straws, then bend the wire to the desired angle. (Do not use these connectors if there are toddlers around.)

You can also make connectors out of pieces of corrugated cardboard cut just large enough to fit snugly into two tubes. Bend the cardboard in the middle for angle pieces; tape the straws where necessary for added strength.

(Hint: It's easier to start with a free-form sculpture than a realistic form—just until you get the hang of the medium.)

Safety Reminder

Small Parts

Required:

- Straws
- Paper clips
- Corrugated cardboard
- Tape
- Scissors

Strawberry Baskets Forever

Safety Reminder

Small Parts

Required:

- Strawberry carton(s)
- String
- Twistems

Ah, the strawberry, that luscious fruit of summer. But what to do with those indestructible green plastic baskets? You can't recycle them, and few stores will actually take them back.

Turn 'em into toys. Strawberry cartons make great cages for toy animals and dinosaurs. When strung together with twistems and a piece of string, they also make an excellent train.

You can make a nifty crane out of the cartons, as well. Turn a carton right side up, then connect all four opposite sides with pieces of string, crossing at the middle, leaving about two inches of slack. Now attach about four feet of string at the point where the two shorter pieces of string cross (see illustration). Drape the string over a chair, and you have a crane ready and able to hoist toy cars, toy people, small blocks, and other goodies to the seat of the chair.

The baskets also make good toys for an indoor sandbox; they're great for sifting macaroni and rice. Outdoors, strawberry cartons make terrific sieves. Start a rock finding expedition and clean your soil at the same time.

Streamers

Whether you're planning a birthday party or your kids simply want to have a festive time, streamers are just what the doctor called for. And they're easy to make, too.

Simply affix two pieces of different colored crepe paper, about four feet long, to a chopstick—or to unsharpened pencils or a wooden spoon handle. Roll up the streamer, then show your kids how to wave their arms about to unravel the streamers and create dazzling color displays.

Another variation: have your kids wave two streamers, one in each hand. To make the most intriguing two-handed streamer shows, make sure that the two streamers contain different colored crepe paper.

Encourage your kids to constantly change the crepe paper and experiment with different color combinations. For added excitement, suggest that they swirl to music. (*The Stars and Stripes Forever* seems to work well as background music.)

Required:
- Unsharpened pencils, chopsticks, wooden spoons
- Rolls of crepe paper
- Tape

Styrofoam Stencils

What can you do with those infernal Styrofoam trays you get at the grocery store or with your take-out order? Clean 'em thoroughly, then make stencils.

First, take a tray and have your child draw a picture on the bottom using a ball point pen. Press the pen deep enough to make an indentation, but not deep enough to cut through the sheet. You can also trace a toy animal, truck, person, and so on. If you opt for the tracing method, you might want to first use a pencil, and then go over the lines with the pen.

Once you've etched your drawing into the Styrofoam, use a brush to apply a thin coating of tempera paint. If you apply too much paint the indentations will fill up, and you won't get a clear image when you press the Styrofoam to a piece of paper, which is the next step. Your drawings should appear as white lines on a solid color background.

As a variation, have children write their names or messages. You can also use the technique to make greeting cards or name tags.

Required:

- Styrofoam trays
- Pencil
- Pen
- Tempera paint

Sun Shadow

Here's a way to have some unusual fun in the sun.

Find a few sheets of paper that, when taped together, will be about three times your child's height in length. On a sunny morning, take the combined sheets of paper outside and weigh the corners down with a heavy object. Make sure the paper is aligned on an east-west axis, then have your child stand on the middle of one edge. Trace his or her footprints on the paper (for future positioning), then trace the outline of his shadow. At different times of the day, have your child step back into the footprints, and again trace his or her shadow.

Discuss what happens to your child's shadow—how it shortens and lengthens and moves around the paper as a result of the changing position of the sun.

You might even expand the activity by making a human sundial and marking the hours at appropriate points on the drawing. And the best thing is, it will never need winding.

Required:
- Large sheets of paper
- Pencil or crayon

Super Bubble Bath (Or, Double Bubble Trouble)

Safety Reminder

Supervise Closely

Required:

- Bubble bath solution
- Bath

No rules here—and not even much in the way of instructions. Just double (or, if you're feeling particularly frisky, triple) the normal dose of your child's favorite bubble bath. Turn on the tap and let the fun begin!

You can do this any time of day. The fun of a super bubble bath lies primarily in the potential for intricate bubble sculptures: the bubbles can be piled in clumps and clouds quite easily, then blown away in an instant. You'll probably find yourself joining in the fun as well. For our part, we can attest to the fact that a parent or two can actually construct a passable larger-than-life-size bust of Abe Lincoln (without top hat, of course) out of bubbles.

Just don't sneeze.

Super Memory

You and your child can memorize a list of items instantly—backwards, forwards, or in any order. The secret: special words that remind you of numbers—and, therefore, of the list sequence. Our words will almost learn themselves for you; each rhymes with the number it represents.

1: Sun
2: Shoe
3: Knee
4: Door
5: Beehive
6: Sticks
7: Heaven
8: Plate

Required:
• Your time

You want to remember this list: book, mailbox, horse, stamp, radio, cup, oatmeal, shirt. Use "peg" words to lock them in your mind with unlikely images. (Yours will work better than ours, but read on.)

Think about every image that follows. A *book* is burning to a crisp because the sun is inside it. You drop your shoe into the *mailbox* and must hop all day. A huge *horse* steps on your knee—ouch! You can't open your bedroom door because a big postage *stamp* has glued it shut. You turn on the *radio* and are stung by bees swarming out of the beehive inside it. You use sticks to stir a *cup* of tea. A halo (heaven) floats above your steaming bowl of *oatmeal*. You strap plates on your chest instead of a *shirt*.

What was number five? (Beehive. Bees. Radio!) What number was the cup? (Cup. Tea. Stir. Sticks. Six!) Kids love this game—and with a little practice, they can amaze you!

Tabletop Hockey for Two

Safety Reminder

Small Parts

Required:

- 8-10 hardcover books or blocks
- 2 popsicle sticks
- A small wad of paper

Most kids love those tabletop air hockey games—but they're expensive, and they burn up a lot of electricity. Here's a simple, fun alternative that doesn't cost a thing.

On a large tabletop, help your child line up enough books or blocks to form the outside walls of a mini-hockey rink. Use as many books or blocks of the same thickness as possible so that the walls will be relatively level.

Leave a space between two of the books at either end of the "rink" to form the goals. (Hardcover books work better, since the "puck" will ricochet better off a hard surface.) Then take a couple of popsicle sticks and a small wad of paper; these are your sticks and puck, respectively.

Each child can take turns shooting under a predetermined time limit.

Who needs ice?

Tambourine a la Bottlecap

Do you have a budding percussionist on your hands? Here's a great way to build a tambourine with just a couple of easy-to-find items.

All you need is a small piece of wood, four bottle caps, a hammer, and a couple of nails. (The hammer and nails are for grownup use only.)

Let your child watch as you hammer the nail through each bottlecap and into the block of wood. Make sure you don't hammer the nails in all the way—leave some room for the bottlecaps to shake around. Four seems to be the optimal quantity to use, but you can vary this if you wish. Consult your musician—he or she may have decoration ideas.

An instant rhythm section. Cha-cha, anyone?

Required:

- Small piece of wood
- 4 bottle caps (not the twist-off kind)
- Hammer (for adult use only)

Telephone

Here's a classic game for four or more you'll probably remember from your own childhood days.

Everyone sits in a circle on the floor. One person whispers a message of eight to ten words to the person immediately to his or her right. That person continues the cycle by repeating the message—or some approximation of it—to the next person in the circle. The fun comes, of course, when the final person in the circle passes along his or her rendition of the message. The final messages are generally garbled in ludicrous ways. (Younger kids, of course, tend to aid the garbling process.)

In one game we know of, the message "I sent you a big peanut butter sandwich, but you never ate it" became "Half's into pigs; be a lot better if they hand witches every breakfast." We weren't sure we really wanted to know what that last one meant.

Required:

• Your time

Ping-Pong Ball Game

Here's a do-it-yourself game that will challenge your child's dexterity—and provide great fun at the same time.

Take a piece of corrugated cardboard about two feet by a foot and a half. The side of a box will do. Cut four or five holes slightly larger than a ping-pong ball—make sure the holes are staggered across the board. (Remember that cutting is a grownup job.) Now score the four edges of the board, so you can fold up each side about an inch to create a frame. Tape the corners together so the walls hold.

Place a ping-pong ball at the bottom edge. The object is to maneuver the piece of cardboard so that the ball reaches the other side without falling into one of the holes. You can vary the difficulty of the game by using more or fewer holes, and by placing them closer or further apart. You can also tape various cardboard "bumpers" onto the board, or remove the frame so that the player has to worry about keeping the ball on the board as well as out of the holes. And for the ultimate test of skill, try playing the game with more than one ball at a time!

Required:

- Scissors (for parents' use only)
- Piece of corrugated cardboard (2' by 1½')
- Tape
- Ping-pong balls

Safety Reminder

Sharp Object

Required:

- Stiff paper
- Crayons, markers
- Straight pin
- Cardboard
- Pencil with eraser

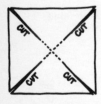

Pinwheel

To make a pinwheel, take a five or six inch square of stiff paper, then have your child decorate it with stripes, circles, lines, color blobs, and whatever else he or she wishes. Fold the decorated paper diagonally both ways. Now comes the assembly (a grownup job). Cut along the diagonal lines to within an inch of the center (see illustration). Then bend four corners down toward the middle, overlapping them so you can pin them at the center. Push a pin through the pinwheel and then through a tiny square of cardboard, then stick the assemblage into the eraser at the end of a pencil. Make sure the pin allows the pinwheel to move freely; bend it back for safety, making sure there is no sharp point exposed. (Do not give the pinwheel to toddlers or younger children.)

Save the pinwheel for a windy day, or use it with the weather ace activity (#348) to determine which way the wind is blowing. Your child can even experiment with different sizes to see which moves the fastest.

Pipe Cleaner Fishing

This is variation on Magnet Fishing (#182) requires a bit more skill. Even so, younger kids can still enjoy it, and the game can be customized to various levels of proficiency.

First, make a kid-sized fishing pole, as described in Magnet Fishing. Instead of attaching a magnet to the string, though, affix a pipe cleaner or twistem. Bend it into a hook shape. For added fun, decorate the "poles" with yarn, foil, or household materials, being careful not to obstruct them. You can also attach a key to the line as a weight or "sinker."

Make fish out of cardboard, or clip pictures of fish from magazines and paste them onto cardboard backing. Punch a hole in the front of the fish, pass a twistem through the hole, and then bend it into a loop. (You can control the skill required by increasing or decreasing the size of the loops in the fish.)

Spread the fish out onto the floor, then have your kids cast their lines from a couch or low table (either makes a great "dock" or "fishing boat").

Required:

- Yardstick or tub
- String
- Masking tape
- Pipe cleaners
- Twistems
- Cardboard

Optional

- Yarn
- Scrap foil

Pitching Ace

Parents usually do not appreciate it when children who are baseball enthusiasts want to practice their sidearm delivery in the house. Here's a way to let your kid work on his or her slider on a rainy day—and keep things more or less intact in your home.

Required:
- Socks
- Pillow
- Rubber band

Step one is getting rid of the ball—the standard baseball, that is. You'll want to replace it with a safe, disaster-resistant variety. . . namely, two socks rolled together and enclosed by a third sock that's tied shut with a rubber band. (By the way, this is a great way to put nonmatching socks to some constructive use.)

Now for the target. Home plate is unrealistic and, at sixty feet and six inches, too far away for most junior aces. A big fluffy pillow at about fifteen feet away is a good bet. Hit the pillow and it's a called strike; miss, and it's a ball.

All that's left to do is to clear away any breakables, pick up the dugout phone, call your pitcher in from the bullpen, and play ball!

Pizza Delivery

In some parts of the country, pizza delivery has always been in vogue; in others, it's making something of a comeback. Wherever you live, your child can have the fun of making and delivering homemade play modeling clay pizzas good enough to well, admire.

First, whip up a batch of play modeling clay (see #247 for a regular recipe, or #248 for supreme clay good for deep dish pizza). Give your child a rolling pin to make a thin "crust," and a cookie sheet (or paper plate) to bake the pizza in an "oven." (A cardboard box will do. Cut a big door in front and use crayons or markers to make dials, burners on top, or anything else that's stove-like.) Of course, your child will need to sprinkle the pizza with cheese—egg noodles will fit the bill.

Before baking, your child might want to add some specials—pepperoni (large buttons that cannot be swallowed), ziti noodles for variety, and anything else that looks appetizing.

Supply a pad to take orders, then just wait for that knock on your door announcing the delivery of tonight's delicacies.

Required:

- Play modeling clay
- Cardboard box
- Markers
- Paper pad

Optional:

- Large buttons
- Ziti

Place Mat Magic

This can be a nice transition from dinner to other evening activities, and may make it a little easier for your kid to bypass the tube during what is rather charitably referred to as "prime time."

Make sure you have a good stock of pictures clipped from magazines, catalogs, and newspapers on hand. After the table is set, each family member secretly selects a picture from the stockpile and hides it under his or her place mat. When dinner is over, one person gives clues about his or her picture. Whoever guesses correctly gets to chant a magic phrase and lift the person's place mat. Shazam—a picture of the mystery animal or object materializes in front of everyone's eyes! The action then passes to the next person at the table.

Another variation entails having one child set the table and select pictures for each person's place mat. This keeps the child in the limelight during the whole exercise, and forces him or her to remember what picture resides under each mat. It also gets your table set . . . well, sort of.

Required:

- Pictures clipped from magazines
- Place mats
- Sit-down dinner

Planet Mobile

Does your child have a basic understanding of the solar system? If so, he or she will enjoy having a planet mobile in his or her bedroom.

To make the mobile you'll need to create a series of papier-mache spheres (see #230). The trick is to create the spheres in the right proportions. This is easily done by using balloons as forms for the larger planets; for the rest, it's a matter of forming spheres of the right size by hand. (Do not let young children play with balloons.)

Your mobile should use the following dimensions (in inches): Mercury (3/8 of an inch); Venus (15/16); Earth (1) Mars (5/8); Jupiter (11); Saturn (10); Uranus (4); Neptune (4); Pluto (1/4). (This is also the order of the planets, from the closest to the sun outwards.) Be sure to insert a hook made out of a twistem or pipe cleaner to each sphere.

When the paper is completely dry, paint the planets. You can make snug cardboard rings for Saturn. Attach strings to the pipe cleaner or twistem loop, then tie the planets to a dowel or yardstick (or affix to hooks on the ceiling). The whole mobile is now ready for hanging or night viewing. Get out your flashlight!

Safety Reminder
Balloon

Required:

- Balloons (adult use only)
- Papier mache (#230)
- Twistems
- Tempera paint
- Cardboard
- String

Plant Map

Your child has no doubt seen many pictures of plants not found in his or her backyard. Where do they grow? Here's how to find out.

Gather a map of the United States and pictures of different plants and trees. A travel magazine can get you off to a good start, although common magazine ads are often filled with lots of good pictures. Say you find a picture of wheat fields; cut out a portion of the picture and place it in the Midwestern states. Find a cactus; plunk a cutting down in Arizona. Place palm trees in Florida or California, and so on. (You can also try this with an international map.)

In addition to pointing out where the plants grow, you might also discuss the qualities of the various plants and their fruits and vegetables: discuss the prickliness of the cactus and sweet taste of pineapple.

Of course, the more you know, the more fun your child will have. A trip to the library or local bookstore might be in order.

Required:

- World map or atlas
- Pictures of plants

Play Modeling Clay

Safety Reminder
Stove

Here's a classic hit with kids (and parents) of all ages. It's easier to mold than clay—and easier to clean up after, too.

The cooking part is for grownups only. Combine 1½ cup flour, 1 cup sugar, and 1 tablespoon powdered alum. (You can find alum in the spice aisle.) Add 1 tablespoon oil and 1 cup boiling water. Stir the mixture until cool, then knead in food coloring. (Your child will love to help out.) Once the clay is ready, give your kids cookie cutters, rolling pins, a garlic press, spatulas, or anything else that can be used for shaping and cutting. Pass out play dishes, pans, flatware, and so on, in case your children feel like throwing a party.

The stuff can last for months. Always keep the clay in airtight containers when it is not in use—otherwise it dries out. (Fortunately, you can rejuvenate even the most crusty play modeling clay by resealing it in a container after sprinkling it with water. After a day or so, take it out and knead it. It will be as good as new.)

(See #248 for a slightly more intricate recipe that produces clay with a finer texture.)

Required:

- Flour
- Sugar
- Oil
- Alum
- Container
- Cookie cutters
- Kitchen implements
- Food coloring

248

Safety
Reminder

Stove

Required:

- Flour
- Salt
- Water
- Cooking oil
- Cream of tartar
- Kitchen utensils

Play Modeling Clay (Advanced)

I f your child enjoyed the easy play modeling clay recipe (#247), here's a more challenging formula that yields firmer clay with a nicer texture. The advanced recipe doesn't require a Ph.D. in chemistry, but you will need strong arms and wrists.

In a saucepan, blend together 3 cups flour, 1½ cups salt, 3 cups of water, 2 tablespoons cooking oil, 1 tablespoon cream of tartar, and a few drops of food coloring. Cook the mixture slowly, (an adult job) stirring constantly until the clay comes away from the side of the pan and you can no longer move the spoon (that's where the muscles come in). Remove the mixture from the pan; when cool, knead it for 3-4 minutes until smooth, and you're ready for action.

Pass out the play modeling clay to your kids, and provide them with a rolling pin, cookie cutters, jar tops (to cut out circular pieces) and various kitchen utensils that can be used to shape the clay. A garlic press can also produce fun and interesting patterns.

Keep the play modeling clay in tightly sealed containers. If it does dry out, add a few drops of oil or water, and you'll give it a new lease on life.

Play Office

If you or your spouse work in an office setting, this activity will naturally appeal to your child. It involves creating a junior office.

First, you'll need a desk. If you have a kid-sized table, place a couple of shoe boxes at the back edge. These can be in- or out-trays. If you don't have a table, an upright sturdy cardboard box will do. Save up a few days worth of junk mail—this could be important correspondence for your junior executive—and place it in the in and out trays.

Provide crayons, markers, scratch paper, an old checkbook, tape, a calculator, an appointment book, and anything else that can be safely used by your budding executive.

Want to go higher tech? Make a computer out of a cardboard box. Draw a screen with markers or crayons, cut a slot at the bottom (your disk drive), then make up some cardboard diskettes. For a keyboard, find a piece of cardboard about two feet long and eight inches wide; draw in keys. Anything else? A telephone, of course. Now stop by for some business talk. Maybe even a power lunch.

Required:

- Small table or cardboard box
- Junk mail
- Crayons, markers
- Toy telephone
- Shoe boxes
- Office paraphernalia

Playroom Observatory

This simple activity simulates the experience of viewing the moon and planets through a real telescope.

You'll need a mailing tube at least two inches in diameter (art supply and stationery stores usually carry them). Find a large box (at least two and a half feet long) that can stand on one end. Cut a hole about two inches from the top of one side, then another eight inches down on the opposite side. (Remember: cutting is a grownup job.) The holes should each be just big enough to snugly hold the tube. This is the "tripod" (see illustration).

Next, draw or affix small magazine pictures of the planets, the moon, comets, etc. on squares of paper. (And you wondered what you were saving those back issues of *National Geographic* for.) Aim the telescope towards a window during the day, or towards a lampshade at night (*not* a bare bulb). Hold a drawing or photo over the open end, and have your child sit and look through the telescope. Ask him or her to describe what's in the "sky", then move on to another card (you might want to read some basic astronomy so you can provide some impressive facts).

Of course, you can save a few surprise drawings and photos for last—like a flying saucer piloted by your child!

Required:
- Mailing tube at least 2 inches in diameter
- Box at least two and a half feet long
- Magazines for clipping
- Paper
- Pens, crayons

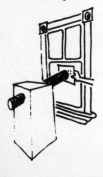

Pop Stick Architecture

Would you throw out a perfectly good piece of wood? Then why toss out popsicle sticks? They make excellent building materials, as you'll see in this activity.

The first part of the activity is a thankless job requiring someone who will spend the time eating popsicles to generate a supply of sticks. When that mission is accomplished, it's time to put the sticks to work.

Your child can use nontoxic glue to build houses, train stations, even boats or submarines. The only limit is his or her own imagination—although you can help by offering some initial hints on what makes for good solid construction. Upside-down steeples, we have found, are not reliable edifices. (For complex structures, it might be best to let "subassemblies" dry thoroughly before moving on.)

Many children decide to go for the abstract when it comes to popsicle stick construction, and that's okay, too. Even junior Frank Lloyd Wrights have to start somewhere.

Required:
- Popsicle sticks
- Nontoxic glue

Portrait Painter

With this activity, you can save a bundle on a family portrait and provide great fun for your child, too.

Make an easel by placing a stiff piece of cardboard on the back of a chair. (You may want to cover it first.) Provide your child with a large sheet of paper, crayons, markers, or paint. Affix the paper to the cardboard with tape. A smock and special painter's hat (see Paper Hats, #226), will complete the accoutrements.

Required:

- Large sheets of paper
- Crayons, markers, or paints
- Large sheets of posterboard or cardboard
- Dropcloth

Now assemble the family, and allow your child to decide what people should wear and where they should stand or sit. (This can lead to some wild-looking group scenes.) For individual portraits, let the child decide on the pose, facial expression, and so on.

When your child is done painting, make frames from large sheets of cardboard or posterboard; you might have to tape or glue the paintings to a sheet of cardboard to keep them from bending. Write the date and the subjects on the backs of the masterpieces—your kids will appreciate it when they're adults.

Today, the family room. Tomorrow, the Louvre.

Post Office

Most kids find the post office fascinating. If your young child has never been to one, you might want to do a quick field trip before trying this activity.

An open-backed chair makes the simplest postal window; you can get more elaborate with a large cardboard box. Either way, provide the postal clerk with a kitchen or bathroom scale to weigh the mail. A sponge soaked with non-toxic ink and rubber stamp (or a homemade stamper—see #255) will also be fun.

Speaking of stamps, your kids can decorate postage stamp-sized pieces of paper and affix double-stick tape to the backs. Now the P.O. will be ready for business.

Bring in junk mail envelopes, used envelopes, small parcels (food boxes wrapped in kraft paper from bags), and similar items. For older kids, provide a map of the U.S. or world, and let them decide the appropriate postage based on distance. (This is a good opportunity to teach a little geography.) Younger kids will probably tell you that all the postage is the same. Just grin and pay up.

(See also: Philately Fun, #234.)

Required:
- Envelopes and boxes
- Paper
- Crayons or markers
- Tape (double stick)

Optional:
- Scale
- Small boxes

Potato Heads

Making a potato head is an age-old activity that still adds up to great fun for kids.

Take a large baking potato and clean it up with a scrub brush. Now supply your child with clay or Play-Doh to make a nose, a mouth and ears. Pieces of felt can also be used to make eyes, a mouth, a mustache or beard. Use short lengths of toothpicks (cut them for your child and supervise their use) to affix the clay, paper, and felt to the potato. An old plastic scrub pad makes for a good shock of hair. If you purchase several potatoes, you and your child can make a whole potato head family. The girl potato heads might enjoy a ribbon or bow.

Now then, how about a nice defrocked baked potato or two for dinner?

Required:

- Baking potatoes
- Clay or Play-Doh
- Colored paper
- Felt
- Toothpicks
- Ribbons or bows
- Scrub brush

Potato Print Shop

Safety Reminder

Supervise Closely

Believe it or not, all you need to start a home print shop is a bag of potatoes and a few common household items.

First, slice a potato lengthwise. Give your child a potato half for each letter in his or her first name, and a felt pen. Tell him or her to draw one letter BACK-WARDS on the inside of each potato half. (You may have to help out here, depending on the age of the child.)

The next step is strictly for you. With an X-acto or sharp knife, strip away the potato surrounding the letter, down to a depth of a quarter of an inch or so. When you're done, you should have the organic equivalent of a rubber stamp.

Next, pour some thick tempera paint in a shallow container. Have your child dip the raised letter in the paint, then press it on paper. Voila! Instant print. Do the same with the remaining letters, and your child will have printed his or her name.

Of course, your child can draw just about anything on the potatoes, depending on his or her skills (and your skill with the knife). Abstract patterns work fine, too.

We have it on reliable authority that Gutenberg's mother started him out with this activity.

Required:

- Large potatoes
- Felt-tip pen
- X-acto or sharp knife
- Tempera paint
- Paper

Potato Sack Race

Safety Reminder

Supervise Closely

Required:

• Old pillow cases

Optional:

• Timer
• Couch pillows

Most of us don't have access to authentic burlap potato sacks, so pillow cases will have to do if you plan to set up an old-fashioned potato sack race. (Use cases that can be sacrificed.) Each child simply steps into the pillow case with both feet, pulls the case as high as he or she can, holds the edges with both hands, then starts jumping towards a finish line. This is best done outdoors in a soft grassy area. Indoors, select a carpeted room and move all furniture to the side. Close off steps—the sacks don't make good parachutes. Monitor the proceedings closely for safety.

You can greatly enhance the game by coming up with zany rules. For example, the first one to actually cross the finish line *before* a timer goes off loses. Or, every hopper must sing a certain song three times before crossing the line. Try setting up an obstacle course involving couch pillows indoors, or a sprinkler outdoors.

(Adult supervision is required for this activity.)

Pots and Pans

Here's an activity that uses the giant dice you created in activity #117.

Mark each face of one of the dice with colors. Arrange a half-dozen pots and pans on the floor. Put a piece of colored paper in the bottom of each pot or pan, or tape a piece of colored paper to the side, so that each pot matches one of the colors on the dice.

Now you and your child can take turns rolling the die. Whatever color shows up, try to throw a bean bag or foam ball into the container with the matching color (see #19 for instructions on how to make a bean bag).

As a variation, designate one of the sides of the die as a "wild card", so you and your child can throw the bean bag or ball into any of the containers. Older children can invent their own scoring systems.

To increase the challenge, you may want to arrange the pots and pans so that the smallest are closest, and the largest are farthest away. Of course, your child can simply arrange the pots and pans randomly if that seems most appropriate.

Required:

- Giant dice
- Pots and pans
- Colored paper
- Bean bag or foam ball

Safety Reminder

Stove

Required:

- 1 package of yeast
- Sugar
- Salt
- Egg
- Flour
- Coarse salt

Pretzel Mania

Kids love to make things in the kitchen, especially goodies that their parents later proclaim to be edible. This recipe for making pretzels is ideal for children of all ages.

Soften a package of yeast in 1½ cups lukewarm water. Add 3/4 teaspoons salt and 1½ teaspoons sugar. Mix in 4 cups flour, and knead the mixture into a soft, smooth dough. Cut the dough into small pieces. Here's where the sculpting fun begins. Encourage your kids to roll and mold the pretzel dough into alphabet letters (spelling their names, if possible), animal outlines, building outlines, jungle-gym sculptures, wild designs, or whatever else catches their fancy. In another bowl, beat an egg; then brush the contents onto the pretzel shapes. If you use salt, sprinkle a dash of salt (preferably coarse grain) on each pretzel.

The cooking part is for grownups only. Bake the pretzels at 425 degrees for 15 minutes, or until golden brown. Once the pretzels have cooled, you and your kids can initiate the last and most important step: eating them.

Quarter Journeys (Or, Where to Go From Here?)

Safety Reminder

Great Outdoors

Required:

• Quarter

This is a wonderful activity when you have a little time and the weather's fine.

Perhaps you've taken journeys around your neighborhood, but we'll bet you've never taken one like this before. As you and your kids step out of the front door of your home, one of you takes out a quarter and flips it. If it comes up heads, begin your journey by turning left; if it comes up tails, turn right.

The "where-on-earth-will-we-end-up" feeling is great fun—and as long as you accompany your children on these quarter journeys, you'll never get lost. Right?

Just don't lose the quarter.

Rainbow Art

This activity requires a full-length black or dark blue crayon, as well as any number of other crayons of any color.

Provide sheets of paper (recycle the unused backs of paper from your workplace.) Have your child use different colored crayons to make dense streaks or bands of color, one atop the other. Or use the crayons to make contiguous color patches. Either way, your child should finish by applying a dense layer of black or blue crayon that covers the sheet completely—so the colors are hardly visible.

Now show your child how to "draw" with a spoon handle, gently peeling off the top layer to expose the underlying colors. He or she can also draw or trace a toy animal, doll, car, or other design on the black or blue layer, then use the spoon end to remove the black or blue crayon that remains inside the outline.

The result: rainbow art fit for the Met.

Required:
- Paper
- Crayons

Read *Me* a Story

Y ou spend enough time reading books for your child. How about turning the tables and having your child read aloud for your benefit?

This activity is actually most fun with kids who *can't* read. Hand them a favorite storybook, let them open it to page one, and sit back. You'll find they spend a great deal of time perfecting the inflections and tones necessary to reach the key words in the story, and will "fill in" the parts in between quite adequately.

Don't be too picky about your child's improvisations. Maybe "Once upon a time the big thing was talking to another late thing and the doggie FOUND IT" isn't a classically correct mode of narration—but if you get the idea, it still counts. (Some of the younger readers will even make up new words for you!)

Now: sit up and pay attention. And share the covers.

Required:
• Storybook

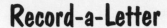

Record-a-Letter

Required:

• Cassette recorder

• Mailing materials

Relatives who live far away are usually hungry for news about (and from) the children in the family. The traditional route to solving this problem is to have the child write a letter—and usually a pretty uninspiring one: "Dear Grandma How are you I am fine Love Sarah."

This activity is more fun for the child and the relative. Sit down with a cassette tape recorder and have your child do the following:

Read a favorite story. Prereaders can do a decent—and very entertaining—imitation of reading. You can provide background music by humming or singing if you like.

Describe his or her room. Spend extra time on favorite projects, new pictures, or gifts from the relative in question.

Talk about the next major holiday. If it is to include a family gathering with the relative, so much the better.

Sing a favorite song. You can provide percussion effects in the background with a wooden spoon and an oatmeal container.

Your child can help you stamp and mail the cassette. Prepare yourself for a very enthusiastic response!

Restaurateur

Our son serves up a mean Play-Doh dinner, so we encouraged him to go public with it. The result: "Noah's Place," our local playroom cafe.

Your child can set up his or her own bistro, too. All you need to provide is a set of plastic dishes and cutlery (use safe utensils with no sharp points or edges), some empty spice and food boxes, and Play-Doh or clay.

You can set up a special table—or let your kids serve you at your kitchen table. You and your spouse can dress up (or down) for the occasion; gauge the ambiance of the place before asking to be seated for dinner. Groups of kids can take turns being chef and waiter/waitresses.

One of the most fascinating parts of this activity will be making the menus. Younger kids can use pictures of food from magazines, glue them on a large piece of paper, and establish prices (don't be surprised if everything costs the same). You can then write in the names of the foods. Older kids might want to write up their own fanciful fare. Roasted socks with banana sauce, anyone?

Required:

- Safe, unbreakable plates and cutlery
- Play-Doh or clay
- Food boxes/containers
- Large piece of paper or poster board
- Crayons and markers
- Magazines/pictures of food

Reverse Tic-Tac-Toe (Or, Three *Not* in a Row)

Required:
- Paper
- Pencils

Here's a new twist on an old classic your kids are sure to enjoy.

In reverse tic-tac-toe, the object is *not* to get three in a row. It's a refreshing change, and one that requires a little new thinking for those of us who are used to the old game. (Kids adapt to it with remarkable ease, however.)

Other than the change in the point of the game, there is only one rule change: The person who goes first *must* take the center square. This puts that player at a slight disadvantage for the current game—it all evens out after a couple of matches. (You'll probably remember that the center square was the most coveted spot in regular tic-tac-toe.) Players alternate taking the first turn.

Try it yourself—it's a fascinating exercise in reverse thinking!

Reverse Writing

Sure, your older kid can write his or her name in the normal way. But what about in reverse?

Reverse writing doesn't affect some symmetrical letters (such as A, H, or M), but it does force you to take a new approach with nonsymmetrical ones (such as J, Z, or R). And, of course, the sequence of the letters must be backwards, too. Have your child try writing a sentence the normal way, then in reverse—without checking it in the mirror halfway through! The mirror is only for use in decoding completed messages. (Besides, it's interesting to see which words or letters didn't quite make it into reverse-writing.)

Hold this book up to a mirror to decode the following reverse message; it will help get your child started.

Required:

- Paper
- Pen or pencil

S2IHT ᗡA𐐬Я UOY NAƆ

Rhyming Game

Want to encourage the budding poet in your child? Try this activity.

Select a common word, then ask your child to think of as many rhymes to that word as possible. (This is an excellent game for younger children developing language skills.) Following is a list of sample rhymes for the word "critter"; it will give you an idea of the potential play value.

Required:

• Your time only

bitter
fitter
fritter
glitter
jitter
knitter
quitter
skitter
twitter

(And some more advanced samples . . .)

babysitter
counterfeiter
rail-splitter
steamfitter
transmitter

Rice Maracas

Children love noise, especially when they're making it. Here's a fun activity that allows your child to make noise that will help teach the fundamentals of rhythm.

Take two paper cups of equal size and stand them side-by-side. Fill one of the cups approximately 1/4 to 1/2 full with uncooked rice. Place the empty cup on top of the full one so that the rims are aligned. When the cups are in place, secure them by wrapping tape around the rims two or three times. Now you and your child are ready to start a mambo band with your rice maracas.

You might want to start by showing your child how to get a variety of sounds and rhythms out of the maraca simply by slowing down or speeding up the shaking motion. After your child is comfortable with this, you could make a maraca for each hand and show how to make music by shaking the instruments at different speeds.

One, two, three—rhumba!

Required:
- Rice
- Paper cups
- Tape

Roman Numerals

Does your child know how to write numbers using Roman numerals? There are only a few basic symbols (I=1, V=5, X=10, L=50, C=100, M=1,000) and only two rules: putting a number of lesser value before one of greater value *decreases* the amount of the second letter by the amount of the first; putting a number of lesser value after one of greater value *increases* the value of the first by the amount of the second. Have your child take a look at the following sample rundown of numbers, then try a few on his or her own. (The system does take some getting used to; people are often tempted to write 9 as VIIII—but as you can see, there is no such animal.)

Required:

• Your time only

1=I	40=XL
2=II	50=L
3=III	77=LXXVII
4=IV	94=XCIV
5=V	100=C
6=VI	1,776=MDCCLXXVI
7=VII	(1000+500+200+50+20+5+1)
8=VIII	1,999=MCMXCIX
9=IX	(1000+[1000–100]
10=X	+[100–10]+[10–1])

Now: what would be the Roman numerals for . . .

300	1,199
99	1,552
1,001	

The Root Stuff

With this activity, you can show your kids the wondrous growth of roots right on your kitchen counter.

Take a potato and insert three toothpicks into the center of the potato on three sides (see illustration). Use the toothpicks to support the potato over a glass filled with water. About half the potato should be immersed. In a week or so, the potato will begin to root into the glass. Shoots will also grow into the air from the dry side. You can also do this with an avocado pit. Just aim the pointed side of the pit upwards. Roots will grow downward, and a central shoot and leaves will grow upward— nature in miniature!

Finally, you can grow roots and a shoot with half a pineapple—just lop off the top and immerse the bottom in a bowl of water. (You'll need a larger bowl and stronger support system).

Whatever vegetable or fruit you choose, use the activity to explain how roots absorb water for the plant and anchor it in the ground. But don't get too hung up on the educational aspect— rooted potatoes, avocados, and pineapples are simply neat to look at, too.

Required:

- Potato
- 3 toothpicks
- Glass

Optional:

- Avocado pit
- Pineapple

Rub-a-Leaf

Nature provides an abundant variety of arts and crafts supplies. Take the common leaf. In autumn, your kids can press leaves in a book between pieces of wax paper, (see #172) then use them to make collages.

But you don't have to wait until leaves turn color and fall to the ground before using them in your home art activities. Pluck a few healthy leaves, and place them under a piece of tissue paper or thin writing paper. Then rub the paper with a crayon—this will reveal the leaf's outlines, stem (or petiole) and veins.

Leaf rubbings are great to make and look at, but they also serve as a means of learning about different kinds of trees. If you don't know an oak or maple from a *liriodendron tulipifera* (tulip tree), you may want to obtain a tree identification guide.

You can also use the leaf rubbings to teach a little plant physiology, pointing out that the veins in the leaf, like the blood vessels in our bodies, carry the nutrients that enable the plant to live.

Finally, consider making a scrap book of leaf rubbings from trees in your area. This is another way to remind your kids about the common bonds they share with their neighbors.

Required:
- Wax paper
- Fresh leaves
- Tissue or thin paper
- Crayons

Optional:
- Tree identification guide

Rubber Band Jump Rope

Safety Reminder

Supervise Closely

Required:
• Rubber bands

Most households have a box, drawer, or plastic bag that holds the spare rubber bands that come with newspapers, groceries, and other products. Pick out the heaviest of the bunch and knot them together to form a long strand (the longer the better!). Bear in mind that the thin rubber bands snap easily; stick with fat ones.

Now you're ready for action. Rubber band ropes make for great jumping for two or more; try tying one end to a door handle if you haven't got a threesome. How did those playground rhymes go? The action doesn't stop there. You can have your own limbo contests (remember that how-low-can-you-go game?) or high jump competitions using the rope.

This toy is simple, free, responsible, and (most of all) fun—what more could you ask for?

(Parental supervision is recommended with this activity; the jump rope can snap back at you. Younger children should not play with rubber bands, as they present a choking hazard.)

Rule for the Day

Can your child go a full day without using the word "yes"? Or sitting on the couch? Or using any word beginning with the letter W?

Who knows; it's fun just to try. Following are some more silly rules. See if your child can follow them from sunup to sundown.

Required:

• Your time

Always enter the kitchen hopping for three steps.

Address siblings by their full name.

Open all doors with left hand.

Say the alphabet before sitting down anywhere.

Snap fingers each time own name is mentioned.

Walk with book on head for five minutes at least six times.

Count backwards from 10 each time a mirror is passed.

Do ten jumping jacks every time telephone rings.

Avoid using words "I" or "me" (very difficult)!

At the conclusion of such Herculean labors, you may want to include a rule of your own: all participants are entitled to a homemade treat!

Old-Fashioned Quill Writing

A lot of people today think computers and word processors have spoiled us—and left penmanship an art of the past. But if you can get your hands on a chicken feather (or, better still, a turkey feather), you can take your child back to a bygone era, when maybe, just maybe, writing was more a matter of deliberate, reasoned placement of words and thoughts than it is today.

Take the feather and cut the tip at a slant before giving it to your child. Then provide a dish of tempera paint thinned with a bit of water. A little explanation will be in order, of course; explain that this is how many people once wrote (and, in some other cultures, still do). Let your child practice with some scrap paper first—it will take a few tries to learn to load the quill correctly. When your child has the hang of it, you might provide a nice piece of homemade stationery for that special correspondence to a favorite relative. (See Old-Fashioned Papermaking, #214.) Be sure to let the writing dry before you fold and/or mail it.

Required:

- Chicken or turkey feather
- Tempera paint (thinned)
- Paper

One-Sided Paper (Or, The Mobius Strip)

Required:

- Paper
- Safety scissors
- Tape

A one-sided sheet of paper? Impossible! Or is it?

Meet the Mobius strip, an ingenious little arrangement that comes as close to being one-sided as anything in this dimension. As your child watches, cut a long strip of paper from a standard sheet.

We'll call one side of this strip A, the other B. To make an ordinary loop, you'd tape the ends of the strip together. With a Mobius strip, you twist one end so A meets B, then tape at the connection. Follow the surface; you'll find the form really does have only one side.

Cut it down the middle of the strip and you'll get another, larger Mobius strip, with *two* twists. Cut it again and you'll get two strips linked together!

Oobleck

Imagine the perfect play glop—non-toxic, easy to make, easy to clean, and hours of fun. Look no further than your pantry. All you have to do is mix cornstarch and water in the right proportions. The resulting "oobleck" is a unique play material; the surface is hard and crusty, but scoop it up and it's fluid enough to pass through a strainer. As your kids mush the oobleck between their fingers, it continually changes from hard to semi-liquid, almost magically.

To make your own oobleck, simply add two parts cornstarch and one part water in a tub or dishpan. Stir the mixture until it begins to thicken.

Now let the rumpus begin. Supply your kids with spoons, plastic shovels, funnels or various kitchen utensils (you can clean them with soap and water afterwards). To create unusual effects, let your kids swirl in a teaspoon or two of different food colorings. Whatever variations you try, the oobleck will endlessly transform in shape and texture, providing non-stop entertainment.

Required:
- Cornstarch
- Water
- Tub or dishpan

Optional:
- Food coloring
- Kitchen utensils

Organic Mobile

As we have seen elsewhere in this book, nature is the ultimate arts and crafts supply center. This activity entails collecting common natural items and making a mobile.

Have your child look for cones, acorns, large seed husks, interesting twigs, or, at the beach, pieces of driftwood or small sea shells. Anything that won't rot is a candidate for the mobile. Collect several small but sturdy branches for supporting rods, as well.

After your search, sort your collection on a table and experiment with various layouts. The mobile can hang from one branch or from several small branches (as in the illustration). In any case, let your child do the arranging; if the mobile looks like it may have balance problems, suggest alternative arrangements.

Once the layout is settled, tie the objects to the strings whenever possible; use nontoxic white glue when you can't. Let the glue dry overnight before affixing the strings to the branches. If you're creating a multi-level mobile with several different branches, you might want to use fishing line—but handle this part of the job yourself, as fishing line is not meant to be used by children.

Required:

- Acorns, cones, and other natural objects
- String
- Glue

Orienteering

H ere are some games that make it easy for your child to learn to distinguish north from south and east from west.

The first job is yours; you'll first have to figure out your home's north-south alignment, if you don't know it already. Checking a local map is one way; looking at your shadow at 12:00 noon is another (it points north at that time). Aim your child to the north, then show that south is opposite from north, east is to the right of north, and west is opposite from east. Now ask your child to point in the various directions. Reverse the game, making sure to intentionally flub a few, just to make sure your child has the idea.

Once the basic idea is clear, try giving instructions like: "Walk two steps north; now jump three times to the east; now walk backwards five steps to the west; now face south," and so on. You can also turn this into a treasure hunt by making a map based on steps and directions.

Finally, spend a sunset with your child and ask which way the sun went down. Then see if he or she can figure out the direction in which it rises—without having to call for a family outing at five in the morning.

Required:
• Your time only

Optional:
• Local map

Our Favorite Mud Pies

Summer isn't official in our house till our son makes his first mud pie. His recipes are simple; your child can adapt them. Just supply a bucket or watering can, a small shovel or stick for stirring, and a little patch of your garden or yard. The rest will come naturally.

Once your child's mixture achieves the desired texture, the fun can begin. Here are some of our household favorites.

Try classic mud pies—supply a baking tin (an aluminum foil pie tin headed for the recycling bin is a good choice), scoop in the mud pie filling, and let it stand in the sun until dry and ready to serve. Small rocks, twigs, or a handful of grass can make a nice garnish. Then there's mud taco chips. Pour a thin pie so it will crack upon drying and naturally break into pieces. How about mud pie lasagna or meat loaf? Excellent fare for those warm summer nights.

And if your child isn't sure what to serve? Well, you can never go wrong with all-American mud pie burgers and fries. . .

Required:

- Soil
- Water
- Buckets
- Shovel
- Pan

Palindromes

Palindromes are words or phrases that read the same backwards and forwards.

Your older kids will enjoy looking at the following classic palindromes and proving their remarkable qualities to themselves. After a while, you can help your children come up with a few palindromes of their own.

Required:
• Your time

Madam, I'm Adam. (Supposedly the first words ever spoken by humans, although how this sentence could have been used before the development of English remains a mystery.)

A man, a plan, a canal—Panama! (Teddy Roosevelt knew the way to immortality: have someone write a palindrome about you.)

Able was I, ere I saw Elba. (Napoleon this time. Might take some explaining.)

Not so, Boston. (Composed after the infamous 1986 World Series.)

He won a Toyota now, eh? (Now, how about constructing a palindrome around the words "Volkswagen" and "fährvergnügen"?)

Paper Airplanes

Making a paper airplane is a snap—if you know the right folds. Just follow the illustrations when you make your own. First, fold a piece of paper in half, then fold down the corners (see Figure A). Fold the paper in half again, as shown in Figure B, then fold each side down to the center as shown in Figure C. Fold down the sides again as shown in Figure D—you've just made the wings, which should be about 4 to 5 inches across at the widest point. Put a small piece of tape across the top of the wings to keep them from separating.

Once your child decorates the plane, the craft will be ready for its first trans-living-room flight.

Required:

- Piece of paper
- Tape

Optional:

- Crayons or markers

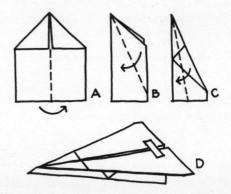

Paper Baskets

Here's a generic "blueprint" for making paper baskets that can be used in a variety of activities.

Cut a square piece of paper, 6 inches to a side. Fold in 1½" on all four sides. Make a cut at each corner, as shown in illustration (a). You can tape, glue, or staple the sides and form the bottom of a basket. Now cut a strip 3/4 of an inch wide and 8 inches long. Affix the strip to opposite sides. (You can make baskets any size, and use stiffer material, but this is an easy way to get started.)

Your child can decorate the basket with crayons or markers (easier done before you make the folds) or with tempera paint. Also, you can make slits in the bottom of the basket and insert strips of colored paper to create a "weave" effect.

Your basket making activities are limited only by the paper in your house!

Required:

- Paper or thin cardboard
- Tape, glue, or stapler
- Crayons, markers, or tempera paint

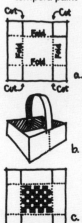

Paper Chains

You probably remember these from grammar school. Paper chains are the construction-paper links that make for festive decorations at holiday time—or anytime your child wants.

Cut a number of small strips of construction paper about six inches long and one inch wide. (Use safety scissors.) The strips should be uniform in size, but of different colors. (Monochromatic chains are boring.)

Connect the two ends of the strips with a small piece of transparent tape. Then link the next one inside it and connect it in the same fashion. Repeat . . . and repeat . . . and repeat. Deck the halls with links of construction paper!

Beware: this is addictive.

Required:

- Construction paper
- Safety scissors
- Adhesive tape

Paper Cutting

If you have a stack of scrap paper, you also have the potential for endless fun at your fingertips. All you need is a pair of scissors to begin some high art paper cutting. Here are some techniques.

The simplest activity is to take a piece of paper and fold it in quarters or eighths. With your scissors, cut out small triangles or make little nicks along the edges. (Children should only use safety scissors). Unfold the paper, and you'll have a sheet with intricate patterns. Your child can decorate the paper around the patterns, or you can place the cut-out sheet over a piece of colored paper or foil to create a colorful piece of art.

Alternatively, you can trace a bowl or plate, cut it out, then fold it and cut shapes and triangles along the edges. You can then use the same decorating methods just described.

Hang the finished paper cutouts in your family gallery or tape them to a window. Or, attach strings and dangle them from a stick or tube to make an instant mobile for your family room or child's bedroom.

Required:
- Scrap paper
- Safety scissors

Optional:
- Scrap foil or wrapping paper
- Tape
- String
- Hanger

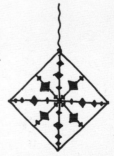

Paper Hats

Required:

- Piece of newspaper

Paper hats are are just plain fun to wear. They're also pretty inexpensive, and the raw materials are plentiful. The hats can be used with many of the activities in this book that call for costumes.

For a large adult hat, take a single full sheet of newspaper, crease it along the fold line, then fold down corners to the center line as shown in illustration (a). Next, separate the 1½-inch edges remaining at the bottom, and fold up to each side. Open the hat and you're ready to boogie.

For a child's hat, open an adult size hat as if you were going to wear it. Then collapse the hat, bringing the front and back points together to form a square—see illustration (b). Separate the two points and fold each up to the top point. Crease well and open to wear, then secure with a piece of tape at the top if necessary.

For a firefighter's hat, fold only one of the points up to the top. Open the hat, wearing the long side to the back. Now *that's* a hat!

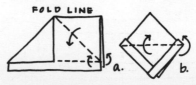

Paper Helicopters

Safety Reminder
Small Parts

I f you don't have any maple trees near your house that can supply you with seedling whirligigs, you can make your own helicopters out of paper to imitate nature.

Cut a strip of regular-weight paper 2 inches x 8½ inches. (Remember that cutting is a grownup activity.) Make the three cuts indicated by the solid bars in illustration (a). Make cut A to form the blades of the helicopter. Fold at the dotted line, one blade towards you and the other away from you. Make cuts B and C to allow you to fold the other end of the strip into thirds, lengthwise. Then fold up the bottom by ½" or so twice, and secure with a large paper clip for added weight. See illustration (b), and keep paper clips out of young children's hands.

Decorate the blades to make whirls of color, then drop the helicopter and watch it twirl!

Required:

- Piece of paper
- Large paper clip
- Scissors (for adult use only)

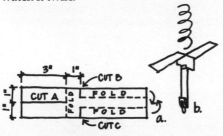

Paper Plate Masks

The excitement of dressing up for Halloween need not come only once a year. A paper plate and some decorating materials can provide plenty of fun any day of the week.

It's easy to make a paper plate mask. Cut out the eye holes (remembering that cutting is a grownup job), then let your child draw in the features for the mask with crayons and markers. If you want to get a bit fancier, use materials like cotton balls or yarn to make hair or beards, pipe cleaners to make whiskers, or antennae, and sand paper or emery boards to make eyebrows and mustaches. You can also cut out ears, horns and other features from cardboard and glue them on—the possibilities are almost limitless!

Finally, affix a safe handle to the bottom of the mask's interior. A chopstick, a spoon, a paper towel tube, or a cardboard tube from a coat hanger will do. Your child is now ready to play. With enough kids and a sufficient stock of paper plates, you might end up with a one-of-a-kind zoo.

Required:

- Paper plates
- Crayons or markers
- Cotton balls or yarn
- Sandpaper or pipe cleaners
- Cardboard tube or chopstick

Paper, Scissors, Rock

Here's a game for two that has doubled as an emergency conflict-resolver among kids for decades. Once your kids try it, it's a good bet they'll become addicted . . . and they may even enjoy deciding who goes first, who gets what, what happens next, and so on.

The whole game is based on the three hand positions shown in the illustration—paper, scissors, and rock, respectively. Each position is superior to one of the others and inferior to the remaining one. Put more simply, paper always covers rock; rock always dulls scissors; scissors always cut paper.

Now then. Suppose the issue is who's going to go first at a certain board game. The two players each make fists, pump hands twice, and on the third pump show one of the three hand positions. Conflict resolved! (You might want to try this at work the next time someone asks you for something when you're under a tight deadline.)

Paper, Scissors, Rock is great as a game for its own sake, too.

Required:
• Your time

**Safety
Reminder**

Plastic Wrap

Required:

- Newspaper
- Flour
- Water
- Mixing bowl
- Tempera paints
- Other materials
  for form

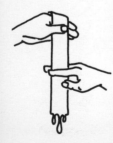

Papier-Mache

It's nothing short of amazing what you can do with some old newspapers, a little flour, and some water. Put them all together, and it's called papier-mache; here's the basic technique.

Tear a good quantity of long newspaper strips, about one to two inches wide. Then find (or make) a form; a wide cardboard tube can be used to make a tunnel, and a cardboard box is a good form for a building. You can also make forms out of wood and other materials. As you choose your shapes, remember that you will have to remove the form when your project is complete, so cover well with plastic beforehand. (This is a grownup job.)

In a mixing bowl, combine water and flour until you have a paste that's thin enough to coat the paper strips. Experiment with small quantities of the mixture first; if it's too thin, the paper will turn into soggy mush. Dip the paper into the paste; show your child how to use two fingers as a squeegee to prepare the strips. Wrap the lightly coated paper around the form, crisscrossing to make overlapping layers. When the creation is finished, place it in a warm, dry area. Once it is completely dry, remove the form and provide your child with tempera paints to decorate it.

Parachutes

You can make a simple parachute that will mesmerize your child as it drifts back to earth. Here's how.

Start with a piece of white cloth or a handkerchief and four strings *of equal length*. (The string length is very important). Before making the parachute, encourage your child to decorate the material with markers or water-based fabric paint. These are available through most arts and crafts stores; be sure to supervise all use of paint closely.

Once the decorations are done and the fabric is dry, tie the strings to the corners of the parachute. Then take the loose ends and attach them to a key chain ring or a loop made from a pipe cleaner or twistem. Finally, run a separate string from the loop to a small lightweight toy or doll.

Drop the parachute from a chair or down a stairwell. Your child can catch the parachute in midair or direct it to a "landing site" or target. If you attach a small cardboard box to the strings instead of a toy, your child can "test" various objects to see which reach the ground the fastest.

Safety Reminder

Small Parts

Required:

- Square piece of material or handkerchief
- String
- Small toy
- Key ring, pipe cleaner, or twistem
- Markers or water-based fabric paint

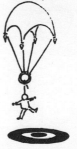

Parental ESP

This game will amaze your kids, and give you a few thrills, too. All it requires is two conspiring adults—a "Pointer" and a "Guesser."

The Guesser leaves the room; a child picks an object. The Guesser then returns and the Pointer motions to various objects, one by one, asking the Guesser if that is indeed the object that the child has chosen.

Unbeknownst to the child, the Guesser and the Pointer have previously agreed that the object the child has chosen will always follow another agreed-upon object in the room—say, the sofa. Thus, the Guesser always knows that as the Pointer indicates objects in the room, one by one, the object *after* the sofa will be the one that the child has chosen. (In the event that your child selects the telltale object, the Pointer and Guesser should develop a code, like two blinks, and adjust accordingly.)

Do it right, and your kids will think you're psychic. Just be sure to share the secret at some point so your child and a cohort can astonish their friends.

Pen Pals

Most children enjoy receiving and sending mail. Here's how you can set up your own correspondence system.

First, tell a relative or the parents of one of your child's friends that you'd like to start a pen pal arrangement. The only rule: each party should respond within five days. If everyone is game, get things rolling by taking some dictation from your child (unless he or she can read and write). The letter might describe some special events that have recently taken place—a visit to the playground, a vacation, something in school, etc. The letter might contain more information about life in the household and community.

Let your child sign the letter, seal it into an envelope, and affix the stamp. Walk together to the mail box, and let your child mail the letter. When the response arrives the following week, you'll have another activity ready to go. Note: you can also set up "household pen pals" between siblings, or between parent and child. And you'll save on stamps.

Required:
- Paper
- Envelopes
- Postage stamps

Philately Fun

W hat's philately? A highfalutin way to say "stamp collecting." And stamp collecting is, in addition to being among the world's most popular hobbies, one of the simplest to start—because just about everyone gets mail.

Granted, your child probably won't be starting out with any special issues from Monaco or San Marino, but you can help him or her get a good start with domestic stamps you receive. Have your child tear away the part of the used envelope that has the stamp, then soak it in water for approximately 30 minutes. After that time, the stamp should separate easily from the paper.

The next step is to mount the stamps: For a beginner's collection, gluing or taping them onto sheets of paper will probably suffice. More advanced philatelists will want to purchase the pregummed hinges that can be detached from the back of the stamp easily.

How many different kinds can your child find, soak, detach, and mount?

(See also: Coin Collection, #51; Post Office, #253.)

Required:

- Used envelopes with canceled stamps
- Dish and water
- Paper
- Glue or tape

Phone Words

M ost parents want to be sure their children know their phone number inside and out—just in case. Why not make the task a little easier (and more fun) by helping your kid translate your phone number into a word or sentence, using the alphanumeric keypad on your phone?

You and your child can puzzle out the word or phrase together—it's a little bit like cracking a code. Just to refresh your memory, here's a summary of the letter/number combinations:

Required:
• Your time only

1: (no letters)	6: MNO
2: ABC	7: PRS
3: DEF	8: TUV
4: GHI	9: WXY
5: JKL	0: (no letters)

(You'll have to ask the phone company what happened to Q and Z; it looks like there's enough room for them . . . but that's another issue.)

Sure, it's great to have a phone number like MILKMAN—but what do you do if you can only come up with words like PLAKHED? Don't be afraid to use the same techniques advertisers use to get numbers to stick in our heads: Keep the numeric prefix, and go for something like 497-BOOK. Try forgetting that!

Photographic Memory

Here's an activity that will test your child's memory. Select a picture from a favorite storybook or a magazine, then let your child study it. Then, while holding the book so only you can see it, ask questions to see how well he or she can describe the picture.

Required:

• Story books or magazines

Gauge your questions to your child's age and abilities; with young children, ask simple questions: "What color was the teddy bear?" "Was there an animal in the picture?" Increase the complexity and challenge by asking more difficult questions: "How many animals did you see?" What were the people doing?" You can also regulate the difficulty by varying the amount of time that your child has to view the picture.

Challenge older kids by briefly showing them several pictures, all at once or sequentially. Then ask questions about the details of each picture—the people, the setting, what the pictures seem to be all about. Throw in a few ringers to test their mettle: If one of the pictures shows only a yellow house, ask about the white house and see what happens. When you've finished your questions, show your child the picture and discuss it; as the old saying goes, a picture is worth 1,000 words.

Photography Studio

This activity gives new meaning to the term "instant photography."

Take a large cardboard box and cut a good-sized square hole in one end. Now cut a round hole in the opposite side, just big enough to hold the tapered end of a yogurt container snugly. Cut the bottom off the yogurt container; insert the cup into the hole. You've just made a precision "lens." Cut a slot in the side or bottom of the box, near the end with the square hole. Draw a button on the side of the box; this will activate the "shutter." Finally, drape a towel over the end with the square holes, and place the "camera" on a chair.

Before opening the studio, gather up some photos of the people who will have their portraits taken. Explain how old-fashioned cameras required photographers to drape a piece of cloth over their head. Your child should do the same with a towel, and press the shutter button when it's time to take the picture. To "process" the pictures, your child simply pushes the appropriate photo(s) (gathered earlier) through the slot from the inside. Hand drawn sketches will work, too. Say cheese!

Required:

- Large cardboard box
- Yogurt container
- Towel
- Family photographs

Safety Reminder

Small Parts

Required:

- Milk jug

- 4 plastic film canisters, medicine vials, or a wooden dowel

- Markers

- Length of ribbon, pipe cleaner, or twistem

Piggy Bank

Take a look at a milk jug from the side—what animal comes to mind? How about a pig . . . or a piggy bank?

To make a piggy bank, take an empty plastic milk jug and cut a slit in the top, big enough for a quarter. (The cutting is a grownup job.) Next, you'll need some legs. Your child can glue on 35 mm plastic film canisters, short lengths of wooden dowels, or medicine vials.

On to the face. Have your child draw eyes with markers—or draw them on paper and glue them on. The same approach works with the mouth. The top of the bottle makes a perfect snout—just add nostrils to the cap. (Keep the cap out of the reach of little ones. You might want to glue one end of a short piece of string to the top, and tie the other end to the handle.) A piece of ribbon glued on to the bottom of the jug will make a great tail, as will a pipe cleaner or twistem.

The piggy bank is now ready for action. Supply some starter coins (again, not for young ones), and your child is on his or her way to saving up for college tuition.

(This activity is not intended for use by children under four years of age.)

Make Your Own Record

Your child can be a recording star—overnight! Well, just about.

Sit down with your child and have him or her list six or seven favorite songs; if necessary and appropriate, you can help by writing down the words. (Obviously, if your three-year-old already has "Twinkle, Twinkle, Little Star" down pat and can't read, you won't need to worry too much about this step.)

Next, get the family cassette recorder out and start your recording sessions. If the spirit moves you, you and/or other family members can provide some impromptu instrumental backing with oatmeal containers, wooden spoons, kazoos, or whatever else may be kicking around the house. Don't worry too much about getting the rhythm right; it's the thought that counts.

Next step: playback! Most kids are entranced by the sounds of their own recorded voices—yours probably will be, too.

Now then, about that contract . . .

Required:
- Cassette tape recorder

Optional:
- Paper
- Pencil or pen

Map Puzzle

Required:
- Map of the U.S.
- Cardboard
- Non-toxic glue

Optional:
- Map of world

Would you like a jigsaw puzzle of the U.S. for your kids—free? (Well, almost free.) You need a map of the country, like the kind in the back of in-flight airline magazines. Of course, you can always sacrifice a high quality, full-size map—but why not get a little extra for your fare? Color weather maps (such as those featured in *USA Today*) work, too.

Affix the map to some thin pieces of cardboard with nontoxic glue. For young children, cut the map into four or five sections, roughly corresponding to the regions of the country. If that's too easy, break it down into groups of states: New England, the mid-Atlantic states, Pacific Coast states, and so on. The highest level is to cut the map into individual states.

Older kids might also be challenged by a jigsaw puzzle of various continents. Start off by breaking the continents down into large regions—then cut out individual countries. It really is a small, small world, after all.

Maple Seedling Olympics

If you live near maple trees, then you can sponsor autumn whirlygig races when the seeds have dropped to the ground. If you find the right shaped seeds, they should twirl like helicopters when you toss them into the air.

After you and your child collect a handful of aerodynamically fit seeds, take them up to a porch or the top of your steps. (Watch players and observers in high places carefully.)

Here are some games you can play. See which seedlings go the farthest, which ones stay in the air the longest or the shortest, which ones can land closest to a designated spot, or which ones are the "twirliest."

Keep the focus on the seedlings—determining which shapes perform best—rather than on whose seedlings "win" a game.

Required:

• Maple seedlings

Mapping the World

Does your child understand the connection between maps and the real world? Here's a way to find out—and help develop his or her understanding of spatial relationships.

For young children, start off simple, with a map of their room. On a piece of paper, draw the outline of the room. Then sketch something obvious, like the bed, dresser, etc. Ask where the window, door, or other unmistakable objects would be located. Continue the process until you have the whole room mapped out. You can test whether your child really grasps the idea by using the map for a treasure hunt. Try the process with other rooms in the house, then graduate to a map of the entire floor of your house or apartment.

Move on to your backyard, neighborhood, the park, and so on. As you escalate the complexity, be sure to give lots of familiar landmarks (the grocery store or playground, for instance.)

For older children, you might use commercial maps or atlases of larger areas. Feeling adventurous? Explain, briefly and clearly, that we all live on a sphere whizzing around the sun. Now that should stimulate some lively discussion!

Required:
- Paper
- Pencils

Optional:
- Commercial maps or atlas

Marble Raceway

That old standby, the cat's-eye marble, can provide nonstop entertainment for kids—all you have to do is set up a marble racecourse.

The core of any marble raceway consists of paper towel tubes sliced in two, lengthwise. You can connect the tubes to create a series of straightaways, or join them to build a maze. Here are some ideas for building your Marble Grand Prix. (Do not let toddlers participate in this activity; they may consider marbles tempting morsels.)

Glue straight tubes at a slight downward angle in a shallow flat box, trimming the sides as necessary to provide a continuous course. You can boost the challenge by cutting holes, slightly larger than a marble, along the tube. The object then is to get the marbles to the bottom without having them fall through any of the holes. (Each player's ability to tilt and manipulate his or her box becomes key here.) The more holes you cut, the greater the challenge.

You can also experiment with cutting and connecting the tubes at odd angles to provide a more interesting course. If you build a maze-like structure and elevate one end, your child's marbles will roll like the water in the old Roman aqueducts!

Safety Reminder
Small Parts

Required:

- Paper towel tubes, sliced lengthwise
- Marbles
- Glue
- Tape
- Shallow box

Safety Reminder
Balloon

Required:

• Paper bags

• Crayons or markers

Optional:

• Papier mache supplies

• Balloons

• Foil

• Felt

Masks and Helmets

M asks aren't just for Halloween—they're for everyday play!

The easiest way to make masks, of course, is to cut holes in paper bags, then decorate them with crayons or markers. (We are all well aware of the potential suffocation dangers of plastic bags.) For more sophisticated masks, use the papier-mache recipe (#230) with balloons as forms. Leave eye and mouth holes, then pop the balloons when the paper mache is dry and decorate with tempera paint. (See Dinosaurs on Parade, #76, for detailed instructions.) You might also want to glue a felt liner to the inside of a papier mache mask for comfort. Very large balloons can be used to make full helmets!

Here are few favorites in our household: animal masks (pipe cleaners make great tiger whiskers); clown masks (ping-pong balls can be fashioned into perfect clown noses); astronaut or deep sea diver helmets (paper towel tubes make excellent air hoses); and robot masks/helmets (be sure to decorate with scrap foil—and use straws for antennae). The ultimate winner: our son's self-portrait mask.

Matching Game

This activity, like #58, #196, and #209 gives your child an opportunity to "flex" his or her memory. The matching game, however, adds a special twist.

Take an egg carton and place one object in each of six of the egg holders. For example, the first egg holder might contain a paper clip, the second a toy car, the third a grape, and so on. Show your child the contents, close the lid, then provide a second, empty egg carton.

Your child's mission: find similar objects to the ones in your egg carton, and put them *in the same position* as the carton you're holding.

To increase the challenge, expand the number of items and/or decrease the viewing time—or have your child race against the clock.

If your kid becomes too proficient at the game, have him or her try to duplicate the items in *two* egg cartons—that should be a challenge!

Required:
- Two or more egg cartons
- Common household objects

Milk Jug Catch

If you're looking for a new sport, just turn to your refrigerator. If it contains two plastic milk jugs (the one-gallon size), you're in luck.

For this activity, you'll need two empty jugs. The first part is for grownups only: cut the jugs in half horizontally. Be careful—slicing them is tricky. Make sure there are no rough edges left. When you're finished, you'll use the top portions as "mitts." (Save the bottom part for household containers; they're great for holding small toys, blocks, Legos, etc.)

The object is simply to toss a ball to your partner, who will catch it with the milk jug and toss it back to you without touching it with the hands. You do the same. With young children, a large, soft ball (low bounce) or bean bag will be appropriate. Older kids with more coordination and strength may prefer a tennis ball or racquetball. You can adjust the difficulty by increasing the distance between the players or getting more people to play the game.

See—milk really does build strong bodies, and in more ways than one.

Required:

- Two or more milk jugs (one-gallon size)
- Small ball or bean bags
- Cutting implements (for adult use only)

Mirror, Mirror (Or, Follow Me, Follow You)

T his activity requires two players (or sets of two); if you can pair off sets of children, great. Otherwise, you'll need to get into the act.

And "getting into the act" is a good way to describe this mirror exercise; it's a favorite warmup among actors and other performers. Two persons stand face to face; one initiates an action, and the other follows in turn. The aim, however, is not a "follow-the-leader" game, but rather a joining of the two sets of movements. If the two people work together, slowly and smoothly, they will eventually reach a state in which both partners (or neither, depending on how you look at it) are leading the exercise simultaneously.

Follow hand wave to hand wave, blink to blink, bend to bend. How close to mirror-perfect can *you* come?

Required:
• Your time

Mnemonics

We all learned mnemonics in school at one time or another to help us remember categories, names, spellings, and other tricky bits of information. Here are some common memory aids that fall into this category.

Required:

• Your time only

For the colors of the rainbow: ROY G. BIV (Which stands for: red, orange, yellow, green, blue, indigo, violet.)

To spell the word "geography": George Eliot's old grandfather rode a pig home yesterday.

For the categories of the animal kingdom: Kind pigs care only for good slop. (Which stands for: kingdom, phylum, class, order, family, genus, species.)

For the notes on the lines of the musical treble clef: Every good boy does fine. (Which stands for: E, G, B, D, F.)

Encourage your child to make up his or her own mnemonics for remembering names, addresses, and other important things—like the flavors at the local ice cream parlor.

Mom and Dad on the Job

In some cultures, kids know exactly what their parents do during the day, because they're right there. In our high-tech modern world, though, work is a black box—Mom and Dad vanish in the morning and return at night. This role play activity will help your child understand what you do all day . . . and it may give you a few laughs, too.

Required:
• Clothes

Have your children act out a typical work day for Mom or Dad. Let them start off by wearing some article of clothing—a hat, your shoes, a tie, a scarf, a piece of jewelry—something that gets them "dressed" for work. Do your kids buzz around the house madly as they get ready to leave? Once on the job, ask your kids to do what Mommy and/or Daddy does during the day. If they're stumped give them some hints: "I talk to people on the phone." "I take food to hungry people." "I carry paper and pencil and look at machines." "I sit in meetings."

Does it look silly? Fast-paced? Familiar?

Monster Bubbles

Safety Reminder

Supervise Closely

Required:

- Wire coat hanger or pipe cleaners
- Pan
- Dishwashing soap
- Corn syrup

Kids have been entertaining themselves with soap bubbles for years. You can introduce a new twist on an old theme by making your own bubble mixture and wands.

Start off with the bubble mixture. In a small mixing bowl, combine six cups of water, two cups of *Joy* dishwashing liquid, and three-quarters of a cup of corn syrup (to give the bubbles added strength). Make the bubble mix four hours in advance of play time, then pour it into a shallow pan.

Wands can be made out of pipe cleaners or reshaped wire coat hangers. Leave part of the hanger as a handle and stick the ends into the cardboard tube from a pants hanger. (For safety's sake, do not let your child use the coat hanger wand—let him or her chase after your masterpieces. Also, be sure to curl the ends back to avoid exposed sharp edges.) A wand with a six-inch bubble area can make bubbles the size of a watermelon. Just dip the wand into the pan, and, in one smooth motion, wave your arm. Once you get the hang of it, you can create blimplike bubbles that will drift lazily across the sky before descending. Toddlers, especially, will delight in chasing after your creations. (Note: keep mix away from carpets, floors, and lawns.)

Morse Code

Once you know Morse code, you can send all manner of secret messages by clicking two spoons together, tapping on walls, or even using a flashlight. Learning the code itself is relatively simple—try copying it out for your child, then having him or her go over it with you letter by letter. Flash cards are great too! Need help? Just click three shorts, three longs, and three shorts.

A •–	S •••
B –•••	T –
C –•–•	U ••–
D –••	V •••–
E •	W •––
F ••–•	X –••–
G ––•	Y –•––
H ••••	Z ––••
I ••	1 •––––
J •–––	2 ••–––
K –•–	3 •••––
L •–••	4 ••••–
M ––	5 •••••
N –•	6 –••••
O –––	7 ––•••
P •––•	8 –––••
Q ––•–	9 ––––•
R •–•	0 –––––

Required:
• Your time

Optional:
• Spoons
• Flashlight
• 3 x 5 cards

Musical Chairs

A classic. Here's a refresher course on this fast-paced favorite.

Find a quantity of chairs equal to one less than the number of players, and place the chairs in a circle with the seats facing out. Now set up a tape player with a cassette that has an upbeat song. Of course, before tape players came in, live instrumentation was the order of the day—if you happen to play an instrument, you can go one better by taking the low-tech approach and supplying the music yourself.

When the music starts, the players circle around the chairs; when it stops, they must find someplace to sit. Whoever's left standing at the end of a round must leave the game—and take a chair. The final round, in which the last two "survivors" eye each other nervously in anticipation of the move towards the final seat, is likely to be a free-for-all. In such cases, the music master acts as referee. And his or her decisions are final.

Required:

- Chairs
- Tape player and cassette (or instrument)

My Best Friend

Does your child have a close friend from school or daycare—someone who's a very special friend? If so, why not create a personalized greeting card to mark that fact?

Give your child safety scissors and construction paper, then help him or her cut out a rectangle of appropriate size. (You may have to handle the cutting if you do not have a pair of safety scissors handy.) Then ask your child to think of what makes his or her special friend, well, special.

Do the two of them share toys together? Like to play the same games? Have a common history together (birthday parties both have attended, for instance)? Enjoy the same types of food? Look forward to the same holidays?

Whatever makes the friendship special, have your child record it on the card (or take notes yourself if your child is a prewriter), then let the decoration begin.

The next step is just for your child, and it's the most fun of all: passing the love along.

Required:

- Construction paper
- Safety scissors
- Crayons
- Pen or pencil

My Own Place Mat

Is your child tired of staring at the same old place mat each meal? If so, try this activity.

First, cut out a piece of stiff cardboard to the desired size of the placemat. If the cardboard is not a color you want, affix a sheet of white paper over it with double-stick tape or a few dabs of nontoxic glue. Now have the child decorate the paper with crayons or markers, or pictures cut out from magazines. Dried leaves (#172) or flowers (#110) can also make for neat decorations—just make sure they're completely dry.

When the artwork is completed, cover it with clear contact paper (a grownup job). The top and bottom edge of the contact paper should wrap around the cardboard an inch or so to make a good seal. Trim the corners as necessary before folding so that you can get a good seal on all the corners, too. For kids prone to spills, you might also want to cover the bottom for complete protection.

The only thing left to do now is sit down and have a meal.

Required:

- Stiff cardboard
- Double-stick tape or nontoxic glue
- Crayons or markers
- Clear contact paper
- Safety scissors
- Magazine pictures
- Clear contact paper

Mystery Clues

Here's something you can do while fixing a meal—or doing anything that prevents you from hunkering down on the kitchen or playroom floor at the moment. (This activity is also a lifesaver when you're just too beat to do anything but talk.)

First, pick a theme, such as animals. Then say: "I'm thinking of an animal that stands on two legs, has a short tail..." and so on. Encourage your child to ask questions ("Is it big or small?" "Does it have fur or smooth skin?" "Does it like water?") When you answer the questions, provide just the right lack of information to keep your child guessing and requesting more clues (but not enough to cause frustration). Reverse the questioning, and have your kid give you clues about an animal or object that he or she selects.

You can tailor the game to your child's interests and abilities. For older children, consider using historical events or issues being discussed in school. The possibilities are virtually limitless!

Required:

• Your time only

Name Game

$\mathbf{M}$any kids love to make funny names. This activity is sure to generate a barrel of belly laughs.

Start off with a name—yours, for instance. Say your first name, then think of the first letter of your last name. Each player must substitute an animal or a common object beginning with that letter. So "Steve Bennett" could become "Steve Beanpole" or "Steve Balloon." Then shift to the second letter of the name and continue until the last name has been completely reworked.

If the action slows down, you can encourage your kids to use outside resources. Even the youngest kids can use picture books to give them ideas, assuming they know their letters. (Alphabet books are ideal.) Older kids should try to use junior dictionaries.

A variation on this activity involves having each player repeat the full list—like "Steve boxcar elephant newspaper noodle engine twinkle toes." Older kids may even be able to make a whole new sentence. How about: Steve barks extremely nonsensical news every third Tuesday?

Required:

• Your time only

Steve Beanpole!

Name Poster and Book

What's in a name? Everything from animals and cars to furniture and space ships—if you play this game. To play, the child must have at least some spelling or prewriting skills. (You might have to help more if your child is just beginning to learn to write.)

On large colored pieces of paper, write or have your child write the letters of his first name—one letter per sheet. Next, ask the child to look through magazines and find items that begin with the various letters. Clip the pictures, then have your child glue or tape the pictures to the appropriate sheets. Get out your box of crayons or markers and invite your child to decorate his name posters as well. Then find a place in your child's room where the works can be proudly displayed and updated during future magazine hunts.

As a variation, your child can create name posters or books for each member in the family. Nice gifts for any occasion.

Required:
- Paper or cardboard
- Magazines

Nature Display

Even the most meager backyard or path through the neighborhood has something to offer in the way of natural wonder.

To conduct a nature walk, simply collect leaves, flowers, twigs, acorns, fruits, rocks, and whatever else interests your child. Take along a "special" bag or basket for your collections.

Tell your nature explorers to collect only what they need; when they remove parts of plants, they should only remove a small piece and do so without injuring the rest. Be sure not to take too many flowers, either—remember, that's how the plant reproduces itself.

When you return home, make a display box for the collection. To do so, take an empty cereal box, tape the top shut, and wrap it in plain paper. Then cut through the cardboard and paper on the front, leaving a half-inch border. Decorate the box, prop it up, and fill it— glue lightweight nature treasures on the inside back, and heavier ones on the bottom.

Required:

- Bag or basket
- Nature collection
- Cereal box
- Paper
- Tape
- Bag or basket

Neighborhood Historian

Do you know the history of your neighborhood? If you live in an older part of town, this activity will be especially enlightening—and entertaining—for you and your child. Take a notebook and/or tape recorder and visit some of the older residents on your street, block, or road. Have your child ask the following kinds of questions:

What was the land used for before the houses and stores were built? Were there farms? Woods? Fields?

What stores used to be in the neighborhood? Did people gather in them to learn the local news? What sorts of things were talked about?

What were the names of the families in the area? What were their kids' names? What sorts of games did the children play?

Were there any momentous celebrations, like parades, Fourth of July celebrations, and so on?

Record the answers while your child does the interviewing; later, the two of you can place them in a permanent book. You might also want to take pictures of the interviewees and include them in the book, as well. Show it off. This activity is a great excuse to introduce yourself to your neighbors!

Required:
- Paper and pencil
- Notebook

Optional:
- Tape recorder

Neighborhood Travel Guide

W hat are the main attractions in your neighborhood? Your child might have some interesting thoughts on the subject. Here's how you can make a travel guide based on your child's local knowledge.

First, take a walk around the neighborhood; have your child serve as tour guide, pointing out interesting flowers, trees, buildings, stores, parks, and so on. Our son was particularly excited about a small open pipe on a telephone pole near our house—it made a fine home for algae after rainstorms and served as the basis for many discussions about plant growth.

You can document such "hot spots" by: jotting down descriptions in a notebook for later discussion; helping make a photo essay; annotating a map of the area (or have your child draw one); capturing a neighborhood walk on tape; or collecting samples—leaves from your child's favorite tree, a napkin from the ice cream parlor, etc.—or helping your child place them in a scrapbook.

Share the results with family, friends, and anyone else you meet who lives in your area. Chances are they'll be inspired by learning what makes your community special.

Required:

- Paper
- Crayons or markers

Optional:

- Camera
- Tape recorder
- Scrapbook or notebook

Number Alphabet

2092131448449108590390712 1521914

Could your child memorize a long number like that? Sure. The key to all memory is to find a way to make random information meaningful. We can do that for *any* number by employing the following simple number alphabet.

Required:

• Your time only

DIGIT	SOUND	HINT
1	t,d,th	"t" has one downstroke, looks like 1
2	n	"n" has two downstrokes
3	m	"tip over" the 3; it looks like "m"
4	r	Last sound in "four": r
5	l	Sideways "L" perched on top half of 5
6	sh, ch, j	6 curves like J, but in reverse
7	k	7 looks like a *key* on end
8	f, v	Handwritten "f" looks like 8
9	p, b	9 and "P" almost mirror images
0	z, s	Zero starts with "z"

Everything is based entirely on how something *sounds*, not how it's spelled. Vowels (and W, H, and Y) are wildcards; that means that 712 could be "cotton" or "kitten". (But "kitten" could *only* translate as 712.) Try some number alphabet flash cards; before long, your child will be able to recognize the number at the top of this page as "Once upon a time there were four rabbits: Flopsy, Mopsy, Cottontail, and Peter."

Number Hunt

This simple game can be played in any room, at any time.

Call out a number, then set your child loose to find objects that represent the number from around the house. For instance, if you're making dinner, and want to keep your kids within view, have them look for kitchen implements. A rolling pin has one roller and two handles, and so would qualify for either "one" or "two." A fork might have four tines, a refrigerator two handles, and so on.

You can also invent numerous variations. For example, have your child find one object in each room of the house that matches the number you call out. If your child can't find an example, give hints to steer him or her towards an object that qualifies.

Finally, if you really want to keep 'em occupied, suggest that when you call out, say, "three," your kids have to find *three* objects that represent the number three, and so on for all the numbers you call out during the game.

The more you play the game, the more you'll refine your own powers of observation. Quick: How many rows of bristles does your toothbrush have?

Required:

• Your time only

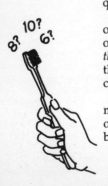

Obstacle Course (Indoor)

You can boost your children's agility by turning your living room or playroom into an obstacle course.

Your course might consist of the following kinds of challenges: crawling under or over chairs; crawling under a table without disturbing any balloons dangling on strings from the bottom; sliding under or crawling over a string stretched between two table or chair legs; crawling or slithering through a tunnel made from couch pillows; or stepping on a series of pieces of paper taped to the floor. You can also challenge your kid by having him or her go through the course while holding an empty toilet paper tube in each hand. Another "handicap": wearing a large hat while maneuvering through the obstacles; if the hat comes off, it's back to square one. Other possibilities include silly rules like jumping up and down three times after completing certain "stations," or singing a song at a certain point in the course. The variations are almost endless, but whatever you do, design the course from the perspective of your child. To do this, of course, you might just have to get down on all fours and try it yourself—watch that back!

Adult supervision is required for this activity.

Safety Reminder

Supervise Closely

Required:

- Furniture
- String
- Couch pillows
- Paper and tape
- Household objects

Obstacle Course (Outdoor)

Safety Reminder

Supervise Closely

Required:

• Lawn furniture

• Hose or length of string

Optional:

• Sprinkler

• Spoons

• Beach ball

• Plate and ping-pong ball

• Water balloons

I f you've tried the indoor obstacle course (#211) and the weather looks cooperative, try moving to the great outdoors. Here are some obstacles sure to delight your kids:

Crawling under lawn chairs, or slithering under a chaise lounge.

Walking or hopping with one foot on either side of a garden hose that's twisted and curved in a tortuous track.

"Tightrope walking" along a piece of string laid on the ground that doubles back on itself and takes twisting turns.

Dodging an oscillating sprinkler (this can be combined with any of the above).

To add some spice to the activity, have your child try making it through the obstacle course while holding a beach ball or balancing a ping-pong ball on a plate. If that's no problem, pass along an armful of water balloons!

Adult supervision is required for this activity.

Old-Fashioned Hopscotch

E ven if you were a great hopscotch
fan in your youth, if you're like most
of us you've forgotten the rules by now.
Here's a refresher course.

Draw a chalk hopscotch pattern on the
ground (see illustration); you can use
tape indoors. The first player tosses a
marker (a stone or bean bag will do)
onto square 1, then hops on one foot *over*
square 1 to square 2, landing on one foot.
(Note: Young kids may have to land on
two feet.) The player then hops on one
foot to square 3, and then lands with one
foot in 4 and the other in 5. He or she
then hops again and lands on one foot in
6, and, with another leap, lands with one
foot in 7 and one in 8. The player then
jumps and turns around, and, with feet
still in 7 and 8, reverses the hopping
pattern—bending down on one leg
while in square 2 to pick up the marker.
From there it's a single hop onto square
1 and out.

If the player succeeds in making it
through all the squares, he or she tosses
the stone or bean bag to square 2. If it
lands in square 2, the jumping process
is repeated, this time skipping square 2.
If the marker doesn't land in the designated square, or the player loses his or
her balance, it's the next player's turn.

Required:
- Chalk
- Stone

Optional:
- Masking tape
- Bean bag

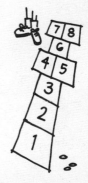

214

Safety Reminder

Supervise Closely

Required:

- Blender
- Water
- Wire screens
- Towels
- 2 plastic containers
- Newspapers, torn in strips

Old-Fashioned Paper

This activity (best for older kids) requires accesories and some patience, but it is well worth it. The first steps are for grownups. Fill a blender to the two-thirds mark with lukewarm water. Turn the blender on "low"; then drop in approximately ten narrow strips of torn newspaper. *Do not* use glossy paper or anything resembling a magazine or shiny advertising inserts. Blend until goopy. (Caution: do not let children use the blender!)

Now take two pieces of wire window screen. They should fit inside two identical shallow plastic containers, each with the bottom cut out in a rectangle the size of the piece of paper you want. Put the screens in between the openings of the nested containers, then place the whole arrangement in the sink. Pour the pulp from the blender onto the top screen. Let the moisture drain into the sink. Remove the top container, then remove and set the top screen (and the pulp) on your counter. Now place the other screen on top of the pulp, cover with a plastic bag, and roll carefully with a rolling pin. Remove covering (but not the screens), then weight the pulp down with a thick dishcloth and a heavy weight. Let stand. (Drying times will vary from one to three days.) When dry, carefully peel away your sheet of homemade paper—and get out that quill! (See #215.)

Kids' Circus

If your child likes the circus, you can sponsor one right in your own living room or play room. Here are some suggestions:

Make a Big Top by throwing a sheet over a table—or place six chairs in a circle, then drape a sheet over the backs. Fill the tent with plenty of stuffed animals (the performers). If you have face paints, you can make your child up as a clown; one of your T-shirts and shoes will make a fine outfit. You can also provide some boxes for the stuffed animals to sit in. Connect the boxes with string, and you have a circus train. Turn some round plastic containers or cups upside down when it's time for the tricks to begin. If your child has a stuffed animal tiger or lion, make a cage, then unleash the beast so your child can perform feats of daring.

Of course, you'll need some refreshments, so whip up some popcorn. Then hand out tickets—which your child has decorated—to other siblings, friends, relatives, etc.

At our house we have one important rule—all circus performers also perform cleanup duty. That's show biz.

Required:

- Sheet or blanket
- Stuffed animals
- Boxes
- Plastic containers/cups
- String

Optional:

- Face paints
- Adult T-shirt and sneakers

Kitchen Camping

If you like the idea of the great outdoors, but cringe at the thought of
sleeping under the stars, we have good
news for you—you can "camp out" with
your kids in the safety of your own
home with nothing more than a sheet, a
few towels or blankets, and a flashlight.

Required:

- Sheet
- Large towels or
  blankets

Optional:

- Flashlights
- Toilet paper
  tubes
- Markers/paint

Throw the sheet over your kitchen or
dining room table and voila—instant
tent. Fashion a sleeping bag for each kid
from a large beach towel or blanket.
Pass out flashlights (with rechargeable
batteries), then turn out the room lights.

You can spice up the great campout
by making a "campfire" from toilet
paper tubes decorated as logs. In that
case, you might as well go all the way
and let your kids "roast" marshmallows
over the "coals." Toddlers and preschoolers will simply enjoy the fun of
hanging out in the enclosed space. Older
kids might want to lead an expedition or
tell ghost stories. You can oblige by providing the necessary sound effects . . .
and a hand to hold if the need arises.

Kitchen Finery

Safety Reminder

Small Parts

R eady for a surprise? Your pantry is chock-full of good stuff for making jewelry. Here are a few suggestions.

Pasta can be strung on a piece of yarn or string to make bracelets, necklaces, headbands, and other finery. To make a pin, glue the pasta onto a piece of cardboard, then tape a paper clip onto the back—and use the paper clip to attach the cardboard to your kids clothes. (Keep paper clips out of very young hands.) To enhance your kid's pasta craft sessions, pick out interesting macaroni shapes the next time you're at the grocery store; look for stars, tubes, pinwheels, etc. You can also make the pasta more fun to work with by dyeing it with food coloring before assembling it on the string. Other food items, like peanut shells, can also be used to make jewelry.

The finery can be worn by your kids, of course, but it can also serve to make a fashion statement with the stuffed-animal set. Finally, don't forget that jewelry can become art—your kids can make collages of their work rather than wearing it. Let friends and relatives admire the creation!

Required:

- String, yarn
- Pasta

Optional:

- Food coloring

Kitchen Trace

170

Your kitchen is a wonderful source of objects that can be traced and transformed into fanciful works of art. On scrap paper, use crayons, pens, or markers to trace the following kinds of objects, then add features.

Overturned colanders and woks can be used to sketch funny faces—the handles also make great ears. Pans are good for the same purpose—the handles can be long necks for clown-like creatures. Plates make good outlines for faces, as well as perfect outlines for balloons and wheels. So do cups, saucers, and the lids from plastic containers.

Square containers can be used for the outlines of houses and buildings, while whisks, large forks, and spoons can be traced for trees. An aluminum foil container makes a good train, car, or bus outline. Don't forget cookie cutters—they're not just for cookies.

Go through your kitchen drawer with an eye to materials well suited for tracing. You're bound to find all sorts of gizmos with interesting shapes. And when your child shows his or her precocious artwork to Grandma or Grandpa, who's to know that the flamingo on one leg is really a French garlic press in disguise?

Required:

- Paper
- Pens, pencils, or markers
- Kitchen containers and utensils

Knuckleheads

Y our child has two good buddies right at the end of his or her wrists—knuckleheads!

Knuckleheads are shy creatures, but they are easily revealed by making a fist, then turning your hand sideways. Extend your thumb across your index finger as shown in the illustration. See the space between your fist and your thumb? That's actually a mouth. As you move your thumb up and down, the mouth moves.

Show this to your child; for added effect use nontoxic washable markers or face paints (which can be purchased at most toy stores) to create eyes, a nose, lips, a moustache, eyebrows, and other features.

What can a knucklehead do? Lots of things. Just give him or her a stage, like a table top, and get ready for songs, orations, editorials, knock-knock jokes, and other forms of entertainment.

Two or more knuckleheads can assume various characters in a play (ad libbed or prewritten) put on by an older child—one knucklehead might be the parent, and the rest the children. The possibilities are endless!

Required:

• Nontoxic washable markers or face paints

Leaf Pressing

O ne way to capture the unique spirit of fall is to press different kinds of leaves and then use them for artwork.

When you go leaf hunting, you and your child should look for the freshest specimens possible. Collect as many different leaves as you can find (get a tree-identification book if you feel that will be helpful). You'll also want to take along a protective carrier. Two pieces of cardboard with a masking tape hinge will do just fine.

Immediately after returning home, insert the leaves between several sheets of newsprint. Place the newspaper between two cardboard covers, then weigh down the covers with a large book. The leaves shouldn't touch each other on paper.

In a week or so, the leaves should be dried out. Your child can glue them to paper and make a record of the expedition. You and your child can also trace the leaves and draw in the veins. Perhaps you will want to glue them to a folded piece of paper—your child can then make a special card for a friend or relative.

Required:
- Cardboard
- Newspaper
- Large book

Lean 'em! (Or, Having Fun With Cards Even If You Can't Read or Count Yet)

Here's a card game for two or more that even nonreaders can enjoy.

Take a pack of playing cards and distribute them evenly among the players. Take turns tossing them against the base of a wall; the objective is to get your card to lean upright, not fall flat. Do it, and you win all the cards that have been thrown against the wall. Miss, and your card becomes part of the "pot."

For older kids, suggest challenging rules. For example, have your child pick a card, face down, from the deck, and then toss it without looking at it. Only hearts or diamonds that lean on the wall count—any others must be thrown again.

Shuffle 'em—and lean 'em.

Required:
• Deck of cards

Lemonade Stand

Here's a summertime classic that's sure to bring a smile to your neighbors' faces.

Outside of finding a safe location you can monitor easily, setting up shop is simple. Chances are there are a few cardboard boxes you can press into service; you can make a sign with a sheet of butcher paper and some markers. Add a cash box with a dollar or so in change, and stand back!

You may want to pass along this classic recipe for lemonade (and referee the manufacturing process):

Eight cups water
12 tablespoons lemon juice
1 teaspoon salt
1½ cups sugar

1. Mix.
2. Chill.
3. Serve over ice.
4. Taste test.
5. Smile.

Required:

- Cardboard boxes
- Butcher paper
- Markers
- Cash box and change
- Water
- Lemon juice
- Salt
- Sugar

Letter Exchange

Here's a fascinating game for two that can make for hours of fun if your children have some spelling ability.

The first player calls out a letter—let's say "A". The second player must then call out another letter, but this time, the player must be prepared, if challenged by the other player, to use the two letters in sequence in a legitimate word. (A household dictionary is a good arbiter of what can be considered a "legitimate" word; if it shows up, it counts.)

Required:
• Dictionary

Play will usually proceed for four or five turns before one of the players is either unable to come up with another letter without actually finishing a legitimate word—or emboldened to challenge a word. Here are turns from a sample game. (Player 1:) "T." (Player 2:) "R." (Player 1:) "A." (Player 2:) "I." [If Player 2 had used "P" instead, the game would be over, since "trap" is a real word. But since the combination is now T-R-A-I, Player 2 must come up with a new letter that continues the sequence and does not result in a whole word.

Letter/Number Addup

Here's a simple game that requires only a working knowledge of the alphabet and numbers.

Cut out 26 small squares of paper and have your kids write a letter of the alphabet on each one. Now toss the papers into a hat. Ask your kids to remove them, one-by-one, and write numbers, in sequence, on the backs of the paper. Let's say the first letter chosen was Q; it would have the number 1 written on the reverse. If the second letter was A, it would have the number 2 written on the reverse, and so on. Now record the letters and their number values on a separate sheet of paper.

The game itself is simple; each player must think of words containing as many high-scoring letters as possible. If E, C, F, and A have values of 5, 21, 6, and 9, respectively, the word FACE will score a total of 41 points. Set a time limit, give each kid a pad and pencil, and let them start coming up with words. When the time limit expires, tote up the numbers and announce the winner!

Required:

- Pencil
- Paper
- Safety scissors
- Hat

Library Fun

Bookworms will love this activity. First, have your child gather up his or her favorite books. Provide small envelopes (extras from junk mail), or make your own by folding construction paper into a pocket. Tape or glue the envelope to the inside back cover of each book. Then write the title of each book on an index card or small piece of cardboard, and place it in the pocket. Stand the books on a shelf or sofa.

At this point, your child-turned-librarian is ready to open the doors of your family library. After browsing, borrowers can present their library card (made from expired credit cards or pieces of cardboard) and sign the checkout card; the "librarian" stamps the envelope with a rubber stamp or scribbles the due date on the envelope, and then places the checkout card in his or her file (any small box will do).

Older kids can have fun developing a card catalog and more sophisticated book "checkout" systems. They can also manage a fine cash box. Don't forget to return your books on time—you may find the fines prohibitive!

Required:

- Books
- Index cards or plain cardboard
- Card file or box
- Envelopes or paper

Optional:

- Rubber stamps

Lip Reading

If you can talk without making any sound, you can help your child understand the world of the hearing impaired.

Set aside a time—say, five minutes—where your child can speak normally, but you can only move your lips silently. Can the two of you communicate? Which words or sounds are easiest for your child to understand? Which are most difficult?

Required:

• Your time only

You should make a point of "speaking" slowly and with exaggerated mouth movements—this will simplify things for your partner. If the game goes well, try reversing the roles; let your child talk ... and you do the interpreting.

If your child gets better at it, he or she may be able to share this activity with a friend or sibling. The house may be a little quieter... for a while.

Don't let your kids get too good at this though. They may start translating the umpire-manager confrontations during televised baseball games.

Little Kids' Bingo

Safety Remind

Small Parts

Required:
- Paperboard
- Markers, crayons
- Tokens
- Goodies to eat

This version of bingo is well suited to groups of pre-readers. Fashion a stack of bingo cards from a piece of paperboard (the kind you get with shirts from the dry cleaners works well). Use a marker or crayon to divide each card into four sections. Each section should be designated by a different color, and each card should be unique.

Next, cut up small squares of cardboard and color them so they correspond to the cards, but with only one color per square. You'll need a total of three squares for each color you chose to place on the cards. Place the squares in a bag and shuffle them.

Have the caller reach into the bag and call out the color he or she has picked. (Alternately, you can use one of the giant dice described in activity #117. If you do, make sure that all the colors on the score cards are represented on the face of the die.)

Whenever a player hears a color on his or her card, he or she covers the corresponding square with a token. Whoever fills up all four squares first calls out "BINGO" and gets to trade in each token for a grape, raisin, or other goodie. Take turns so that each child can be the caller. At the end of the game, you may opt to let everyone eat the leftover goodies. (See also: Big Kids' Bingo, #22.)

Living Room Sandbox

W hat do you do when your child yearns to play in the sandbox, but it's the middle of winter? Bring the sandbox indoors, of course. Take a large plastic tub; place it on a canvas or plastic drop cloth (if you have one) to make cleanup easy. Fill the tub with rice, small pieces of pasta, cornmeal, oatmeal, or a mixture of the above. Then give your child all the essential sandbox utensils: cups; large spoons; strainers; sifters; funnels, and anything else good for digging.

The youngest kids will enjoy manipulating whatever you put in the sandbox. Toddlers and slightly older kids will also enjoy playing with cars, trucks, or animals in the sandbox. (Cornmeal can make an especially fine desert or beach setting.) Small pasta makes a great environment for toy bulldozers, backhoes, cranes, and other construction toys.

Of course, toy animals are natural for indoor sandbox play. Encourage your child to make mountains, valleys, and other terrain fit for toy dinosaurs, jungle animals, and other denizens of the toy box.

When your child is done playing, don't forgot to cover up the sandbox or transfer the contents to a jar. No point in letting real critters share in the fun.

Required:
- Large tub
- Rice, cornmeal, oatmeal or pasta
- Kitchen utensils

Optional:
- Drop cloth
- Toy cars, trucks, animals

Macaroni Cards

Safety Reminder

Small Parts

Why should your kid bother with those stuffy preprinted greeting cards? When holidays, birthdays, or other special events roll around, have your child put together a deluxe macaroni card.

These are cards that use dry, uncooked macaroni noodles (or any other variety that suits your child's fancy) as decorative elements. You glue them into place with nontoxic glue, let them dry (a couple of hours will usually suffice), and then decorate the cards and the noodles with tempera paint. They make quite a statement! (Only one warning is in order: If you plan on mailing the cards to a friend or loved one, be sure to use adequate cushioning; it's no fun if the noodles crack. Popping the card into a standard envelope will only invite the wrath of the Postal Service's automatic sorting machines.)

The cards are perfect for birthdays, Mother's, Father's, or Grandparent's Days, Hanukkah, Christmas, or just about any other occasion—including no reason at all.

Required:

- Paper
- Macaroni
- Glue
- Tempera paint

Magnet Fishing

Safety Reminder
Small Parts

Required:

- String
- Masking tape
- Small magnets
- Large non-swallowable paper clips

Optional:

- Yarn
- Scrap foil
- Styrofoam trays
- Large cardboard box

How about going fishing from the comfort of your living room? Find a yardstick, wrapping paper tube, or other kid-sized "fishing pole." Attach two to three feet of string to the pole with tape, then tie a small horseshoe magnet onto the other end. Try decorating the magnet with yarn or scrap foil to make colorful "lures." (Use only large, nonswallowable baubles.)

Next, make fish out of cardboard or paper, or cut pictures of fish from magazines. Place a large metal paper clip on the front of each fish, then place the fish on the floor and set your kids loose with their gear. (Keep paper clips out of very young hands.) Younger children will delight in fishing from a sofa pillow "boat," or even a large box. Older kids can fish against the clock or follow silly instructions with each new fish caught ("wiggle like a worm," "hop up and down three times," and so on). They'll also get a kick out of fishing from a shopping bag or with their eyes closed. (See also: Pipe Cleaner Fishing, #241.)

A backyard or back-porch alternative: Make fish out of Styrofoam trays, attach the paper clips, then place them all in a water-filled pan or tub. Nothing beats the real thing!

Magnet Sculpture

Magnet sculpture is easy to do and can provide nonstop entertainment for your kids.

To create any kind of magnet art, you'll need a strong bar magnet and some small metal paper clips. (Not for very young children.) Magnetize the paper clips by rubbing them on the bar in one direction. Once they've acquired a magnetic field, your kids can stand them end-to-end vertically, connect them horizontally, and create any number of shapes.

Required:
- Strong bar magnet
- Small metal paper clips

Optional:
- Iron filings

Suggest all kinds of sculptures: a scarecrow, letters or numbers, a dog, or other simple forms. Kids can also experiment to learn how many they can connect, and whether or not they can push one paper clip with another clip without touching. This is a great opportunity to explain magnetism to older children. Put the magnet under a piece of paper, and sprinkle some iron filings on top (you can obtain them from a hobby or hardware store, or perhaps from running your magnet through the nearest dirt pile). The filings will arrange themselves in a pattern that reflects the magnetic field. Explain that the magnet has a positive and negative pole, and that opposites attract, while likes repel. Just like so many other things in the world.

Mail Call

If your kids love getting and sending mail, this activity might become an instant favorite.

Find a large cardboard box that, when placed on end, is nearly as tall as your child. Cut a flap at the top and bend it toward you to create a door. Fashion a handle out of cardboard and tape it to the door. Cut another door in the lower front of the box—this will be used for retrieving the mail.

Provide your child with lots of re-cycled envelopes from junk mail or bills. Obsolete stationery from the home or office can also be used. If any of the junk mail has come with stickers, offer these as stamps.

Let your kid(s) write on the envelopes; they will want to include letters and drawings, pictures clipped from maga-zines, or anything else of importance. In a group setting, the children can take turns collecting the mail from the box putting it into a mail pouch, and deliver-ing it around the house. Older children might want to read their letters aloud.

Best of all, you can rest assured that the living room mail system operates flawlessly in rain, sleet, and snow—and all without rate increases.

Required:

- Cardboard box (and tools for adult to cut it)
- Envelopes from junk mail
- Obsolete envelopes and stationery
- Crayons and markers
- Magazines

Make a Bird

I s it a bird? Is it a plane? If you do this activity right, it should *look* like a bird.

Take a sheet of paper and have your child draw the outline of a bird, or trace one from a magazine picture. You can now fill in the shape by using nontoxic glue to affix the following kinds of materials.

Feathers. If you live by or visit the seashore, bird feathers should be plentiful.

Leaves. If you live in an area where the leaves change color in the fall, collect different colored leaves and press them in a book to dry them out (see #172). When dry, use the different colors for different parts of the bird: for instance, red for the head, yellow for the neck, brown for the body, and orange for the wings. Glue the leaves in an overlapping fashion to create a feathery look. When the glue dries, you'll have a piece of nature art to display proudly.

Required:

- Paper and pencil/crayon
- Glue
- Feathers, or leaves

Make a Book

Who hasn't thought about writing a book? You and children can become instant authors. Here's how.

Browse through magazines, junk mail, mail order catalogs, brochures, and other printed material for pictures of things that interest your child. Next, organize the pictures so they form a simple story line, then tape or glue the pictures onto sheets of paper. Staple or string the pages together or put them in a notebook.

For pre-readers, you can make up a story together, prompting them with questions like "Where did the doggie go?" or "What do you think the boy did next?" Keep it short—your child will delight in being able to "read" his or her story back to you and to brothers and sisters.

Older kids will likely make up their own stories with no problem. If they're learning to read and write, you can help them with the spelling of troublesome words.

Stand back and enjoy where the story goes. To use the language of publishing, you're acting as production manager, not editor!

Required:

- Pictures from magazines and other sources
- Nontoxic glue
- Paper
- Stapler or hole punch and notebook

Invent-an-Animal

This activity will definitely stretch your child's imagination to the limits.

Pose different requirements for animals, and see how your child solves them. For example, how about an imaginary animal that lives on the land, but likes to submerge himself in water. The animal can't hold his breath—and must inhale air. What kind of beast might fit the bill? Some possible answers: one with nostrils on top of his head, or a nose like a trunk that works like a snorkel, or a snorkel tube on his back.

How about an animal that can fly fast *and* run fast—wings would get in the way of fast running, and long legs might get in the way of fast wings. Possible answers: an animal with wings with feet on the tips, or legs that actually change into wings.

Have your child assign a name to some of the creatures and sketch them if he or she is so moved. Collect everything in a "strange zoo" notebook—and add this to your child's collection of creative works.

Required:
- Paper
- Crayons or markers
- Notebook

I've Got a List

A rmed with just a pencil and paper, your child can exercise both logic and imagination by coming up with lists; all you have to do is provide the categories. (You may have to act as scribe for prewriters.)

Following are some ideas. Ask your child to find and list things in the immediate environment that . . .

Required:
- Pencil
- Paper

> . . . *are stacked on top of something else.*
> . . . *are smaller than a breadbox.*
> . . . *are bigger than a breadbox.*
> . . . *were given to the family.*
> . . . *run on electricity.*
> . . . *touch the floor.*
> . . . *can be reused or recycled.*

You can customize the activity to your child's age and ability simply by adjusting the target number of items being sought. Five or six will be challenging for very young listmakers; older ones will be able to come up with many more. After a while, your child may even volunteer some surprising categories of his or her own!

Jet Races and Others

This activity involves absolutely no skill; "winning" is a matter of pure luck.

Use string, yarn, or tape to create targets or finish lines on the floor. Then blow up a balloon for each child (you can also play this with a single kid). Count down from three—at "go," everyone lets fly with a balloon. The object will depend on your surroundings; you may opt to try to get the balloons to land in a target zone or cross the finish line.

For variety, you might choose to decorate lightweight paper bags, blow up the balloons inside them, and release. Hint: the bags must be as light as possible—trim or tear away any excess paper not needed to hold the balloon.

Another twist on this idea involves attaching a two-inch length of straw to the empty paper bag. Pass an 8- to 10-foot-long piece of string through the straw, then stretch the string between two chairs. Pull the bag to one end, blow up the balloon inside the bag (but do not tie it) and then let go. Do this with two sets of chairs at a time, and presto: balloon raceways!

Have fun, but don't take things too seriously—it's all just hot air.

(This game is intended for older children only. Younger children should not play with balloons because of the possibility of suffocation.)

Safety Reminder
Balloon

Required:

- Balloons
- String, yarn, or tape

Optional:

- Crayons or markers
- Paper bags
- Straw

**Safety
Reminder**

Stove

Required:

• Flour

• Salt

• Water

• Poster or
tempera paints

Optional:

• Cookie cutters

• Plastic
containers

Judy's Clay

This recipe for homemade clay allows you to "fire" any objects your children make in your kitchen stove. (A grownup job.)

To make Judy's Clay, have your child mix four cups of flour, one cup of salt, and 1¾ cups of water. When the material has a nice even texture, roll it out, then let your child get down to business with some shaping activities. Supply cookie cutters and plastic containers for making imprints (plastic strawberry baskets make neat patterns). If the kids are making ornaments or other treasures to be hung from a string, remind them to punch a small hole in the object.

Once your kids are done with their masterpieces, bake the clay at 200 degrees for about three hours. It's important to keep the temperature low and the baking time long; you're evaporating the water. (Again: managing the oven is not for kids.) Once the objects have cooled, use poster paint or tempera paint to decorate them.

Thanks go to Judith Burros for this recipe—her kids' homemade clay Christmas ornaments are just as good today as they were 20 years ago.

Juice Bar Delight

In the summertime, your kids may be used to slurping down lots of frozen "pop" bars. The only problem is, these treats have minimal value (most are essentially colored sugar water). Plus, they're expensive. Why not make a project out of making your own juice bars with your kids?

All you need are a few paper cups, some reclaimed, washed plastic spoons, and a bottle or two of your favorite fruit juices. Pour juice into the cup, set the spoon in (it will freeze at an angle, but that adds to the character), and place the cup in the freezer. Approximately two hours later, run the cup under warm water and you'll have a delicious home-made frozen treat.

Your kids will eventually find themselves experimenting with various juice combinations, some of which will be quite tasty. We can vouch for apple/cranberry juice bars; other, more adventurous flavors proved too intense to sample. You'd flinch, too, at a gourmet tomato juice/pickle drainings/peach nectar bar.

Required:
- Juices
- Paper cups
- Spoons
- Refrigerator

Junior Robot

Everybody loves a friendly robot. And you can make a quick and easy robot suit out of some readily available kitchen supplies.

Starting at the top, fashion head gear out of a paper bag. Make holes for the robot's eyes, nose, and mouth. For a more mechanical look, take two yogurt container tops and cut out the bottoms. Tape the remaining circular frames around the eye holes. You can also cut out the bottoms of small paper cups, then tape the cups to the mask. Fashion an angular nose from cardboard. (Of course, you can simply have your child sketch in facial features with crayons and markers.)

Next, cut out armholes and a neck hole in another paper shopping bag. Glue on paper towel tubes, straws, plastic container lids, coffee cup lids, packing materials, and other mechanical-looking objects. Wrap a cereal box in kraft paper, add some dials, and tape or glue it to the torso shopping bag; this is the control center.

Finish the outfit with kraft paper sleeves and pantlegs; your child is now ready to bring the robot to life.

Required:

- 2 shopping bags
- Crayons and markers
- Paper towel tubes
- Plastic containers and lids
- Cereal box
- Kraft paper

Just in Time

How many times a day do you find yourself saying, "Just a second," "Just one minute," or "Just a few minutes"? What do these ideas really mean to your child? To find out, try these time games.

Find a clock or watch with a second hand. Then have your child close his or her eyes and start counting, "One hippopotamus, two hippopotamus," and so on, explaining that it takes about one second to say each "hippopotamus." Now see if your child can mentally count off the seconds—and tell you when ten seconds are up.

Now move on to longer periods of time. Show your child how long it takes for the second hand to move around the clock, explaining that the full circle is one minute. Then explain that two revolutions around the clock are two minutes. (Even if your child can't tell time, he or she may be able to comprehend the idea of the second hand going full circle.) Try having your child let you know when one or two minutes are up. Then hold the watch or clock out of sight and have your child guess when a minute has passed.

By the way, how long did it take you to read this?

Required:

- Watch or clock with second hand

Keeper of the Cans

Do you live in a region that requires deposits on beverage containers? If so, your child can use this "hidden money" as part of an ongoing project that will help him or her learn about managing resources and helping others.

Appoint your child "keeper of the cans" and ask him or her to select a charitable organization or community group that would benefit from a donation from your family. (You may have to help younger children select an appropriate charity; your local chapter of the United Way is always a good candidate for giving.) Your child's job: to find a secure space for the receptacles, to keep them neatly stored, and to keep a running total of the amount of money your family is setting aside in the form of deposits. After a week or two, accompany your child to the deposit redemption center, help him or her transfer the cash into a check or money order and oversee the mailing of the proceeds. If the organization you and your child select is close, you may be able make the donation in person—even more satisfying.

Required:

- Beverage containers

- Secure, safe storage space

- Pencil

- Paper

Kiddie Bank

L ots of kids seem to think that the
bank is where anyone can go to get
any amount of money needed, free.
Would that it were so easy!

Your children might enjoy playing
teller in your living room bank. And they
can learn about counting currency, too.
All you really need for a teller's window
(or automatic teller machine, for that matter) is an open-backed chair—although
you can always create something a bit
more elaborate out of a cardboard box. Of
course, you'll need to make stacks of play
currency, unless you have a Monopoly
set you can raid temporarily for this
game. Coupons and junk mail inserts
make excellent currency; see also Currency Games (#68). You can usually get
an extra checkbook cover for free from
your bank, and you can always use some
slips of note paper for a few check deposit
slips. And for customers with savings
accounts, any small notebook will do.

Finally, provide some "coins" (we
suggest the large childproof tops from
aspirin bottles—they're big enough to
be safe when used by small depositors).
You may also want to supply a small
zipper bag for customers who make
large cash deposits.

Join in the fun: open an account yourself. Just don't expect any complimentary toasters to come your way—kid
bank officers run a pretty tight ship.

Required:
• Play money

Optional:
• "Coins" from
  aspirin bottles
• Crayons
• Notebook

Kids' Celebrations

W ho says only our elected officials can declare new holidays? Your child is just as capable of deciding what days we should honor events, people, and animals. Here are some of the major holidays we've come to observe in our house:

Required:

• Pen or pencil

• Calendar

Green and Blue Day (April 16)

Blue and Green Day—a *very* different affair (May 2)

Rubber Band Day (June 19)

Lemonade Week (July 2-8)

Lego Week (August 19-25)

Be Kind to Your Pillow Month—pillow fights at specified hours only (October)

Bubble Month—at least one Monster Bubble (#198) a day (June)

L.. our child create his or her own own write them on a calendar. By the way, have you decided what you're going to wear this coming Toadstool Day?

Indy 500 Balloon Race

Safety
Reminder

Balloon

Here is a great balloon activity you can sponsor without having to find a helium tank.

Tape a short length of plastic straw to the top of each balloon. Set up pairs of chairs a room-length apart, and cut string long enough to stretch between the backs. Feed the string through a straw on one of the balloons, then tie the ends to a pair of chair backs. Repeat this procedure for each player, then start the clock. This time everyone will have to blow the balloons while walking. One important rule: Players may not touch the balloons in any way.

On your mark, get set, blow!

(This game is intended for older children only. Younger children should not play with balloons because of the possibility of suffocation.)

Required:

- Large balloons
- Straw
- String
- Chairs

Initial Game

Required:
- Paper
- Pencils

Here's a game that requires only a few sheets of paper and some pencils. Draw a vertical line down the left-hand side of one of the sheets; on the left-hand side of that line, write the alphabet. When you're done, think of a letter at random. On the right-hand side of the line, write that letter across from the letter A at the top of the page—then continue alphabetically until you pass Z, start again at A, and exhaust all 26 letters. Duplicate the sheets for as many people as are playing. You should then be left with two or more identical sheets with columns along the left-hand side that look something like this.

AQ	EU	IY
BR	FV	JZ
CS	GW	KA (etc.)
DT	HX	

The challenge is to come up with as many celebrities, historical figures, or friends *known to all players* as possible—with initials that match your list. For instance, GW could translate to George Washington; DT might be your family friend David Tucker.

Have the person who made the list call out the initials. Everyone can work together to think of people to match each pair. Finally, count how many you come up with at the end and go back and fill in the impossible pairs with silly entries like "Henry Xissinger."

Instant Orchestra

The following easy-to-play musical instruments are tried-and-true winners guaranteed to get toes tapping and heads bobbing. Your kids may not always be in tune, but isn't that a matter of opinion?

Have your child gather and assemble:

The basic comb-and-tissue-paper organic synthesizer. Wrap a comb with two or three layers of tissue paper and switch on. Have your child hum with gently parted lips and hold the synthesizer to his or her mouth. No electricity required.

The empty oatmeal container drum. These days the cardboard cylinders come with plastic lids; purists prefer the standard cardboard-lid model. A wooden spoon is the drumstick of choice.

The pop-bottle wind ensemble. One or more plastic pop bottles will yield superior tone; all the musician has to do is blow gently across the top of the spout. Add water to vary the tone.

On the count of three . . .

Required:

- Comb
- Tissue paper
- Oatmeal container
- Wooden spoon
- Pop bottle

Optional:

- Water

154

Instruction Manual

M ost anyone can drink a glass of water, make a bowl of cereal, or tie shoelaces. But how about writing detailed *instructions* for others to follow on how to carry out such tasks?

For small kids, you can take dictation on such matters as how to stack blocks, open an envelope, or close a door. Then try reading the instructions back—and see if your child actually completes the task in question when following the instructions to the letter. "Put the shoes in the closet." may seem like a pretty clear command, but if the closet door is closed your child should probably give instructions on turning the knob, opening the door, turning on the closet light, etcetera.

Older kids can try describing advanced tasks like jumping rope or making a paper airplane.

How about explaining how you tie your shoes? That's a *very* tough one—try it yourself!

Required:

- Pen or pencil
- Paper

International Capitals

Do you know the capital of Uruguay? You will when you're done with this activity. Or at least your child will.

Have your child name any country he or she can think of—then try to name the capital yourself. Now it's your child's turn—name a country (not too obscure), and see if he or she can come up with the capital.

Of course, you'll need to have an almanac or atlas handy to verify the accuracy of guesses. Once you get the easy ones like Great Britain (London) and France (Paris) out of the way, you'll be ready to tackle toughies like Zaire (Kinshasa) and Guatemala (Guatemala City).

By the way, the capital of Uruguay is Montevideo. But you knew that.

Other international capitals: Canberra (Australia); Ottawa (Canada); Havana (Cuba); Abidjan (Ivory Coast); Moscow (Soviet Union); Madrid (Spain); Stockholm (Sweden).

Required:
• Your time only

International News

E ven if your child can't read or write, here's an activity that will provide both entertainment and information about other cultures.

On a sheet of scratch paper, write the name of a country followed by the words "Times" and "News," as in Japan Times or Japan News. Now work on some "articles" with your child. First ask what your child knows about Japan—the language, food, where it's located on the map, etc. Then write a few sentences about each topic. If you can find a sample of Japanese writing, let your child imitate it. And be sure to affix any pictures relating to the country you might find in magazines. (Note: You don't have to become an expert on the countries in question—just a few general facts will get you going. If you really get into the activity, a good almanac or a travel guide on the featured countries will give you lots to talk about with your child.)

As you create more newspapers for different countries, combine them in a notebook: Find a picture of a globe you can put on the cover, and you'll have the world in your play room.

Required:
- Paper
- Pens, crayons, or markers

Optional:
- Notebook
- Picture of globe

Improbable Cuisine

O ur son and his friends often delight in suggesting some rather strange foodstuffs. You and your child can too, just to pass the time away (or while waiting for a meal to finish cooking). Here, with apologies to vegetarians, are some favorites from our household:

Required:

• Your time only

> French fried snake toes on whole wheat bricks
> Glazed mouse antlers on rye socks
> Peanut butter and lizard wings on phone books
> Fish feet with banana chairs
> Cold hippo feathers
> Hot chicken fins on fence posts
> Bird tusk pie with mouse flippers on top
> Camel wing stew

And the list goes on. How many improbable entrees can *your* child come up with between now and dinner? What about a frog ear and Swiss on dark flannel?

Improvised Card Games

A deck of playing cards can provide hours of entertainment for your child—without your having to explain how to play poker or blackjack.

Required:

• Playing card deck

Show your child all the marvelous pictures of people and symbols contained in a deck of cards. Then suggest that your child develop a game of his or her own using some of the following ideas: matching all cards of the same color; grouping cards with pictures or cards with numbers; comparing two cards and guessing which has the higher value; and so on.

The most entertaining game for you, however, may well be the not-uncommon one in which your child invents complex rules that seem to change with each new hand. At least it keeps everyone alert.

Watch out! Your child may play a two-suit stomp on your latest discard, then pick up all the black cards and proclaim, "Bingo."

In the Bag

Safety Reminder

Small Parts

M ost of us negotiate the world by means of sight and sound—so much so that we often ignore the rich textures about us. This game will help your kids stay tuned to the rich world of touch, and have plenty of fun in the process.

Place a number of common objects into a paper bag. You might select favorite toys and/or stuffed animals; household objects such as sponges or kitchen utensils; food items such as celery stalks, carrots, cucumbers, and so on. Then have your children feel inside the bag without looking and try to identify the objects. Give clues, if needed, and gear the selection of items in the bag to your child's experience and abilities.

You can increase the challenge by having your kids identify similar objects by touch. For example, show them several toy cars (or: dolls, blocks, keys . . .) that are roughly the same size and shape, and then drop them into the bag. Ask the children to identify the different items by touch alone. Perhaps they'll prove that the hand can indeed be quicker than the eye!

Required:

- Paper bag
- Household items

Indoor Safari

Is that a floor lamp or a giraffe with a lampshade on its head? Only one way to find out—ask your child to act as safari leader.

Your child can conduct a safari right in your living room (or any other room in your house); it just takes a little prep time. First, take paper and cut out various sets of footprints. Draw some feet with pads and claws for lions and tigers; hoofs for gazelles, zebras, and antelopes; feet with "thumbs" for gorillas and monkeys; and big round feet for elephants and hippos.

Next, make a pair of binoculars for each member of the safari by taping together two toilet paper tubes. (You might want to cover them with black paper first.)

Lay out a trail of footprints leading to different parts of your house. Perhaps the hippos and elephants have headed toward the bathtub for a drink. The monkeys may be hiding in your hanging plants. And the tiger family may be lounging in a den made from couch pillows.

Make sure you all keep your cool when looking for the animals—too much noise and they may head for the hills.

Required:

- Paper
- Toilet paper tubes

Ibble Dibble

Do you speak Ibble Dibble? It's more fun than Pig Latin, and twice as impossible for the uninitiated to understand.

Here's how it works. Simply insert the nonsense sound "ibble" before every vowel sound, so the word "strawberry" comes out sounding "stribble-aw-bibble-air-ibble-ee." For words that begin with vowels, all you do is substitute the sound "dibble" at the beginning of the word.

Let's see how Ibble Dibble works in a sample sentence. Suppose you wanted to say, "If you are able, give me back my bubble bath, Sibyl" in Ibble Dibble. That becomes "Dibble-if yibble-ooo dibble-are dibble-ayb-ibble-ul, gibble-ive mibble-ee bibble-ack mibble-eye bibble-ub-ibble-ul bibble-ath, Sibble-ib-ibble-yl." The trick is to remember that you're looking for every vowel *sound*, and you're not paying any attention to the way the word is spelled. Everything is phonetic, so "bubble" has two vowel sounds.

Gibble-et dibble-it?

Required:
• Your time

Ice Cream Vendor

146

Safety Reminder

Small Parts

Required:

- Large cardboard box
- Sheet of cardboard (or box flaps)
- Thin cardboard sheet
- Ice cream cones
- Toilet paper tubes

With this activity, you can help preserve an endangered species—the old-fashioned ice cream cart.

Take a box at least two and a half feet long by a foot and a half or so wide and high. Cut a flap midway down on top, and fold it back to create a door into the body of the box (see illustration). Cut out wheels about five inches in diameter from a piece of heavy cardboard. Affix the wheels with brads or pipe cleaners so they turn. (If you use brads—those metal joint connectors—be sure to keep the pointed edges inside the box, and remember that small, swallowable parts should be kept away from younger children.) The wheels are really just for decoration; mount them so they just touch the ground. Have your child decorate the cart with crayons, markers, or tempera paint.

All you need now is the inventory. Make some ice cream cones: roll up thin cardboard to make the cone, and tape or glue a wad of paper on top for the ice cream. Don't forget popsicles: tape recycled sticks to toilet paper tubes. Of course, you'll want to provide some napkins. This kind of ice cream can get pretty messy!

Guess the Object

Here's a game sure to intrigue kids of all ages. Collect four or five objects (more for older kids) made out of various materials. For example, choose something made out of hard plastic (such as a ping-pong ball), something made out of wood (a block), a metal object (a toy car), a soft object (a stuffed animal), and, finally, something made out of cardboard (a small box).

Show these objects to your child, and let him or her touch and explore them. Then have your child turn around. Place one of the objects in an opaque plastic container with a lid; remove the rest from view. Make sure there's enough room for the object to move around freely in the container. Now let the child shake the container and rattle the object. Ask him or her to try and guess the object based on the sound.

Once your kids get good at this game, you can try placing more than one object in the container at a time, or have them race against the clock to identify an object.

One of the nice features of this activity is that you can really never run out of new objects to play with—just about anything of the right size is fair game.

Required:

- Common objects of different materials
- Opaque plastic container with lid

Half and Half

This is a fascinating way to write secret messages. You'll find you and your child can use it to facilitate all manner of sensitive communications about classified meetings, updates on the latest news around the house, or even— perish the thought—whether it's time to perform the "Secret Cleanup" on your child's "Secret Bedroom."

Required:
- Paper
- Pencil

Take a piece of paper and fold it lengthwise, but leave the two portions unequal; this will leave about three-quarters of an inch of paper protruding at the top. The trick is to write a message along the top, so that half of the writing appears on the three-quarters of an inch of protruding paper, and half appears below it.

After you've composed your secret message, fold the paper several times randomly. (This is to hide the secret fold from those who haven't yet won "Eyes Only" clearance.) Unfold. Only by repeating your initial folding procedure exactly will your message be readable!

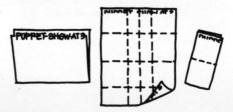

Hand Shadows

All you need for this activity is a darkened room, a lamp, and a little imagination.

Adjust the lamp until the shadows it casts are clear and the lamp itself is out of everyone's way. (You don't want any accidents arising from the sudden movements of enthusiastic audience members.) Then try the following shapes— or make up your own.

A flying bird. Link your thumbs and wave your fingers as you move your hands in an upward diagonal path.

A quacking duck. Join your two hands together, interlocking your fingers. Then extend your two index fingers and turn your hands so your palms are parallel to the floor. Tap your index fingers against one another.

A butterfly. Place your thumbs side-by-side; keep your fingers together. Touch your palms together, and then return them to their original position. Repeat. Amazing how many pets you have between your fingers!

Required:
- Darkened room
- Lamp

Hat Trick

No, this has nothing to do with hockey. The trick is to make your cards land inside the hat.

Just about any hat will do—a beat-up derby, a cowboy hat, even a baseball cap. Set the chapeau on the floor in the middle of a large room and pass out equal amounts of playing cards to all contestants. (You can also use blank three-by-five cards—just make sure everyone gets the same amount.)

Now have the players take turns throwing cards. (It's tougher than you might think—but remember, you can always adjust distances to match the skill and patience levels of the players.) Anyone who gets a card in the hat gets to keep tossing. The player with the most cards gets to start the next round.

In the unlikely event that one player manages to toss all his or her cards directly into the hat without missing even once, all other players get the chance to duplicate the feat. And let's face it—anyone who can get twenty in in a row really does deserve a tip of the hat.

Required:

- Hat
- Playing cards

Have It Your Way

What's the ultimate game for children? One they make up themselves.

Supply your child with pieces of cardboard uniformly cut to the same size. (The cardboard you get from the dry cleaner works well.) You'll also need a piece of heavy posterboard (good for a game board), crayons, markers, very large buttons (these are great tokens, but they should be kept out of reach of children under three years old). Finally, provide giant dice (#117), pieces of scrap paper, and a timer. Now set your child to the task of inventing a game of his or her design. If your child has trouble getting going, draw a snakelike path of squares to color and talk about special instructions to put on the squares . . . or pick up the pieces of cardboard and explain how to play fish. Be patient—at some point, a unique game will emerge.

If all else fails, you can teach your child to play Tegwar, a game described in detail in Mark Harris's novel *Bang the Drum Slowly*. Tegwar stands for The Exciting Game Without Any Rules, and it's most fun played with a grownup who thinks there must be some kind of system at work.

Required:

- Large piece of posterboard
- Pieces of cardboard and paper
- Crayons and markers
- Buttons
- Dice
- Timer

Heart Song

Children enjoy learning about the inner workings of their bodies, and pulse rate is an easy way to get them thinking about their circulatory system.

Required:
• Your time only

First, explain that the heart is like a pump. If you don't have a stethoscope handy, have your child put his or her ear on your chest to hear the "lub dub" sound. Next, describe the circulatory system as many hoses that carry blood from the heart to the lungs and all parts of the body, then return to the heart.

Show your child how to take a pulse reading at his or her wrist or neck (or your wrist or neck). Demonstrate how various activities cause the heart to speed up or slow down: running, jumping, lying down on the floor to take deep slow breaths, and so on. Younger kids will appreciate their pulse simply going faster or slower; for older kids, watch the clock, say start and stop, and let them count. (You can do the multiplication to determine the rate.)

You might want to save this activity for a rainy day: Test your child's pulse with lots of activities . . . then end with a nice long rest on the floor or couch.

Heavy Stuff

Does your kid think a pound of bricks weighs more than a pound of feathers? This activity can clue you into your child's understanding of the physical world.

Make a scale by placing a dowel or cardboard tube across two chair seats. Leave two feet in between. Use books to keep the dowel or tube from moving. Place a hanger over the dowel or tube, and tie an equal length of string to the bottom of the hanger at both ends. Put a piece of tape over the knots to keep the string from slipping. Next, attach identical strawberry (see #308) or paper baskets to the strings. Attach bits of clay to the hanger or baskets to level the "scale."

Have your child gather a variety of items that can be compared on the scale—say, a plastic animal and a lunch bag filled with paper strips. Or two toy trucks, roughly the same size, one wood and one metal. Explain that the heavier item makes the scale go down further than the lighter one, and that two items that weigh the same will balance the scale. Such is the way of nature.

Safety Reminder

Supervise Closely

Required:

- Dowel (3 feet) or cardboard tube from wrapping paper
- Wire hanger
- String
- Clay
- Strawberry or paper baskets

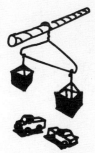

Hello

Your child will probably get a charge out of greeting people in many different tongues. Here's a roundup of "good day" salutations in eight different languages:

Required:

• Your time only

Chinese: Neehow
Dutch: Goeden dag
French: Bonjour
German: Guten tag
Hebrew: Shalom
Japanese: Konichee-wa
Serbo-Croatian: Dobar dan
Spanish: Buenos dias

You can devise all sorts of games with these salutations: use a different one each morning, or have the child make up a story together and see if your child can use all of the greetings in a five minute span. This will create a veritable tower of Babel! Perhaps this little game will stimulate a lifelong interest in learning languages.

Well, we gotta go—or habari za jioni, as they say in Swahili.

Hide It

T his simple "hide it" activity can be played just about anywhere, at any time, with whatever props are available.

Have your children volunteer a few small toy animals, cars, dolls, or similar objects. (Keep swallowable objects away from younger children.) You can use just about anything that's small and can be safely manhandled. Instruct your child to wait in another room (or close his or her eyes). Then hide the objects around the room, and invite your kids to find them. Gauge the level of difficulty to your child's age and abilities. Remember that most kids will look for things at eye-level or lower—you can increase the level of challenge by placing the toys or objects in slightly higher spots. Provide clues or feedback in terms of being "warm" or "cold." Reverse the roles when your child has found all the objects.

When it's your turn, use the game as an opportunity to teach your kids how to give clues. But don't be surprised if your child tells you the exact where-abouts of the object you're searching for—some secrets are just too good not to tell!

Required:

• Small toys or household objects

Safety Reminder

Supervise Closely

Required:

- Eggs
- Bowl
- Watercolors
- Felt-tip markers
- Macaroni, barley

Hollow Eggs

Once upon a time, the name Faberge meant a little more than cologne; it was the name of the man who perfected the decoration of hollow eggs with precious trappings like diamonds and gold. Even though your child's list of materials may be a little more modest, he or she can still create masterpieces that will last a good long while by hollowing out an egg.

The first step is for you to do: Using a pin, carefully make one hole in each end of an uncooked egg. The bottom hole should be biggest. Now comes the part where your child can help—have him or her blow through the top hole, emptying the contents of the egg into a bowl. (Don't eat the raw egg, though.) The hollowed egg shells will be strongest if you allow them to dry for a day before decorating them with watercolors or felt-tip markers. You can even attach precious baubles (well, macaroni or uncooked barley) in place with nontoxic glue, and color them for added effects that would have garnered a nod from Faberge himself.

Home Planetarium

These days, a good planetarium projector costs a little over $300,000. That may be too pricey, but you *can* create a pretty wild—and even educational—light show with nothing more than a flashlight and some common household items.

To make a home planetarium projector, draw a constellation or random star pattern on a six-inch square piece of paper. (A trip to the local library or bookstore might be helpful if you want an accurate star pattern.) The next part is for grownups only: Cut out the stars with an X-acto knife—or fold the paper where you would like each hole and clip with a pair of scissors. Next, remove both ends of a large juice can, and wrap the paper around one end. You can either tape the paper on the end, or hold it in place with a rubber band. Insert a flashlight into the open end, and shine the light onto the ceiling of a darkened room. Shine the flashlight at an angle, onto the side of the can, rather than directly through the paper, to minimize distortion. Have your kids hold the light and rotate the stars around the ceiling. It's fun—and just think about what you can do with the $299,999 you saved on the projector!

Required:

- Flashlight
- Large juice can
- Paper
- Tape or rubber band
- Scissors or X-acto knife (adult use only)

Homemade Dashboards

Required:

- Cardboard box
- Plastic container lids
- Bottle caps
- Brads
- Crayons and markers
- Cardboard tubes

Extracting our son from the driver's seat of our car proved to be one of the greatest parenting challenges we had ever faced. Life became easier when we gave him his own dashboard.

You can make a dashboard, too. Find a sturdy cardboard box at least eighteen inches wide. Next, attach parts—lots of them. (Here comes the payoff from saving all those plastic lids and odd-sized plastic gizmos we mentioned in the Introduction.) Punch a hole in the top of a yogurt container, and affix it to the box with a brad (a pronged metal affixer you can purchase at any stationery store). You now have a free-spinning dial. Put markings on the dial and the box to make a meter. Affix a paper plate the same way—the dashboard now has a steering wheel.

A paper towel tube makes a splendid gear shift lever, and bottle tops make excellent buttons. The more dials and buttons and moving parts, the more interesting the dashboard. Be sure to leave a slot for a key!

We used ours in the car at first, then found that the dashboard can be used for off-road travel, too. Your child can use the dashboard to explore the depths of the ocean, or even the outer reaches of the galaxy.

Homonyms

Homonyms are words that sound the same, but are really different. In this game, you give clues to your child about the two homonyms you're thinking of . . . and see if he or she can guess the words!

Here are some examples: "I'm thinking of a word that describes what a bandage helps do for a cut and the back of your foot." (Heal/heel.) "I'm thinking of a word that's a letter and a drink." (T/tea.) "I'm thinking of a word that has to do with the post office and with people who aren't women." (Mail/male.) Here are some more to get your game started.

Required:
• Your time

Ant/aunt
Bored/board
Bear/bare
Beat/beet
Hole/whole
Meet/meat
Reel/real
Rose/rows
Sea/see
Two/too
Use/ewes
Way/weigh

House Detective

In Hide It (#135), you played the classic "warmer/colder" finding game with your child. Now give your child clues about common objects hidden in your house. Tailor the clues to your child's abilities.

One variation involves beating the clock. Use an egg timer or kitchen timer to create an air of excitement. If several children are involved in the game, make sure that they understand they're competing against the clock, not each other.

For older kids, try making up written clue cards on scrap paper or index cards. ("I am in something square." "I am next to a small bottle." "I am inside the largest thing in the living room.") Each card should contain a single clue; the goal is to see how few clues the child needs to locate the object.

Don't miss the opportunity to call your child's attention to things that have personal stories behind them, such as heirlooms or antiques, or items that bring your family history to life.

Required:
• Your time

Optional:
• Scraps of paper

House of Cards

Playing cards make for wonderful building materials. Here are some games that will entertain your child and build his or her fine dexterity.

Start out with some basic forms. A teepee is easy, and can be turned into a square by propping cards up against the open ends, tilted at a slight angle, and placing two additional cards at the ends of the two new cards. (See illustration.)

Your child will quickly see how delicately the cards must be placed and how easily a house of cards will tumble. Don't breathe too hard – you might undo an afternoon's work!

Once your child gets the hang of card architecture, suggest that he or she make a multi-story building. Other challenges include making a corridor of cards or a bridge.

For ideas on a simpler version of this activity for younger children, see Easy House of Cards (#86).

Required:

• Playing card deck

House of Cups

What to do with those pesky, un-recyclable disposable cups? Save them, wash them, then break them out on a rainy day for the world stacking championship!

Required:

• Disposable drinking cups (saved and washed)

Stacking cards may be fun for some, but stacking cups is sometimes a better bet when it comes to keeping young hands and attention spans engaged. The game is great fun when two or more play, but it can also make an excellent solo diversion.

Perhaps you and your child can take turns placing the cups on top of one another – carefully, of course. If your child gives in to a sudden desire to seize the bottom cup, that's okay.

How high can you make them go before they tumble on their own? How many cups does it take to build a passable reproduction of the Tower of London? Can you stack different types of cups without initiating an avalanche? Only time, patience, and a good chunk of table space will tell.

Household Factory

Manufacturing machinery can be fascinating for kids and adults alike. With this activity, your child can pretend that he or she is stamping out widgets (whatever those are), toys, or common household objects.

Take a large box and tape the flaps down. The box should be fairly sturdy. Cut a flap near the bottom, giving your child access to the inside. (Remember that cutting cardboard is a grownup job.) Cut a square hole in the back large enough for toys to pass through. Now cut a few holes in the top—two should be just the right size to snugly hold toilet paper or paper towel tubes. Decorate with crayons; see Dashboards, #138, for ideas about affixing plastic container tops and other common items to make moving dials.

Collect several toys, stuffed animals, and household items such as radios or clocks. Ask your child to close his or her eyes, then insert one of the items to be "manufactured" through the back. Next, have your child turn the dials, flip the switches, and do other important stuff. When your child decides the item is done, he or she simply opens the front flap, and there, ready for shipment to your house, is—whatever.

Required:

- Large cardboard box
- Tape
- Paper towel and toilet paper tubes
- Crayons or markers
- Dashboard items (see #138)
- Toys, stuffed animals, household props

The Household Gallup Poll

Turn your child into a roving interviewer; supply a clipboard, paper, and pencil, and stand back.

You're about to find out how family members *really* feel about important issues like favorite colors, preferred pets, favorite ice cream flavors, vacation plans, and what time they like to go to bed. You're about to learn the power of the Household Gallup Poll.

The limits to this activity exist only in your child's imagination; after you explain the initial idea of a poll (you may be able to sneak in a little math for the older kids), all you have to do is answer forthrightly, refer the polltaker to other likely respondents, and sit back and wait for the results.

You may find that 100 percent of your kids feel they should be able to stay up later. But you can rest assured that the findings are nonscientific enough for you to pronounce certain results inconclusive.

Required:
- Clipboard
- Paper
- Pencil

RASPBERRY

Gotcha!

This is a fun game for two—you pop hypothetical "hot dog" balloons.

Take four sheets of paper and draw four identical ten-square-by-ten-square grids, labeled with letters for the columns and numbers for the rows. Each player gets two grids. Each grid represents a square of air—one for the player's own balloons, and one for his or her guesses about the other person's balloons.

Before play starts, each player positions the balloons by putting Xs in various squares (see illustration for a sample layout). Each player must use: one balloon that is five squares in length; two that are four squares in length, three that are three squares in length; and two that are two squares in length. (No, the balloons can't turn corners or bend on the diagonal!)

The first player lets fly with an arrow: "A4." The other must respond with either "Hit" or "Miss." (One arrow hit does in any balloon.) All of a player's shots are recorded on his second grid. Play alternates until one player sees his final balloon burst—until the next game!

Required:
- Paper
- Pencils

Grandmother's Button Box

Did you ever play the old childhood favorite, Grandmother's Button Box? If not, this will fill a hole in your past. Here's how to play the game with one or more kids.

Required:

• Your time only

The first person says, "I went to my grandmother's button box and I found a hat (or some other object)." The next person then says, "I went to my grandmother's button box and found a hat and (another object)." The next person adds an object to the previous items until the sequence gets too hard to remember. Have older children keep the sequence alphabetical for an added twist. ("I found an airplane ticket," " . . . a bag full of ribbons," ". . . a carrot," and so on.)

A variation on the game is to have the children think of a pocket instead of a button box. This is similar to the old folk tale about the mitten full of animals in the forest: "My pocket is oh so heavy because it holds a hippopotamus." The next person then adds his or her contribution to the pocket—and play proceeds until no one can remember the whole list, the pocket gets too full, or the giggles get too loud.

Grass Whistle

Good thing this is an outdoor activity—the whistles emanating from these all-natural noisemakers can be a little on the loud side. We have a feeling that will make your kids love them all the more.

Find a fat blade of fresh grass. Now hold it flat between the outer edges of both thumbs so that it forms a reed. (You should be able to see both your thumbnails straight on as you do this.)

Just below the knuckles of your thumbs will be an elongated, oval-shaped opening for you to blow through. Give a toot—you'll be heard practically in the next county.

Helpful hint: The most common mistake in assembling natural whistles is to leave the grass limp between your thumbs. The blade of grass must be taut; you might try pulling the top of the blade of grass over the tip of one thumb before you apply the other one.

Try it—anyone can whistle!

Required:
• Blade of fresh grass

Grasshopper Anatomy

Insects have very different bodies than ours—the problem is that they're so small and move so fast that we usually don't have a chance to see them for very long.

If you can, track down a grasshopper. Then put him in a plastic jar with a screw-top lid and see how many of the insect's body parts you can identify using the list below and the accompanying drawing. (Let your guest go back where he came from after you're finished with the anatomy check.)

Listen—did you hear someone's legs rubbing together?

head (a)
thorax (b)
abdomen (c)
foreleg (d)
middle leg (e)
hind leg (f)
fore wing (g)
hind wing (h)

Required:
- Plastic container
- Grasshopper

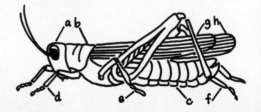

Green Hair

Here's an activity in which you and your child can create people and animal faces with "hair" that grows. Actually, it's grass; it works like this.

Provide your child with used Styrofoam or white paper cups. Have your child draw animal or human faces on them with crayons or markers. You might also provide pieces of cork or felt that can be glued onto the cups to make facial features, ears, beards, etc. (anything *except* hair).

Fill the cups with potting soil and sprinkle the top with a layer of grass seed, which can be purchased from your local garden store. Moisten the dirt and place the cups in a moist area. Make sure the soil doesn't dry out. Within a week or two, your child's cup face will begin to sprout delicate strands of green hair, which will eventually become thick shocks in need of a trim job.

Under your supervision, your child can then switch from gardener to hairdresser, cutting and trimming as he or she sees fit (with safety scissors, of course).

Required:
- Paper or Styrofoam cups
- Markers or crayons
- Grass seed
- Soil
- Safety scissors

Grid Game

This activity is a combination of skill and luck. It also draws on your child's visual memory and powers of observation.

Find a large piece of paper or posterboard (at least three feet by three feet). Draw a grid on the paper with five columns and five rows; each square in the grid should be at least 6 inches across. On the top, put characteristics like "soft," "hard," "smooth," "shiny," etc. On the left side list five colors.

Have your child stand at a designated spot and toss a bean bag onto the grid (see #19 for instructions in making a bean bag). If the bean bag falls in the square corresponding to "shiny" and "red," he or she must find a shiny red object in the house. Tailor the grid so it matches the objects in your house.

You can also create a grid for animals, trucks, and other things your child can name from his or her own experience. For example, an animal grid might contain qualities like "smooth skin," "four legs," "lives in water," etc. The possibilities are virtually limitless—and a grid game a day keeps boredom away!

Required:
- Large piece of paper
- Marker
- Bean bag

Grocery Cart Rembrandt

The next time you need to put together a shopping list, try to leave yourself a little extra time. By avoiding slapping the list together at the last minute, you'll be able get your kid into the act in a creative way—and make the trip itself a lot more entertaining.

Instead of jotting down the items yourself, give your child a big piece of paper and something to scribble with. Now tell your child each item you'll need from the store, and help him or her write—or draw—the item.

Drawing is especially fun, and will provide you with a little fun as you work from your rather unconventional list at the store.

Don't be concerned about those quizzical looks from your fellow shoppers. You've got a grocery list with a difference!

Required:

- Paper
- Pencil or crayons

Grown Up Stuff

Remember dressing up in your parents' clothes when you were a child? Didn't it make you feel strong and proud to wear Dad's jacket or hat, Mom's purse or high heels?

Required:

• Your clothes
• Kids' hats

Encourage your kids to do the same, and prompt them to talk about who they are. For example, suggest that they describe what Mom and Dad do at work, how they relax, how they treat each other, their kids, and their friends, and how they behave around the house, etc.

Now switch roles—put on one of your kid's hats, and act out your child in various situations: happy and sad, serious and clowning, and so on.

Beyond the entertainment aspect, this kind of role playing is a terrific way to get at difficult or touchy issues. You'll learn things about yourself that you can't see during your everyday role as parent.

Kid stuff, grown up stuff—when you get right down to it, isn't it all a matter of what hat you wear?

Easy Trail Mix

Before you and your child head out for an adventure, why not whip up a batch of trail mix—you never know when you're going to need an extra burst of energy.

Pay a visit to your local natural food store, or the natural food section of your supermarket. Purchase raisins and other dried fruit (apples and apricots are great), nuts, carob (or chocolate) chips, and granola.

Provide sandwich bags or plastic containers, and have your child sprinkle some granola into each bag or container to give the trail mix some bulk. Then let your child experiment by adding various proportions of the other ingredients. (You'll probably want to limit the supply of carob or chocolate chips.)

For some reason, trail mix you "cook" on your own – or with a little help from a nearby grownup – is much more appetizing than the storebought variety. Play it for all it's worth. Food is more nutritious when you eat it.

Ready to hit the road?

Required:

- Raisins/dried fruit
- Nuts
- Carob chips
- Granola
- Sandwich bags or plastic containers

Eat Right

Getting kids to eat right is an age-old problem. Now it's more important than ever—many pediatricians tell us that early childhood diet can have a dramatic affect on health later in life.

Required:

- Posterboard/ cardboard
- Pictures of food

To teach your kids about nutrition, make a game of it. Begin by constructing a food chart that shows the four food groups or "Basic Four": Protein, Dairy, Vegetable/Fruit, and Bread/Grains/ Cereals. Cut out pictures of various members of the groups and affix them to a large sheet of posterboard. Explain that to be healthy, we need foods from all of the groups.

Another way of teaching the groups is to take a large sheet of cardboard or posterboard and divide it into four quadrants, one for each food group. Cut up pictures of different foods and tape them to index cards. Make a stack, and have your child place the cards in their proper food group.

Once your kids know the Basic Four, steel yourself and have them categorize everything on the dinner table. How's your diet?

Egg Quiz (Or, What Goes Around, Comes Around)

Here's a little trick you can pass along to your child that he or she can use to surprise friends.

It requires two eggs, one hard-boiled egg and the other uncooked. Have your child bet his or her friend a cookie (or the proverbial "zillion dollars") that, even if the friend repositions the two eggs while your child's back is turned, he or she will be able to select the hard-boiled egg—and crack it open confidently, without fear of messing the place up.

The trick? Hard-boiled eggs spin merrily when you give them a turn; raw ones stop after a turn and a half or so. (Demonstrate the rotation differences before your child performs the trick—otherwise there may be an unfortunate miscalculation and an unpaid debt of one zillion dollars.)

Required:

- Uncooked egg
- Hard-boiled egg

The Eightfold Path

Here's a trick that will make your kids (or anyone else who learns it) look like geniuses. It's actually simplicity itself.

Ask your partner if he or she knows how to fold paper. The answer will be a smug "yes." Then ask if it's possible to fold a piece of paper in half more than seven times. "Of course!"

Required:

• Sheet of paper

But it isn't. No matter what kind of paper you use, any sheet you pass along will be too thick by the time it hits that eighth fold. Try it and see.

Don't ask us why this trick always works—we're told it has something to do with the way fibers lock together in the papermaking process. The point is, it's a reliable principle, whether you're using a sheet of newspaper or a sheet of fancy stationery.

After many attempts at that eighth crease, your partner will eventually decide it's impossible . . . and fold.

Elephant Dance

$\mathbb{A}$n innovative teacher we know once had everyone make elephant head gear and roam the outdoors, attracting great attention from onlookers. Here's how to make your own elephant gear.

Start off with a paper shopping bag. Cut eye holes and a nose hole. Next, roll up large piece of kraft paper, so you have a sturdy tube about two and a half feet long and two inches wide. Cut four lengthwise slits at one end of the tube, so you can fold back four sections like petals on a flower. Insert the "petals" into the nose hole, and tape them to the inside of the bag—the trunk will now remain firmly in place.

Next, cut out a pair of large ears from thin cardboard or posterboard. Affix them to the bag with a piece of wide masking tape running the full length of each ear. Don't worry about making them immobile—elephant ears are supposed to flop around.

Turn your elephant loose for a waltz in your yard—you'll be sure to amaze your friends and neighbors.

Required:

- Shopping bag
- Large piece of kraft paper
- Piece of thin cardboard
- Wide masking or packaging tape

The Enormous Radio

Remember the old-fashioned radios, the ones big enough to sleep four? Try making one out of a large box—appliance boxes work extremely well. (You can sometimes get boxes from floor models at appliance stores).

Make a speaker grille on the front of the box with crayons or markers, or glue a piece of fabric on the front. Add volume control and tuning "dials"; your child can draw the knobs with crayons or marker, or you can glue on yogurt container tops covered with colored paper or scrap foil. Finally, cut a door in the back for your child to climb inside, as well as two side windows to let light in.

Now tune in for some lively radio listening. Your child can sing, recite poems, read stories, present family and school news, or give editorials about the state of the house, the state of the world economy, and the meaning of the cosmos.

Suggest that your child pretend that he or she is a live talk show host. Pick a topic, like the weather or dinosaurs, then fire off questions to the expert in the box. "And just how *did* that large gorilla get to the top of the Empire State Building?"

Required:

- Large box
- Crayons or markers

Optional:

- Fabric
- Yogurt container tops

Family Book of Records

Your family no doubt has some astounding tales of strength, courage, and ability that should be recorded for posterity.

Get a three-ring binder and some dividers (or make the dividers from construction paper). Label the dividers Athletics, Blocks and Toys, Household, and so on. You should also collect a stack of three-hole punched scrap paper. Cover the notebook with kraft (coarse brown) paper, and have your kid(s) decorate it. Now ask questions like: What's the greatest number of blocks that you have stacked? The longest jump? The longest time balancing on one foot? The longest time staring at someone else without giggling? You can also keep the competitive aspect down by asking the same questions of each child, so that children only compete against themselves.

Jot down the feat, the record, the record holder, and the date, and place the information in the appropriate section. (Older kids who can write can serve as scribe). Affix a photograph or drawing if available.

There is only one rule: no one can challenge anyone else's accomplishment for at least 24 hours—that lets everyone have his or her day in the sun.

Required:

- 3-ring notebook
- Scrap paper/hole punch
- Dividers or construction paper
- Kraft paper

Family Calendar

H ere's a way to make a calendar that truly revolves around your child's sense of what's important.

On a large sheet of construction paper, draw a calendar grid for a particular month, a quarter, or the whole year. Select dates that your child is sure to be interested in, such as his or her birthday, the birthdays of other family members, major holidays or travel plans, and so on. Now cut out a flap for each date.

Place a piece of posterboard behind the calendar. Attach the two pieces with double stick tape or glue at the outer edges. Open each flap and draw or affix an appropriate picture or photograph to the second sheet. Then draw a picture for the outer flap, as well.

You can use the calendar to show your child how many days he or she has to wait before a special event. You can also use it to announce outings you'll know about a day or two in advance, such as trips to the zoo, the park, or a visit to a special friend.

Required:

- Large sheets of construction paper
- Sheet of posterboard
- Glue or double-stick tape
- Crayons or markers
- Photographs

Family Coat of Arms

You don't need to live in a castle to have a family coat of arms—your child can design one for you.

Explain that a coat of arms is a special picture for your family (most dictionaries and encyclopedias can show a sample coat of arms). To make one, just supply paper, crayons, markers, and paint. You might want to cut out a shield and some circular objects to trace, as well as a ruler.

Your child can add all sorts of "regal" trimmings—stars, stripes, trucks, animals, or even dinosaurs. Some kids will opt for a strange mix. (Our son decided that our household coat of arms would be Tyrannosaurus rex surrounded by three flowers and standing on a garbage truck.)

When the coat of arms is finished, hang it on the playroom wall. If you have access to a photocopy machine, you might want to make a set for use on greeting cards and have your child provide the crayon power for each unique card.

Required:
- Paper
- Crayons, markers, or tempera paint

Family Flag

What banner does your household fly under? Let your child decide—then make a flag.

You'll need a piece of cloth (you can cut an old pillow case open), some fabric paint (available from most art supply stores), and a wooden dowel or a cardboard tube from some wrapping paper. Young children will probably want to dive right in and start painting whatever surface they can, freestyle. Older kids might appreciate first doing a rough sketch on paper, then copying it onto the cloth before doing the coloring in.

When the fabric paint has dried, roll one side around the dowel or cardboard tube. Secure the material, remove the dowel or tube, and then sew or staple the cloth. (This is a grownup job.) Make sure you also close off the top, so the flag doesn't slip down the tube.

Fly the flag at all appropriate family gatherings and events, such as balloon volleyball (#17) or the Crazy Olympics (#65). And when it's not in use, keep the flag on special display.

Required:

- Piece of cloth or old pillowcase
- Fabric paints
- Stapler or sewing gear
- Dowel or cardboard tube

Optional:

- Paper and pen or pencil

Family Gazette

E xtra! Extra! Read all about Teddy Bear's first tooth . . . the results of the latest toilet paper tube bowling tournament . . . or the first worm sighting of the year in the family garden.

These are only a few of the kinds of things your kids might want to report in a family newspaper. For a simple gazette, you can use the backs of scratch paper and hand write the stories as told by younger children. (Post it on your refrigerator for best circulation results.) Give older children help with writing their own news stories; if you want to get fancy, use a typewriter or word processor to create columns of text.

Older kids will enjoy being reporters and writing their own stories. Pass along the basics of reporting: the five W's (who, what, when, where, and why). Then send them out on assignments around the house or yard to report on things like the state of the family recycling campaign—or to get opinions from family members on hot issues (like favorite meals, toys, or countries).

Remember, in the Family Gazette, life itself is news, and the news is always fit to print.

Required:

- Paper
- Pencils, crayons, or markers

Optional:

- Typewriter or word processor
- Family photographs
- Glue

Family Historian

This activity works well with the Family Tree (#99), although you can do it separately.

At the next family gathering, provide a list of questions for your child to ask the oldest members. If they emigrated from another country, your child can begin with questions about life before and after the move: "Where did you grow up? What did your parents do for a living? What kind of house did you live in? What did you do for fun? What was school like? How did you get here? What was it like to live in a new country? What was different? What kind of work did you do?"

For other relatives, the child can focus on questions about the houses they grew up in, their cities or towns, their friends, their school days, current occupation, interesting travels, and so on.

Write down the answers so your child can focus on the interview. Tape record the interviews, too, if possible. You can attach pictures of the relatives to the write-ups, then place them in a notebook. The book and tapes will become wonderful mementos for everyone in the family.

Required:
• Paper and pencil
• Notebook

Optional:
• Tape recorder
• Photographs

Family Tree

At some point, kids enjoy learning about the network of relationships that makes up their family. They're fascinated and comforted to learn how they fit into the scheme of things, too.

Give your child a large sheet of paper and crayons or markers. Show your child where to draw boxes for various relatives, starting at the top with the oldest living generation. (You might want to use different colors for your side and your spouse's side of the family.) Sound out the names for pre-writers who can write letters, but let older kids write in the family names themselves.

To make the tree more detailed, affix photos of the various people to their names on the tree. If you have enough space on the paper, you might want to write a brief story about each family member; encourage your child to compose as many of the stories as he or she can.

You'll probably find this activity a good opportunity to explain such elusive concepts as grandparents, cousins, aunts, uncles, and second cousins twice removed.

Required:
- Large sheet of paper
- Crayons or markers

Optional:
- Photos of relatives

Fancy Footwork

Sure, you and your child can come up with some pretty snazzy drawings by conventional means. But what happens if you take the more radical step—holding the crayon between your toes instead of in your hands?

Required

- Large sheets of paper
- Crayons

Use a couple of big pieces of construction paper, clear a space on the floor, and give it a try. Before too long, your child may become a foot-drawing expert.

This activity is not only a lot of fun—it also serves as a reminder of the flexibility that is such an essential feature of the human race. Tell your child that people who have lost the use of their hands are well known for adapting themselves to the new situation by learning to write, paint, draw, count, hold objects, and do any number of other tasks with their feet. Stick with drawing for now, though; you might just be surprised at how steady-footed your child is.

(See also: Ambidextry, #5.)

Fantastic Creatures

Throughout our history, we humans have come up with some pretty strange beasts, extravagant creatures that exist only in the imagination. Most of them are fascinating to kids; why not share this list of famous classical "animals" from other worlds and suggest that your child draw pictures to accompany them?

The chimera: Head of a lion, body of a goat, and tail of a snake.

The centaur: Half man, half horse.

The dragon: A huge fire-breathing reptile with wings.

The minotaur: Half man, half bull.

Pegasus: A winged horse.

The satyr: Half man, half goat.

The sphinx: Head of a woman, body of a lion, wings.

The unicorn: Small horse with a long, straight horn growing from the center of the forehead.

Required:

- Paper
- Crayons or markers

Fantasy Baseball

You and your kids can play a nine-inning baseball game in under half an hour. Use the newspaper to get the player names and positions for a couple of your favorite teams. Set your lineups, get a pencil and paper, draw a diamond, and play! Here are results for each of the thirty-six possible combinations resulting from the two dice, which are tossed by the defense.

Required:

- Dice

- Paper and pencil

1-1 Home run
1-2 Infield fly
1-3 Walk
1-4 Single, adv. 1
1-5 Strikeout
1-6 Ground ball
2-2 Double, adv. 2
2-3 Flyout, center field
2-4 Single, adv. 2
2-5 Ground ball
    (Double play if poss.)
2-6 Infield lineout
3-3 (Roll one die again:)
    1,2,3 Error (infielder),
    1 base

4,5,6 Error (outfielder),
    2 bases
3-4 Strikeout
3-5 Flyout, right field
3-6 Ground ball
4-4 1,2,3 Double, adv. 2
    4,5,6 Triple, adv. 3
4-5 Infield fly
4-6 Flyout, left field
5-5 Walk
5-6 Ground ball
6-6 Flyout, left field

This will yield a "game" that is remarkably similar in outcome to real baseball box scores. Add your own refinements. If you want to know which player committed an error, you might employ the following breakdown:

Infielders
1=P; 2=C; 3=1B; 4=2B;
5=3B; 6=SS

Outfielders
1,2=LF; 3,4=CF; 5,6=RF

The same approach would work to determine which infielder handled a grounder or flyout.

Play ball!

Fantasy Baseball (Advanced)

People who play Fantasy Baseball (#102) sometimes hunger for a more sophisticated game; here it is.

The basic principles are the same, but note the pound signs (#) and asterisks (*). If the hitter at the plate hits over .300, read the pound sign outcome instead of the normal result; if the pitcher has an earned run average lower than 3.00, read the asterisk outcome instead. This allows for some players—as in real baseball—to outperform others.

Required:
- Dice
- Paper and pencil

1-1 Home run
1-2 Infield fly
1-3 Walk
1-4 Single, adv. 1
1-5 Strikeout
    (#: Single, adv. 1)
1-6 Ground ball
2-2 Double, adv. 2
2-3 Flyout, center field
2-4 Single, adv. 1
    (*: Strikeout)
2-5 Ground ball
    (Double play if poss.)
2-6 Infield lineout
3-3 (Roll one die again:)
    1,2,3 Error (infielder),
    1 base

4,5,6 Error (outfielder),
    2 bases
3-4 Strikeout
3-5 Flyout, right field
3-6 Ground ball
4-4 1,2,3 Double, adv. 2
    (*: Strikeout)
    4,5,6 Triple, adv. 3
4-5 Infield fly
4-6 Flyout, left field
5-5 Walk (#: Home run)
5-6 Ground ball
6-6 Flyout, left field

In Advanced Fantasy Baseball, you can steal bases. Here's the basic chart, which you can adapt in any way you like to give an advantage to basepath speedsters.

BASE	SINGLE DIE ROLL
2nd	Safe if 1, 2, 3, 4
3rd	Safe if 1, 2, 3
Home	Safe if 1 *thrown twice in a row*.

Fast Talkers

Required:
- Watch
- Paper
- Pencil

Optional:
- Tape recorder

This game is simple. How fast can you talk?

Select a poem or other recitation everyone in your family knows by heart. ("Twinkle, Twinkle, Little Star" and "Baa, Baa, Black Sheep" are favorites around our house.) Get out your watch, yell "Go"—and have one of your kids zoom through the text as fast as possible. No skipping words! Record the various times on a sheet of paper and place them in a notebook—you'll want to know if you set any world records. (See #93 for ideas about a Family Book of Records.)

For a real laugh, try tape recording your speedtalking efforts. You may end up hearing somethingthatsoundsalittle-bitlikethisandfindthatyoumustplayit-backafewtimesinordertobeabletomake-everythingoutdistinctly.

(What language was that anyway?)

Feed the Birds

Safety
Reminder
Stove

There's a lot more to taking care of the birds than simply tossing birdseed onto the ground or into a feeder. Here are two ways to turn your bird feeding into creative fun. If pine trees grow in your area, have your child spread peanut butter on a pine cone and then roll it in birdseed. Affix a string to the cone, and hang it from a tree or a hook near your window.

Still another approach is to make a "suet bell." Save the drippings from meat and mix them with twice as much bird seed and bread crumbs. Now punch a hole in the bottom of a yogurt container and insert a string, leaving about a foot coming out of the hole in each direction. While holding the string so it doesn't coil, pour in the mixture and let it solidify. When it has fully cooled and hardened, slide the yogurt container off and hang your fresh suet bell from a tree. Nature will do the rest.

Whatever you do, the birds in your neighborhood will appreciate the meal, and your kids will enjoy meeting their new neighbors.

Required:

- Peanut butter
- Pine cones
- Meat drippings
- Bird seed or bread crumbs
- Yogurt container
- String

Finger Puppets

L ooking for a way to simultaneously
create a toy for your toddler and
keep your older child decked out for
Halloween? Snip the fingers off a sacrifi-
cial glove and use them to make finger
puppets. Then give the remainders of
the gloves to your older kids—they can
use them for a classic hobo routine or
whatever else the style of the moment
dictates.

Required:

• Old gloves or—
    peanut shells
    Band-Aids
    thimbles

• Decorating
    supplies

Optional:

• Cardboard box

Even if you don't have spare gloves
(or any teenagers, for that matter), you
can make finger puppets out of peanut
shells, pieces of felt, thimbles, and, yes,
Band-Aids. Use markers to draw faces,
and affix yarn or cotton with glue to create hair, beards, and other features.

Try making a theater by cutting a window (6" square or so) towards one end of
a cardboard box. Remove all of the box
flaps from the top except the one at the
same end as your window. Now set the
box on end with the window uppermost
and facing out. Slip your hand under the
flap and have your puppets perform a
show through the window.

Fingerprints

This activity will amaze your child . . . and, just possibly, reveal whose hands have been in the cookie jar.

First, explain that everyone has unique fingerprints. (Even twins.) Then have your child print the entire family. You can use a washable stamp pad or take a pencil and rub it on a sheet of paper to make a pad. Show your child how to hold a "suspect's" finger and gently roll it back and forth on the pad. Then have him or her place the finger on a piece of paper, again rolling it once from one side to the other. This will leave a clear fingerprint. (If you use the graphite method, you'll have to put clear tape over the print—otherwise the graphite will rub off or smudge.) Label the prints.

Next, demonstrate how to dust various objects with corn starch and a small soft brush. You'll get the best prints off hard and smooth surfaces. Blow off the powder (away from your child's face), and presto! You'll see the fingerprints the person who touched the object. Try matching them to the various family members. A magnifying glass will help.

Now 'fess up—aren't those *your* prints on the cookie jar?

Required:

- Washable stamp pad or pencil
- Paper/notebook
- Tape (not necessary if you use a stamp pad)
- Corn starch

Optional:

- Magnifying glass

Safety
Reminder

Balloon

Required:

- One or more flashlights
- 3 balloons (red, yellow, blue)

Optional:

- Paper bag

Flashlight Color Lab

Most kids find colors fascinating. Activity #55 used food coloring to demonstrate how colors are made from the three primary colors; this activity does it with light.

You'll have to sacrifice three balloons—a red, a yellow, and a blue. (Keep balloons out of young children's hands.) Stretch the balloon material over a flashlight and hold it in place with a rubber band. Then, in a darkened room, have your child shine the flashlight on the wall or ceiling. By adding different balloon "filters," you can make a variety of secondary colors. (Blue + yellow = green; red + blue = purple; red + yellow = orange.) If you have several flashlights, you can place one of the primary color balloons over each one, and do the mixing on the wall or ceiling.

A variation on this theme entails using three flashlights with balloon "filters" (one for each primary color), and holding them inside a good-sized paper bag with holes cut in the bottom. This is easiest if you and your child each hold a flashlight within the bag. Aim the holes at the ceiling and move the flashlights inside—you'll create a rainbow-like dance of light and colors guaranteed to delight and amuse.

Flip Book

Did you ever play with a "flip book" as a child? Flipping the book one way and the other makes an image go forwards and backwards. Cut a number of index cards in two. Now decide on a theme, such as a ball bouncing, an airplane taking off, or a bird flying in the sky—whatever interests your child. Next, successively draw the moving objects in slightly different positions on the pages of the book.

For example, if you're using the bouncing ball theme, start the ball in the upper corner of the picture on the first page. Draw a line at the bottom of the page, as well as on all the rest of the pages. With each page, draw the ball a little closer to the line, until it hits the floor and then bounces up again.

Now, have your child decorate a cover. Staple the pages and cover on the left side, putting the first picture in the back and the last in the front. Flip the book forwards and backwards, and the ball or whatever object you choose will magically appear to move. Next time around, let your child try the drawing part.

Who knows—this could be the beginning of a great career as an animator!

Required:

- Index cards
- Crayons or markers

Flower Press

Flower pressing is an old art that will captivate your child.

First, conduct a nature walk and collect a good sampling of small flowers such as violets, buttercups, daisies, or pansies. Place the flowers between sheets of absorbent paper, then put the paper under a heavy book (now you see why the flowers have to be small). Keep the pressure on until the flowers are dried out.

The dried flowers can be used for a variety of decorative purposes, including homemade greeting cards or place mats, or to create works of natural art such as a flower and leaf collages. (See #172 for instructions about drying and pressing leaves.)

Yet another possibility is the flower display, in which you tape or glue the flowers to the back of a shallow box, then stretch plastic wrap over the front and tape it to the back. Label the name of the flower on the back of the box or on a small piece of paper glued next to the back of the box. Display the box where it will be seen by visiting friends and family—they're sure to admire it.

Required:
- Small flowers
- Newsprint
- Heavy book

Optional:
- Shallow cardboard box
- Plastic wrap

Follow the Arrows

Here's an activity that can make for a great surprise—the only catch is that you'll need to set it up after your kid goes to bed for the night. That way, it will be ready the moment he or she wakes up the next morning.

What, exactly, will your child discover? Arrows—lots of them. Place pieces of paper with large arrows drawn on them all around the house; beginning with the first arrow, your child will follow them all around to reach the end—at which point you will have placed a special breakfast treat, tickets for a lobbied-for future family outing, or a birthday surprise.

How intricate should the arrow arrangement be? That's up to you—gauge the design to your child's abilities. Do be sure to put something worthwhile at the "end of the rainbow," however. Failing to do so will lead to a severe erosion in credibility!

Required:
- Paper
- Markers
- Tape
- "Treasure"

Food Face

You probably don't notice half the food advertisements in the magazines you read. Well, pay attention, and start clipping pictures and photographs of fruit, vegetables, eggs, and other food items. (For a jump start, pick up an issue of a magazine with plenty of recipes like *Family Circle* or *Woman's Day*. Better yet, use the supermarket circulars that clog your mailbox.)

Required:

- Magazines, circulars
- Paper
- Markers

When you have a good collection of pictures, let your kids use them to create a face—a banana for a mouth, tomatoes for eyes, grapes for hair, and so on. Use a glue stick or tape to affix the pictures to paper. Or, make a flannel board version (see #85) so your kids can reuse the pictures. Note: to draw the outlines for the faces, you or your children can trace plates, pots and pans, and other common objects.

You can use themes other than food, too, like cars and machines. Use a road for the mouth, headlights for eyes, wheels for ears, and so on. Once you start thinking of ads as sources for this game, you'll notice yourself developing an automatic "clipping reflex."

Forest Crowns and Bracelets

The great outdoors is a great source of raw materials for regal finery.

To make a crown or wreath of leaves, collect some fresh leaves (you'll have the most colorful finery in autumn). Poke a hole in one stem with the stem of another, and feed the stem through. Continue this process until the leaves are chained together. You can do the same thing with clovers and flowers by making a slit at the bottoms of the stems and feeding the ends through one another to make a chain.

Another type of nature finery is the seedling bracelet. To make a maple bracelet, for example, collect a batch of fresh maple seeds (don't forget to play whirlygig with them first), and cut small holes in the end of the stem. Pass a string through the holes and tie it so that it's just large enough for your child's hand to pass through, but small enough to keep from slipping off. Elastic string works best.

The next time you go out walking, watch out—you might be stepping on a precious gem.

Required:

- Leaves, flowers, seeds
- String

Fox and Goose

Snow is a great toy—it's fun and it's free (not counting lost work days and pains from aching backs). This traditional game, "Fox and Goose," can supplement traditional sledding, snow-man-making, and similarly wintry activities. Best of all, it can be played even in a small backyard or driveway.

First, make a "playing field" by stomping out a circle 10 to 20 feet in diameter into the snow (in a driveway, you might have to make an ellipse). Next, make four to eight paths that cross at the center, dividing the circle into a "pie-slice" form.

Now you're ready for action. One person plays the fox and the other the goose. The fox can chase and try to tag the goose, using only the tromped-down circle and pathways. The pathways provide sneaky shortcuts, and fortunately for the goose, the center is "goose haven"—where he or she can't be caught.

Upon tagging the goose, the fox doesn't get a meal; rather, he or she becomes the goose, and the goose becomes the fox!

Required:

• Fresh snowfall

Geography Rorschach Test

E ven people who claim to be "geo-
graphically illiterate" have no
problem describing the physical shape
of Italy.

That's because Italy looks like a boot,
and a boot is a little easier to remember
than some more abstract shape. We call
this the "boot principle."

With a little imagination, you and
your child can make other parts of the
world memorable and unique—by
applying the boot principle. In short,
that principle is to make an abstract
shape memorable by finding some way
in which it resembles a common object.
Trace a state or country outline for your
child, then ask him or her what the
shape looks like. When you settle on an
appropriate object, pass out the crayons
and have your child make the new asso-
ciation a reality.

Our research has shown that Indiana
is actually an old man with a beard,
Florida is a bent sock, and Nevada is a
baseball diamond's home plate—broken
in half.

Required:
- Paper
- Pen or pencils
- Map for tracing

Giant Blocks

This activity requires a bit of storage space. But for the fun your child will have constructing life-sized structures from play blocks, you may find yourself considering getting rid of your furniture—or moving to a larger house.

Required:

- Miscellaneous cartons
- Decorating supplies and materials

Start collecting cartons from your shopping forays, and from goods that you order through the mail or receive as gifts. The recommended size is at least one cubic foot. (Of course, you can go out and buy shipping boxes at your stationery or office supply store. That will give you nice uniform blocks, but it won't help you recycle the endless stream of cardboard boxes that pass through most households.)

Tape the boxes shut, then turn your child loose with markers, crayons, scrap wrapping paper, or anything else that can transform the boxes into kid-style building blocks. When the decoration is done, encourage your child to build walls, towers, houses (you can use a large piece of posterboard for a roof), tunnels, and other structures big enough to climb in (but *not* on).

Hint: leave some of the boxes open on one side. That way you can use them to store smaller boxes and toys, so you might not have to sell off the sofa after all.

Giant Dice

Want to do some educational—and legal—gambling? Here's how.

Carefully measure and cut off the lower portions of two half-gallon milk cartons (about 3¾ inches from the bottom). Slit one of them at each corner, to within an inch of the bottom, and force it inside the other milk carton bottom. This will give you a milk carton cube. Wrap the cube in white paper, neatly and tightly, and tape. Make a second cube the same way.

Next, mark the 6 faces of the cube with shapes, patterns, animals, pictures, letters, numbers, or words. Mark the second die identically. You now have a pair of giant dice. Invent your own games, like seeing who can roll a match. Or, if you're working on numbers, count how many times it takes to actually get a green hat, a boat, a dog, and so on.

For an older child, you could each throw a die with numbers, then have the child add (or multiply) them. Finally, if you're using letters, the object of the game might be to think of a name with the two initials resulting from your throw. By the way, you can always use the milk carton tops for Cereal Box City (#40)—perhaps for a model casino!

Required:
- Four milk cartons
- Paper
- Crayons or markers

Giant Theme Books

Giant Theme Books are big scrapbooks filled with pictures of cars, airplanes, animals, people, and anything else that strikes your child's fancy. They're a lot of fun to put together.

Clip pictures from a variety of magazines and save them in envelopes, then affix them to large sheets of stiff paper with double stick tape or non-toxic glue. Let your child organize the pictures according to his or her own criteria.

Punch three or four holes in the left side of the sheets of paper, then pass a string through each hole to make a loop. The string loops serve as a binding. (You can also get individual rings at a stationery store.) Before binding the sheets, your child may want to make a cover with a sample illustration, and even dictate a title.

Here are a few examples:

My Favorite Cars
People With Moustaches
Baseball Days

Date the books and save them—you'll be glad you did!

Required:

- Magazine pictures
- Large sheets of stiff paper
- Tape or non-toxic glue
- String

Dino Bone Hunt

Would your child enjoy playing junior archaeologist? If so, he or she will appreciate this activity.

Collect as many popsicle sticks as you can find—generating a supply should not be a problem. The sticks are about to become dinosaur bones. If you or your children don't indulge in sugary things, you can use pipe cleaners. Indoors, you can hide the popsicle sticks or pipe cleaners in "digs" such as the crevices between couch pillows, the space between rugs and rug pads, or underneath furniture. Outdoors, you can bury the "bones" in soil about an inch below the surface. Provide some sophisticated archaeological tools—such as a spoon—to uncover the bones and a brush to clean off loose soil.

Once the dig is complete, see if your archaeologist can construct a skeleton; provide nontoxic glue for the popsicle sticks. The pipe cleaners can simply be twisted into spines, necks, ribs, and so on.

When the skeleton is complete, put it in an appropriate display and give it a prominent place in the playroom.

Required:
- Popsicle sticks or pipe cleaners

Dinosaurs on Parade

**Safety
Reminder**

Balloon

Required:

- Papier-mache materials
- Aluminum foil pie pan
- Funnel
- Tempera paint
- Balloon
- Toy dinosaurs

This activity will be a great hit for dinosaur-lovers. Your first step should be to review #230 for the basic technique for papier-mache making.

Every dinosaur landscape needs a volcano. Use a large funnel as the form. When the volcano is dry, let your kids streak red paint down the sides to simulate lava. A cotton ball on top makes for good "smoke."

Next, make a dino cave by wrapping the wet papier-mache mixture around an elongated balloon. When the form dries, have your child pop the balloon; you'll be left with a cave that would please any Triceratops.

Make a primordial lake by using an aluminum foil pie pan as the form. Build up the sides to create a bank; when the model dries, paint it blue and green—ideal for Pleiciosaurus. Inverted yogurt containers make good forms for small mountains, and paper towel tubes can be used to shape prehistoric trees and logs.

The finished pieces can stand alone, or you can affix them to a piece of wood. Either way, add a few toy dinosaurs (or even pictures of dinosaurs from magazines) and your child is all set for a journey to the Jurassic.

Dioramas

Safety Reminder
Plastic Wrap

There's something magical about museum dioramas, those dramatic scenes from faraway places and past eras. It's as though time itself were locked behind the glass. To create your own dioramas right in your home, you and your child will need a box (at least the size of a shoe box), some plastic wrap (keep this away from toddlers), and tape. Place toy people, animals, dinosaurs, cars, or other figures within the box; alternatively, you can cut out pictures, paste them on cardboard, and bend the bottoms back to make stands. Try these ideas:

Jungle scene. Use jungle pictures for the background. Add a variety of toy jungle critters and perhaps an explorer. Try making a thatched-roof hut out of cardboard and popsicle sticks.

Outer space. Make a background with black paper; create stars with white tempera paint. Paste on pictures or drawings of planets and comets. Hang a toy or cardboard spacecraft—and an astronaut or two—from the top.

House scene. Make room scene backgrounds from magazine pictures (*Better Homes & Gardens* is a good source). Add people, toy or cardboard furniture, and other elements.

Seal up the dioramas with plastic wrap and tape.

Required:

- Box (at least shoebox size)
- Plastic wrap and tape
- Construction paper
- Pictures from magazines
- Small toys/figures
- Decorating materials

Do It Yourself Letters

This activity is a great way for kids to learn their ABCs. It will test your ability to master a few tongue-twister words, as well.

First, you need a stock of letters. Cut them out of magazines or newspaper, or write them on small squares of cardboard. (You can also cut letters out of construction paper or make them out of pipe cleaners or clay.)

Required:

• Magazines, construction paper, pipe cleaners, or clay

Make at least two of the common consonants and three of each vowel. One each for X, Q, and Z will generally be enough.

For pre-readers, think of a word (but don't say it) and call out its letters in sequence, one-by-one. Your child can arrange them on the floor or on a table. Give hints as to what the emerging combination spells. (This is also a good way to show how different sounds fit together.) For older kids, reverse the process: give hints about a word you're thinking of and let them spell out their guesses.

Once you're done with the spelling, try this silly variation. Have your child randomly arrange the letters, then you try to pronounce the word. Quick—how many times can you say "mxtizoqreewf" without tripping up?

Doctor's Office

This activity turns going to the doctor into fun by putting your child in the "white jacket." As a patient, *you* can demonstrate that getting treated is painless and fun.

First, you'll need to equip the office with a few essentials, like a scale, a yardstick or tape measure, and a flashlight for examining ears and mouths. You can make a stethoscope out of cardboard (make the earpieces too big to fit anywhere they don't belong); for the smock, provide an old white T-shirt cut down the front with lapels and a pocket drawn on with markers. Finally, provide a few bandages for authenticity.

As a patient, schedule a well Mommy or Daddy visit, including a weigh-in and measuring. Then have your child treat you for various disorders, maladies, or injuries: skinned knees, chicken pox, and/or a runny nose are good candidates. Get your diagnosis and prescription; be sure to talk about how wonderful the visit is, and how much better you feel as a result of seeing the doctor.

You might be surprised at your child's powers of observation; after our last weigh-ins, we were each told to lose 68 gallons. Or else.

Required:
- Scale
- Tape measure or yardstick
- Bathrobe
- Band-aids

Dollar Quiz

Your older child will get a kick out of this quick currency quiz—with a twist.

Hand your child a one-dollar bill and have him or her look it over for a moment. Then ask if your child can find the following objects on the bill:

Required:
• Dollar bill

(1) The Roman numerals for 1776 (MDC-CLXXVI)
(2) Thirteen arrows
(3) Thirteen stars
(4) The word "tender"
(5) A single eye in a triangle
(6) A key
(7) A mushroom

The answers are printed upside down below.

(1) On the back of the bill, at the base of the pyramid. (2) On the back of the bill, held by the eagle. (3) On the back of the bill, above the eagle's head. (4) On the front of the bill, beneath the word UNITED. (5) On the back of the bill, at the peak of the pyramid. (6) On the front of the bill, superimposed over the word ONE as part of the Treasury Department seal. (7) A tricky one. Looking at the front of the bill, fold the top third upwards, just above George Washington's eyebrows. Now make another fold along George's lips and bring the first third of the bill downward. A Washington mushroom!

Doorknob Hangers

Older kids are always looking for a way to add a personal flair to their surroundings. How about a customized doorknob hanger, with a design and message uniquely suited to your kid?

All you need is a sheet of whitish cardboard (lighter is easier to cut). The basic shape is simple: a rectangle with a circular hole near the top large enough to slip over the outside knob of your kid's bedroom. You can handle all the sharp stuff, then pass along the finished blank for your kid to go to work on.

Supply crayons, markers, and anything else that seems likely to aid the creative process—then watch what happens. Any number of intriguing (or bizarre) messages/images may result. Our friends with kids told us of signs that read: RED SOX FANS ONLY; GENIUS AT WORK; DISASTER AREA; NUCLEAR-FREE ZONE; and even YES, I AM REALLY DOING MY HOMEWORK.

For our part, we tried making one that said MAID SERVICE, PLEASE, and hung it, rather optimistically, on our bedroom door. It hasn't worked. Yet.

Required:

- Lightweight cardboard
- Crayons, pens, or markers
- Scissors (for adult use only)

Dots, Dots, Dots

This is an interesting twist on standard painting or drawing activities that will open up a whole new world of color and design awareness for your child.

The rule is simple. Whether painting with a brush, sketching with a pencil or pen, or drawing with crayons, your child can use one pattern and one pattern only: dots. Some children may be more comfortable if a design is sketched in lightly before the dot session begins; alternatively, you can use the designs in a preprinted coloring book. (Art history buffs will recall that Georges Seurat got pretty good results with this technique.)

One twist you can introduce if color is involved is to ask your child to use only primary colors (red, blue, and yellow) and "mix" them by planting various color dots in close proximity. Close up, those look like separate blue and red dots—but back up a few feet, and you'll see a luminescent purple!

Required:

- Paper
- Drawing implements

Draw a Meal

Here's a way to entertain your child while you fix dinner.

Cover the table with a large sheet of paper, then use masking tape to keep the corners in place. Provide your child with a good supply of colored crayons. Have your child draw a place mat where everyone sits, followed by a plate, a napkin, flatware, and a cup.

Now, as you make the meal, explain what you're making. Your child can then draw that particular dish and "serve" it up on everyone's plate. Tell your child to dole out appropriate portions for each member of the family. Continue this for each course you're going to serve up. Don't take it personally if your child's drawings bear no resemblance to food—that's no reflection on your cooking prowess.

Another hint: Don't be too surprised to find blue tomatoes, red green beans, or other inventively colored cuisine on the "plate." It's all part of the fun.

By the way, it should be interesting to see who your child believes eats the most. Now who might that be . . . ?

Required:

- Large sheet of paper
- Masking tape
- Crayons

84

Easy Bird Feeder

Safety Reminder

Supervise
Closely

Required:

- Half-gallon milk container
- Stapler
- Tape
- Chopstick or unsharpened pencil
- Wire
- Pipe cleaners
- Birdseed

Your children will get a kick out of seeing birds dine in their backyard—especially out of a homemade feeder!

Close and staple together the sides of the spout of a half-gallon milk container. Seal the whole top edge with tape, and then punch a small hole about a quarter of an inch from the top. Place a wire or pipe cleaner ring through the hole.

Set the carton upright, then cut two small holes about an inch and a half from the bottom on opposite sides. (Remember that cutting is a grownup job.) Poke a chopstick or unsharpened pencil through the holes, so it sticks out on both sides. This is the perch. One-half inch above the perch on each side, cut a two-inch-square flap that swings up. Fasten the flap in the open position with a wire or pipe cleaner.

Use a funnel to pour birdseed into the flap opening. (You can get birdseed at your local garden or hardware store; if you have a favorite local bird, go to the library and learn what kind of feed it likes best.) Hang the bird feeder by attaching a wire from the loop in the top of the feeder to a tree branch.

Remember: When you invite birds to a backyard feeding party, they'll expect season tickets!

Easy Flannel Board

You can make a flannel activity board simply by stretching a flannel shirt or receiving blanket around a piece of cardboard, and holding it there with paper clips. (A solid color piece of flannel is best, but that may require a trip to the fabric store.)

Now make items that your kids can attach to the board. Shapes made out of felt work very well—the fuzzy fibers from the felt cling tightly to the flannel. Another approach is to cut out pictures from magazines, laminate them with clear contact paper, and then glue felt, sandpaper, or Velcro to the backs.

The youngest kids will love tearing off the pieces and then sticking them to the board again. If you have an extra piece of flannel, you can draw a tic-tac-toe board or some other game pattern on it for older children.

If you've donated a shirt for the occasion, don't fret: it's still a perfectly good piece of your wardrobe. Just don't forget to remove the felt pieces—you might get some strange looks the next time you wear it to the supermarket.

Required:
- Flannel shirt or receiving blanket
- Pieces of felt

Optional:
- Sandpaper or Velcro
- Glue

Easy House of Cards

I f your child is old enough to use a pair of safety scissors, he or she can have a great time building an easy house of cards that will stand up to huffing and puffing!

You don't *have* to use regular playing cards—three-by-five index cards will be missed less and will probably work a little better. All you have to do is cut notches in each card as shown in the illustration. Now the cards will fit together snugly, form structures when joined, and even hold up under a bit of a breeze.

Help your child design simple structures at first before moving on to the real challenges; before too long, you'll wonder why anyone bothers with the shaky, unforgiving house-of-cards techniques of the past.

Can your child make:

A tower?
A driveway?
An airplane?
A model of your house?
A robot?
A castle?

(See also: House of Cards, #141)

Required:

- Playing cards or three-by-five cards
- Safety scissors

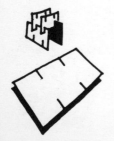

A Day in the Life of...

What do animals really do all day? To find out, just ask your child.

Tell your child to imagine that he or she is a tiger, an elephant, a bird, or some other favorite animal. Then have him or her describe a typical day in the life of the selected animal, starting from the moment the animal gets up to the moment it goes to sleep.

To stimulate creative thinking and imagination, and draw on your child's knowledge about the animal world, you might have to ask questions: "What does the rabbit eat for breakfast?" What does the rabbit play with in the morning?" "Does the rabbit go to work?" "What kind of work does the rabbit do?" and so on. When you've covered all the bases with one animal, *you* try it, and let your child ask questions about the animal.

A variation involves having your child describe the life in a baby of the species. Then he or she can talk about how the mother or father goes about providing care.

(Bet you didn't know that at lunch some animal kids eat people crackers.)

Required:
• Your time only

Describe It

72

This little game requires absolutely nothing in the way of props. You can do it while fixing dinner, when you're getting your kids dressed, or at any other time when your hands are tied. (It's also great on car trips). Look around the room or out the window and pick out an object. Then say, "I see something red about the size of a . . . .", describing its general qualities. Gear the activity to your child's abilities, shifting from over-all "form" qualities like size and shape to more subtle aspects of function—such as what it does and who might use it. ("I see something that can hold water . . .")

With younger kids, take turns being the describer and the guesser. With older kids, invent more complicated rules as the game progresses. For example, if you can stump your fellow guessers and have to tell them the object, you get to continue being the describer. The person who guesses correctly, however, gets to do the describing.

Whatever your rules, keep the re-wards simple and the focus on the game. Don't make the rules too complex. The beauty lies in the eyes of the describer!

Required:
• Your time only

Designer Memo Pad

H ow's your child at drawing rect-angles? How about writing out a simple sentence (or copying one with your help)? If either of these are in the repertoire, you can commission your child to design the family's next memo/message pad.

The drawing part is the most fun. Give your child a black marker (it reproduces best) and have him or her set up the basic scheme on a sheet of paper of appropriate size. The only real requirement is that there be plenty of white space near the center of the page for you to write messages on. A headline is also recommended: "Things We Have To Remember" or "Messages" would do the trick. (Your child may have interesting headline ideas to talk over, too.)

Next, take your child with you to the copy shop. Most will be able to produce the pads in a tear-away format, but you can also use loose sheets.

What better writing pad can you ask for than a Kid Original?

Required:

- Paper
- Crayon (black)
- Nearby copy center

Dictionary Fakeout

This game for three or more is most fun for older kids.

One person takes a (large!) dictionary and finds a strange, nonsense-sounding word within it. Then he or she writes the word—and its true definition—on a sheet of paper. The word itself—but not the definition—is then announced to the group. Each player, including the one who originally found the word must now make up a convincing fictional definition of the strange word. When everyone's done, one person reads all the definitions aloud and asks players to cast one vote for the definition that sounds legit. (Of course, the person who found the word can't vote.) Score five points for every correct answer—then go around the room so everyone gets a turn at finding a word.

Just any dictionary won't do—you need a pretty substantial one. Also, some players may have trouble finding good words. We've supplied a starter list below to get the game going.

"Starter" word list: granadilla (edible fruit of passion flowers); remiped (animal with feet like oars); rill (small rivulet or brook); bobbery (noise or commotion); hebdomad (a week); blatherskite (foolish, talkative person); wahine (Hawaiian for "female"); jongleur (minstrel).

Required:

- Large dictionary
- Paper
- Pencils

BLATHERSKITE

Cryptograms

Cryptograms are coded messages. Here's a simple one based on letter substitution.

All you do is select a new letter to represent every letter of the alphabet. Your master sheet might look like this:

```
ABCDEFGHIJKLMNOPQRSTUVWXYZ
CEKPADJQUVIMLRWXNHBSYZOTGF
```

Required:
- Paper
- Pencil

Using this key, the word "dictionary" would transcribe to "puksuwrchg." (Don't try pronouncing it.)

What can kids do with the key? Operatives can send secret messages to each other. ("Meet me in the living room at five o'clock for ice cream.") Ace cryptographers can try to crack the code. You need to supply them with a fairly long message for this task; finding a solution depends on determining how frequently common letters come up, then making guesses at the remaining blanks. Here is a list, in descending order, of the most commonly used letters in the English language.

ETAONRISH

Even with this aid, cracking the cryptogram is likely to prove pretty challenging the first time around. Help out by passing along a couple of clues for less common letters: "C equals K and L equals M in this message."

Currency Games

Here's a way to give young kids a sense of the complexity of currency—and have plenty of fun, to boot.

Using safety scissors, your child can cut sheets of construction paper into pieces the size of a dollar bill. Now find some stiffer cardboard or posterboard and trace small bottle caps—cut out the pieces for change.

Your child can now open his or her own treasury with crayons and markers. Be sure to point out the details—people, buildings, and, of course, the pyramid-and-eye design on the one-dollar bills. You might also provide non-toxic glue or double stick tape so **your child can** affix pictures cut out from magazines.

If your child has math skills, you can help him or her develop a currency system—one blue bill equals five reds, one red equals 10 gorilla head pennies, and so on.

You can also use the money with several of the other activities in the book, such as Kiddie Bank (#165) and Restaurateur (#263). Just keep it in the house—you don't want a knock on the door from the Secret Service.

Required:

- Paper
- Crayons or markers
- Safety scissors

Optional:

- Glue or double-stick tape

Custom T-Shirt

We all know we're not supposed to draw on our clothing—or are we?

Sometimes it's best to break a rule here and there . . . with appropriate supervision, of course. For the price of a new, blank T-shirt and a set of non-toxic colorfast markers, you can help your child create a personalized garment that will show off his or her artistic and fashion design talents for the best.

A do-it-yourself T-shirt will be worn with great pride.

Clear a space on table or floor, then lay down a number of sheets of newspaper. This will be your work area. Insert a flattened grocery bag into the shirt to keep the colors from soaking through to the other side. Use masking tape to pull the shirt taut, and start in.

Possible designs include:

       My family
       Sunshine
       Favorite animals
       Brothers or sisters
       Our home
       Self-portrait
       My pet

Watch out, Calvin Klein!

Required:

- T-shirt
- Nontoxic colorfast markers
- Newspapers
- Paper bag

The Day I Was Born
(Or, My Very First Birthday)

Required:

- Notebook or blank book

- Writing implements

The day of your child's birth is no doubt one of your most cherished memories. Why not share the story—and make a personalized book with your child, a book describing the events of that day?

All you need is a blank book or notebook and some writing implements. You will provide the basic story line, of course, and help out younger kids with the actual writing. Illustrations and arrangement of photos, however, should be left to the main character.

The beauty of this activity is that it requires you to formalize the passing-down of the story of one of your family's most important moments. You also get a real "keeper" of a handmade book. Hang on to it! This volume will become more and more treasured as the years go by.

(See also: What Else Happened That Day?, #353.)

Crazy Olympics

Safety Reminder

Supervise Closely

Required:
- Your time only

A s the name suggests, the object of the Crazy Olympics is to dream up silly games and sports, such as: hopping on one foot across a room or a stretch of yard; walking backwards while flapping your arms; crawling on all fours while balancing a book on your head . . . and other similar feats of silliness. Encourage your child to dream up games of his or her own, and to combine activities such as hopping, singing, and carrying a ball on a spoon (see #299). Monitor all activities closely for safety!

You and your child can compete by seeing who can do a particular "sport" the fastest (or the slowest). Groups of kids can also have great fun at the "meets," and can be asked to invent their games on the fly. For instance, you might simply set up a start line and finish line, and instruct all the contestants that the object is to walk to the finish line keeping one hand on the ground and one in the air.

Whatever you do, you and your kid(s) could well become trendsetters in the Olympic tradition.

Creature Deck

With a pack of three-by-five cards and a few crayons or markers, your child can create a virtually endless menagerie of crazy creatures.

All you have to do to start is place the blank side of three cards horizontally, one above the other, on a table. Now have your kid draw a head on the top card, a matching body on the middle card, and a set of legs on the bottom card. You now have your prototypes; your kid can now create dozens of matching heads, bodies, and feet that combine in startling and hilarious ways. After ten or twelve creatures, have your kid stop and do a little mixing and matching. A robot head with a furry body and a set of webbed feet? Odder things still await your kid—every new member added to the Creature Deck increases the strange possibilities.

The only word of warning is this: The heads must all be placed on approximately the same spots on all the cards, and the same goes for the other body parts. You may want to help with the first few cards that come after the prototype; before long, your kid will get the hang of it.

Required:

- Index cards
- Crayons or markers

Crayon Rubbings

I f you have a quarter, a key, a bottle top, or any of hundreds of other common household items, you have access to a treasure trove that can be turned into fine art.

Safety Reminder

Small Parts

Peel off the paper from a few crayons. Then place various coins underneath a sheet of blank paper. Rub the crayon over the surface of the coin, and presto—you have a rubbing of the coin. You can keep it as a picture or cut out the rubbings for use with the Kiddie Bank activity (#165) or in other games that involve currency. (You might want to mount the coin rubbings on pieces of cardboard with double stick tape so they'll wear better.) Keys also work well—you and your child can rub a set of keys and then mount them on cardboard for use with a play dashboard (see #138), or for playing house.

Required:

- Coins or keys
- Paper
- Crayons
- Other textured items as required

Don't stop with your pockets, though—your child can make rubbings of just about anything that has texture and fits under a sheet of paper. (Patterned floor tiles are great!) Just keep your credit cards out of sight.

Crazy Nines

Is your child trying to learn the multiplication tables? This activity will help him or her master the nines in nothing flat!

Nine is a funny number. First of all, you can always tell whether a number is divisible by nine—just by adding all the digits together until you reduce the whole mess to one number. If that number is nine, the number you started with is part of the family. It works with 45 (4 + 5 = 9); it works with 5625, too (5 + 6 + 2 + 5 = 18; 1 + 8 = 9).

Now for the fun part. To get the first ten results of the multiplication tables for nine, have your child follow these simple steps.

One. Think of the number you're multiplying nine by. (Let's say it's three.) Now subtract one. (That leaves us with two.) The result is the first digit of your answer.

Two. Now all you have to do is ask yourself, "How much would I need to add to get this to equal nine?" (In this case, seven.) The answer is your second digit.

Three. Give the answer (27)!

Required:

• Your time only

Construction Paper Greetings

Provide your child with a sheet or two of construction paper, a set of crayons or markers, and an envelope, and presto! Instant, mailable greeting card art. And no two are the same.

If you don't have any construction paper on hand, a trip to your stationery store is in order (get some envelopes while you're at it). Fold the paper over and let your child go to work.

Prereaders can work on the decorative or "mood" themes, and you can write in the greeting or slogan later. For kids just learning the alphabet, you can dictate the letters of the words. Let older kids write out their own cards.

In addition to artwork, you can include a pressed leaf (#172) or flower (#110), as long as it's dry, do some sand art (#274), or use a potato stamp (#255).

However your child creates the cards, the recipients are sure to appreciate the personalized effort and message. After all, it *is* the thought that counts.

Required:

- Construction paper
- Crayons, markers, or tempera paint

Optional:

- Pressed leaves
- Pressed flowers
- Glue
- Sand

Safety Reminder

Stove

Required:

- Molasses
- Sugar
- Shortening
- Milk
- Flour
- Soda
- Spices

Cookies You Can Read

ABC cookies are great fun. You can use your own recipe, or try the following; in any case, your child can have fun participating in the cookie making—measuring, stirring, rolling, and so on—and the all-important eating step, too.

First, the heating and mixing (adult jobs). Heat 1/2 cup molasses to boiling, then add 1/4 cup sugar, 3 tablespoons shortening, and 1 tablespoon milk. In a separate bowl, mix 2 cups flour with 1/2 teaspoon of each of the following: baking soda, salt, nutmeg, cinnamon, cloves, and ginger. Add the dry ingredients to the molasses mixture and blend well. Roll the dough on a flour-coated surface until it's 1/4 inch thick.

Now help your child make alphabet letters from strips of dough, perhaps associating an animal or favorite object with each one. (You can do this even without a set of alphabet cookie cutters by using a butter knife to cut out shapes your child traces on the dough.) Kids learning to read can make the letters spell out words. Place the cookies on a buttered cookie sheet and bake them for five to seven minutes at 350 degrees. Allow to cool; serve with milk and eat your p's and q's.

Crayon Copier

Maybe your kid can't quite afford a high-speed photocopier, but this activity will provide the next best thing. All you need is a crayon, a pencil, and a few pieces of paper.

Have your child scribble with a crayon until the paper is covered nearly completely with a solid color. (Don't get too concerned if there are small gaps of white space; the main thing is to provide a consistent coat of color that will transfer to another sheet of paper, and small gaps may even add an interesting stippled effect.)

Now have your child place the sheet, colored side down, on top of a clean sheet of paper of the same size. A drawing created on the rear of the colored sheet will now produce an exact duplicate on the sheet below!

Hint: You may have to tape the sheets in place before your child starts in on the pencil drawing; if the papers shift, the underlying image will, as well.

Reductions? Enlargements? Well, we'll have the design team get back to you…

Required:
- Paper
- Pencil
- Crayons

Optional:
- Tape

Crayon Games

The life of a crayon is a sad one indeed. First regal and stately with fine pointed tip, standing proudly as part of a perfect row, most wind up short, worn, and stubby, their edges dulled, and tossed into an old shoe box.

You can resurrect the once-noble crayon with this activity. Mix up a handful of used crayons of various sizes and spread them on a table. If your child is in the pre-counting phase, ask him or her to arrange them from smallest to largest, then reverse the order.

For your next request, have your child first organize the crayons by color. Then, within each color group, arrange the crayons by size, again going from smallest to largest and then largest to smallest.

Older kids will need more of a challenge. Draw a line and have your child guess the fewest number of crayons of any size he or she chooses it will take to equal the length of the line when the crayons are laid end to end. Then have your child actually line up crayons and see how close he or she came to the right answer.

Required:

• Used crayons

Optional:

• Paper

Compass Explorer

Safety Reminder
Great Outdoors

I f your child has learned the compass directions, he or she may enjoy playing these compass games (you can purchase an inexpensive compass at a camping or sporting goods store.)

Show your child how the compass needle aligns itself with magnetic north, and that by simply rotating the compass to line up the needle with north, you'll know each direction. Once your child has the hang of it, take a walk through the house, yard, or neighborhood . . . and constantly take a directional check.

Next, have your child close his eyes; lead him or her to a different room if indoors, or to a different part of the yard or neighborhood if outdoors. Be sure to change directions numerous times as you guide your child. (And hold hands at all times!) Instruct your child to open his or her eyes, then ask if the child can use the compass to tell which direction north is. (A variation on this activity is to have your child first guess the directions, and then validate the answer with the compass.)

Whatever you do, you'll take heart in knowing that if you're ever stranded, your child will be able to point you in the right direction.

Required:

- Inexpensive compass

Concentration

This game is a TV-free version of the old television game show *Concentration*. (Actually, the show itself was based on an old card game.)

First, rummage through your magazine photograph file (see #112), and select a variety of objects. Glue the photographs onto thin cardboard for strength, and allow them to dry. Cut each picture card in half, then spread the picture halves on the floor or on the table. Mix up the pictures, face down, and arrange them in the rough form of a square.

Each player is allowed to turn over two pieces of cardboard. If the cards match, the player gets to remove them from the playing area. If not, the next person takes over. By memorizing where various pieces are located (initially as a result of trial and error) players have a chance at clearing the board.

Of course, the game can be played solitaire, and the number of pieces should be restricted for younger children. With older kids, try playing the game under a time limit—that will test their concentration!

Required:

- Magazine clippings
- Cardboard
- Glue

Color Mixing

Here's a quick and safe way to turn your kitchen into a junior chem lab!

Provide containers of various sizes, bottles of food coloring, and various "lab" implements—eye droppers, turkey basters, spoons, measuring cups, and so on. Before turning your kids loose in Chem 101, though, be sure to explain that it only takes a drop or two of food coloring to do the job at hand.

The youngest kids will simply enjoy making colors and pouring colored liquid from container to container. Depending on your child's age and abilities, you can also use the activity as an opportunity to explain the primary colors, red, blue, and yellow, and how you can use them to create a multitude of other colors. (Blue + yellow = green; red + blue = purple; red + yellow = orange.) Older kids might want to start a "lab notebook," and record what happens when, for example, you mix twice as much red as blue to make purple. This is also a great way to teach about measurements. Let's see now, one cup equals how many ounces?

Required:

- Food coloring
- Containers
- Eye dropper
- Turkey baster
- Spoon
- Measuring cups

Columbus

If you have a smooth table and an object that will slide harmlessly across it (we use a plastic saltshaker) you can play this game.

Two players sit at opposite ends of the table; one slides the shaker to the other. The object is to come as close as possible to the edge *without going over*. (Explain that, back in the old days, sea explorers used to fear going over the edge of the world—until Columbus came along.)

Required:

• Smooth table
• Salt shaker

If you want to keep score, two slides can equal one game, but we think you'll find that the fun of the activity transcends winning and losing. The real enjoyment comes from letting your shaker go . . . and watching it slide over the lip of the table, then stop just before tipping over!

(Helpful hint: You may want to place some blankets or other padding material on the floor underneath each player.)

Once this activity has begun, you may find that it takes a considerable amount of willpower to stop.

Chain Drawing

This activity for two or more can generate some wild art.

Start off by drawing a line or a shape on a piece of paper. Then ask your child to add a line or a shape of his or her own. Then it's your turn again; continue in this way until you complete a picture. (Try beginning each new turn with a different colored pencil, crayon, or marker.)

With each new line, describe what you see. This can be especially fun if one player is sitting on the opposite side of the drawing, since the two of you will have very different perspectives.

To entertain a group of kids, get a large sheet of newsprint (see Introduction) or posterboard, so the drawings can bend back on themselves and wind around each other. For prolific drawers, have a stack of large sheets of paper ready.

Once you and your kids have finished drawing all the shapes and lines, you can take turns coloring in the spaces. Then ask the artist(s) to think of a suitable name for the masterwork.

Required:

- Paper
- Colored pencils, crayons, and markers

Chain Laughter Reaction

Required:

• Your time only

You can unleash an uncontrollable chain laughter reaction right in your living room. No protective equipment is required.

To spark chain laughter, you'll need at least three people (big or little). One person lies down on the floor. A second puts his or her head on the first person's stomach. A third then puts his or her head on the second's stomach, and so on. The first person says "Ha," after which the second says "Ha, ha" and so on around the chain.

Eventually, a curious thing will happen—the "ha ha ha's" will turn into genuine laughter—perhaps even wave after wave of uncontrollable laughter.

Try reversing the direction when things calm down . . . or, for a test of willpower, see how long everybody can maintain their positions *without* laughing. Someone will inevitably break down, and waves of laughter will once again ripple through the group!

Chain Story

Y ou can use this one anytime you're in a pinch for something that will entertain your kids, but doesn't require much energy. We call it the "chain story," because each person (you can play with just two) contributes a link to a tale in process. You start off simply: "Once upon a time...". (If you're feeling more dramatic, you might try something like, "It was a dark and stormy night...".) Your child then fills in the next part of the story, at which point it passes back to you.

Younger children may have difficulty grasping the concept at first, so you might have to supply several lines of the story. Alternatively, you can adapt the plot from a favorite book to get them going—in which case you might just get the book retold (which is okay, too).

Older kids might enjoy finishing incomplete sentences, such as: "One dark and stormy night a green car with...." Groups of kids can go around the room, each taking the story in a different direction.

Who says great literature can't be written by committee?

Required:

• Your time only

Checker Calculator

Safety Reminder

Small Parts

Required:

- Checkerboard
- Checkers
- Dice

H ere's a great game for kids who are working on their addition skills.

Start with a checkerboard and eight checkers, four of each color. Place all the checkers on one row at the edge of the board, four black on the left and four red on the right. Black moves first, so the player with the red checkers calls out a number between one and six; let's say it's four. Black must now say what number, when added to four, will bring one checker to the other end of the board. He or she then rolls *two* dice; if either of them come up with the correct number, the player may advance to the end of the board and take the checker off the playing surface. Alternate turns; whoever gets rid of four checkers first gets to start the next game.

No batteries required – and no keys to get stuck in place, either. Another low-tech triumph.

Chicago Busmobile Adventure

O ne of our son Noah's favorite creations is the "Chicago Busmobile." It consists of a large dashboard made from a cardboard box (see #138 for instructions on making a dashboard).

When the spirit strikes, we line up our kitchen chairs and take our seats in the bus. Our son collects tickets, then sits behind the dashboard and announces the various stops: the supermarket, the playground, the museum, New York City, Chicago, Australia, downstairs, and the moon. (Be prepared to give directions.)

Your child can invent stops based on his or her experiences. For long rides, try singing the old classic, "Wheels on the Bus." You might also want to take along snacks, and for special excursions, make up special tickets or tokens.

You can also use this activity without the cardboard dashboard—just being at the head of the bus may do the trick for your child.

Required:
• Chairs

Optional:
• Cardboard dashboard (see #138)

Chicken Scratch

You've heard of Pig Latin? Anyone can figure that out. Ah, but Chicken Scratch—that's another story.

Chicken Scratch is a special alphabet that corresponds exactly to the standard English alphabet; it's a code, based on the scribbly arrangement you see in the accompanying illustration. Wherever a letter is placed determines the symbol for that letter. The letter E, for instance, is simply a square box with nothing in it; the letter P, on the other hand, looks like an L with a dot placed inside the two lines.

Get it? Chicken Scratch is a written language only—its sole purpose is to be encoded or decoded on paper. But it sure looks impressive. And if you get good enough at writing with it . . .

Required:
- Pencil
- Paper

Chisanbop

Chisanbop is an easy, lightning-quick calculator developed by a Korean schoolteacher, Sung Jin Pai. Your grade-school kids can learn to use it in minutes. It requires two hands.

Try it yourself first. Place your hands palm-down on a table, fingers spread. That's zero. Now make two fists. Your calculator now reads 99, the highest value. Reading from left to right now, each of the four *fingers* on your left hand equals ten; the left *thumb* equals fifty; the right *thumb* equals five; and each of the four *fingers* on your right hand equals one. Now construct different numbers on your own. Two thumbs folded under could only equal 55; two index fingers, 11.

Let's try a sample problem: 18 + 26. Show 18 by pressing down the left index finger and the right thumb, index, middle, and ring fingers.

Now: Think of 26 as 10, 10, 5, and 1. The first two 10s are easy: Press down the middle and ring fingers on your left hands. The 5 is the only tricky part; you exchange between hands. Lift the right thumb (subtracting 5), then press down your left pinky (adding 10, for a net gain of 5). For the 1, press down the right pinky. Your hands now read 44—the correct answer!

Required:
- Your time

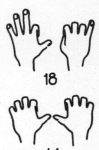

18

44

Cleanup Games

Throughout this book we stress non-competitive forms of play. Here, though, we take exception, and for obvious reasons.

Many parents (us included) believe that children should help clean up the toy messes they make. But instead of turning the cleanup into a battle, you can make a game out of it.

With one child, take a kitchen timer or egg timer and offer an irresistible challenge like, "See if you can put away all your dolls before the timer goes off." The trick is to keep the tasks small and manageable rather than say, "Go clean up the play room."

With groups of kids, assign each a well-defined task, and challenge them to see who can clean up their designated areas the quickest.

At our son's preschool, the children take turns ringing a bell that signals cleanup time, at which point each child tackles a job. And at our house, our son delights in ringing the bell, signaling the before-bedtime cleanup and assigns himself a task, with Mom and Dad finding one as well.

Required:

• Kitchen timer or egg timer

Optional:

• Bell

Clock Time

Here's a way to introduce your younger child—gently—to the idea of clock time.

Use a real clock, or make one out of cardboard. (If you do the latter, use a brad or pipe cleaner to affix the hands so that they're snug, but still movable.)

Now set the clock at whatever time your child gets up. Move the little hand around the clock, and talk about the kinds of things your child does at various times in a typical day. You'll probably also want to introduce the ideas of a.m. and p.m., but remember that this can be confusing for younger children.

Look for magazine pictures that show or represent the activities you've been discussing (like a picture of a box of cereal for "breakfast"). Affix them to the clock near the appropriate hour, or draw a picture of miniature clocks with the hands in the picture corresponding to the magazine picture.

Don't rush teaching your child to actually tell time—our son would look at the clock and say it was "7 pounds." But he somehow knew that "7 pounds" meant a bath was in the near future.

Required:

- Clock
- Paper
- Magazine pictures of daily activities
- Glue or tape
- Crayons or markers

Optional:

- Cardboard, brad, or pipe cleaner

Cloud Watching

How often does your child point to some everyday object and "see" a face, an animal, or other feature? Unfortunately, most of us stopped doing that when we learned it was time to get serious about life.

Here's a way to get unserious. On a warm day, with plenty of sun and puffy clouds, find a stretch of grass, beach, dune, or whatever. Lie down and let the cloud viewing begin.

There are no formal rules for this activity, nothing for you to direct. Everyone simply reports impressions. Don't ask questions like, "Do you see the dog?" One person's cloud dog may be another's cloud frog. Besides, you may frustrate your child by implying that there's a right and a wrong way to see.

It may be short on rules, but cloud watching is a time-honored winner.

(See also: Color Blots, #53.)

Required:

• Warm day, clouds

Coin Collection

Your child's piggy bank may not boast any Indian head nickels or double-strike Lincoln pennies, but there is quite a bit of fun to be had in beginning a basic coin collection.

Safety Reminder

Small Parts

Required:

- Coins
- Cardboard
- Tape

The initial guidelines are quite simple. There are four kinds of coins (not counting extinct items like fifty-cent pieces or Susan B. Anthony dollars): pennies, nickels, dimes, and quarters. The challenge is to find one coin in each main category dated in each of the last ten years. Tape each accepted specimen to a sheet of cardboard and label it appropriately.

That's a total of forty coins—small enough to be manageable, but large enough to provide a challenge. The initial session in which you categorize the coins will be a lot of fun—from there it will be a matter of keeping a watchful eye on the change that passes through your house. (We found a 1949 penny!)

Who knows—you might find that Lincoln doublestrike yet.

(Keep coins away from small children.)

Safety Reminder
Small Parts

Required:
• Quarters

Coin Toss

The common quarter can provide a great time for kids with supple thumbs.

Kids can flip it and try to set the world's record for a high toss. There are two technicalities that must be observed for the record to count, however. The coin must spin in the air, and it must be caught in the palm of the hand before striking anything else.

As a game for two, this can be a lot of fun, and may even necessitate a move out onto the porch, where ceilings won't get in the way. You and your kids can also flip quarters to one another, or take turns spinning a quarter and seeing how long it stays in rotation. If it looks like a winner, check it against the Family Book of Records (#93).

That beat-up old quarter may not look like anything special, but given the chance . . . your kids will flip for it.

(Keep coins away from small children.)

Color Blots

Ink or "Rorschach" blots have long been thought to reveal secrets about the inner recesses of the mind. Whether you believe in this idea or not, ink (or in this case, color) blots can be a blast for you and your kids to make.

Fold a piece of paper in half, then open it up. Place various pools of tempera paint on one side of the crease. Now fold the paper in half again, so the paint smears. (It will take a little practice to gauge how much paint is appropriate for the size sheet you're using.) When you unfold the paper, you'll find all sorts of interesting patterns and colors.

Required:

- Paper
- Tempera paint
- Pen, pencil, or crayon

What does your child see in those patterns? If it's a face, draw the outline (after the paint dries, of course). If it's animal tracks, do the same. If it's a butterfly, draw an outline of the wings and body. Add antennae if you feel the urge! Of course, you may not want to draw anything at all—the color blots may speak for themselves.

Red panthers? Purple cookies? Orange feet? Blue suns? Anything is possible once you let your imagination go to work.

Color ESP (Or, The Crayon Sensor)

You can teach your child to "feel" colors without seeing them—at least, that's what it will look like to friends.

Here's how. Your child will claim to be able to distinguish colors without looking at them. To prove it, he or she will ask to have a crayon of a secret color picked and placed in a paper sack. Your child, without ever having seen the crayon, will be able to identify the color—because in feeling the crayon, the intrepid "ESP expert" can get a fingernail into the side of the crayon, remove a tiny sliver of color, think hard, say some magic words, and *subtly* check his or her nails to identify the shade.

(Younger children may find the temptation to look at their fingernails too great, in which case the child's friend may be politely asked to close his or her eyes for a moment.)

Admit it. You'll want to perform the trick yourself before sharing the secret with your child, won't you?

Required:

- Crayons
- Paper bag

Celery Leaves

Here's a little experiment that's guaranteed to delight your kids while teaching them how fluids move through a plant's vascular system.

Find a robust, leafy stalk of celery. Give the stalk two "legs" by cutting a four-inch slit starting at the base of the stalk. Next, fill a small glass with water. Have your child add several drops of blue food coloring. Fill another glass and add several drops of red food coloring. Place one of the stalk's "legs" in the blue water, and the other in the red water. Let the whole apparatus sit overnight.

The next morning, your kids will be amazed to find that half of the leaves are streaked with blue, while the rest show red! Explain that the food coloring traveled up little tubes in the celery stalk, and that the tubes are used to carry water up from the roots for the plant when it's in the ground.

Afterwards, you can cut the stalk crosswise for your child to help him or her see exactly how the color got to the leaves. Seeing is believing!

Required:

- Leafy stalk of celery
- Two cups
- Blue and red food coloring

Cereal Box City

Cereal boxes (as well as any rectangular cardboard food boxes) make marvelous toy buildings.

Other "prefab" buildings reside in the refrigerator. Paper cream containers make for good houses, and milk cartons make ready buildings with sloping roofs.

To decorate the buildings, wrap the boxes in paper bags, construction paper, or unprinted newsprint (see Introduction). Then draw windows, doors, and other features. You can also cut doors and windows, leaving a flap. (Be sure the cutting implements you provide your children with are appropriate for their age and skill levels, and always supervise any activity involving sharp objects.)

Your budding architects can become city planners by drawing streets and city blocks on a large piece of paper, then placing the food box buildings on the map. Help them become landscape architects, as well—make shrubs out of cotton, grass out of green felt, streetlights out of cotton swabs, and trees out of cups, clay, and unsharpened pencils.

Add a few toy cars, and your kids will be ready for a night on the town.

Required:

- Empty food boxes
- Paper
- Decorating materials
- Safety scissors

Optional:

- Felt
- Cotton
- Cups
- Clay

Bubble Basketball

Safety Reminder

Supervise
Closely

Required:
• Monster Bubbles

We're indebted to bubble fan Norie Huddle for passing this great game along. It puts a new twist on both basketball and bubble-blowing.

Follow the instructions for Monster Bubbles (#198) and get a good-sized bubble floating. Now have your child blow the bubble across the room into a bucket placed some distance away. Of course, the only way to score is to keep the bubble from bursting. This usually means doing a good deal of "low blowing" to keep the bubble going up instead of down toward the floor, then blowing for direction as the bubble descends.

It's a tricky process—but a lot of fun! You can adjust the challenge of the game by situating the bucket nearer or farther from your child, depending on his or her skill level.

Michael Jordan beware!

(Note: The bubble mixture is not kind to some surfaces – keep it away from floors, carpets, and grass.)

Bug Motel

If you read about the ant farm (#11) but don't live in a place with access to ants, here's how to make a "Bug Motel." And as we all know, bugs are *everywhere*.

You and your child can make a bug motel from just about any small box, although an empty oatmeal box is ideal. Use a rubber band to hold a piece of screen over the top, which serves as both a window and a door. You can also cut window holes and tape screens across them to contain the guests. Make sure you provide leaves for the guests, then take your child on a bug hunt with a net or jar.

You might have a policy that guests stay for a day or two, after which they're returned to the wild where they belong. (You could also point out that mixing spiders with other bugs might give the spiders an unfair advantage.)

Running a bug motel will give your child a better appreciation of the little creatures in the world about them. And if you have "insectophobia" and would like to overcome it, this may just be the way to cure it.

Required:

- Empty oatmeal container
- Swatch of window screen
- Rubber band

Business Card Bonanza

You can help your child develop his or her own personalized business card—even if the business it promotes may be a few years away from getting off the ground.

You can use standard paper cut into appropriate sized pieces (3⅜" x 2") and a typewriter, computer, printer, or (to take the economy approach) a decent black pen with which you or your child can simply copy the text over a few times by hand. The resulting cards can be passed along with pride to your child's family, friends, associates, potential backers, and other contacts. Here are a few sample text formats to consider.

Required:
- Small pieces of paper
- Typewriter, printer, or pen

Andy West
Purveyors of Fine Lemonade
Corner of Maple and Elm
Lemonville, Massachusetts 02222
Call 617/555-LMON; we cater to large gatherings

Second Floor Junk, Unlimited
Joe, Proprietor
"No toss, no loss"
Easy answers to your storage problems
508/555-JUNK

Safety Reminder

Supervise Closely

Required:

- Toilet paper tube
- Straw
- String
- Piece of Play-Doh or small toy
- Two chairs

Optional:

- Crayons, markers

Cable Cars

Not that you were considering it, but why go to the trouble of hauling the family to the Alps to watch an aerial cable car when you can operate one right in your own living room?

To make a tram or cable car setup, attach a two-inch piece of straw to a toilet paper tube with glue or tape; make sure the straw is parallel to the tube. Next, have your child decorate the tube with crayons or markers, drawing windows and faces.

Feed a length of string (about 8 feet) through the straw, and attach both ends of the string to the backs of chairs. Make sure that one end of the string is higher then the other, and that the string is taut. Place a weight in the tube—a chunk of Play-Doh* or a small toy will do. Move the tube to the high point, then let it slide down to the low position.

The youngest kids will simply enjoy watching the cable car move from top to bottom. They might also get a kick out of transporting toy animals, cars, etc. from the top to the bottom "station." For older kids, you might want to create two cable car "lines" and sponsor a cardboard tube grand prix.

*Play-Doh is a registered trademark of Tonka Corporation.

Capital Bingo

This game will give you a refresher course and entertain your older kids. Write down the name of each state capital on pieces of index card small enough to fit in or near the state outlines on a map. Spell out the name of the state, let your child find it on the map, then place the capital name by the appropriate state. When all the states have been learned, make a new set of bingo cards with the names of the states—and take turns drawing a capital card from the pile.

Required:
- Index cards
- Map of U.S.

AL: Montgomery
AK: Juneau
AZ: Phoenix
AR: Little Rock
CA: Sacramento
CO: Denver
CT: Hartford
DE: Dover
FL: Tallahassee
GA: Atlanta
HI: Honolulu
ID: Boise
IL: Springfield
IN: Indianapolis
IA: Des Moines
KS: Topeka
KY: Frankfort
LA: Baton Rouge
ME: Augusta
MD: Annapolis
MA: Boston
MI: Lansing
MN: St. Paul
MS: Jackson
MO: Jefferson City

MT: Helena
NE: Lincoln
NV: Carson City
NM: Santa Fe
NH: Concord
NJ: Trenton
NY: Albany
NC: Raleigh
ND: Bismarck
OH: Columbus
OK: Oklahoma City
OR: Salem
PA: Harrisburg
RI: Providence
SC: Columbia
SD: Pierre
TN: Nashville
TX: Austin
UT: Salt Lake City
VT: Montpelier
VA: Richmond
WA: Olympia
WV: Charleston
WI: Madison
WY: Cheyenne

Now—without looking, what's the capitol of South Dakota?

36

Captions

Clip interesting or amusing photographs from the newspaper—then pass them along to your children. Their job: write new captions for the now-captionless images.

Of course, you may have to provide some help for prewriters, but the game can be great fun for them, as well. After the game is through, you may want to bind the images and their new text descriptions into a notebook or album.

One young lady we know suggested the following caption for an informal photograph of a United States Senator: "This man works at a grocery store. He has a very important job putting our food in bags."

Look for photos of:
Animals
People
Automobiles
Buildings
Sports Events
(races are great)
Celebrations

Required:
- Paper
- Pens/pencils
- Newspaper photos

Optional:
- Binder or album

Careers

When asked what he wanted to be when he grew up, our son once answered, "A dinosaur." He's since become more realistic and has decided to specialize in animal feeding at the zoo. What does *your* child want to be when he or she becomes an adult? Try this activity and find out.

Required:
• Pencil and paper

List various occupations in a column on the left side of a sheet of paper, then read them off one by one. (You should only list jobs that your child will know about.) Now have your child act out what a person in each occupation would do; help with hints as appropriate. You can create props as needed from various household items—a briefcase, a lunch box, and so on. At the end of the career session, ask which job your child thought was the most fun and interesting, and note it in the right column of the piece of paper.

Try this activity out every four to six months; date the responses so you can see how your child's interests change. Whoever would have thought that your son or daughter the brain surgeon began life wanting to become a circus ringmaster?

Carrot Top

When you make a salad, do you throw out the stubby end of the carrot—the part with the greens? If so, you're missing out on a great opportunity to show your child how plants grow.

Required:

- Carrot tops
- Saucers
- Water

Save those stubs and have your child place them in saucers that contain just a little water. Keep the saucers near a window, keep the water level consistent, and mark the height of the greens on the first day. Before long, your child will note a measurable increase in height—and be well on the way to a profitable career in carrot green production.

By beginning a new carrot top each day, your child will be able to see the results in an even more dramatic way: seven plants will yield seven different heights at the end of the week.

Note: You will need to use carrots that have not had the greens removed initially; this generally means you must buy them fresh, by the bunch, and not in bags.

(See also: The Root Stuff, #269.)

Brainstorming, Part Two

Here are a couple of advanced brain teasers for older kids—they require some abstract thinking and reasoning.

First, ask your child to imagine that a ping-pong ball has fallen into a short pipe with a sealed bottom sunk into the ground. The pipe is too narrow for your child's hands. Next to the pipe sits a box of cereal, some small magnets, a cardboard tube, a comb, and a bottle of apple juice. How can these be used to retrieve the ping-pong ball? (Answer: pour the juice into the tube so the ball floats up—the rest of the items are red herrings.)

If your child wants a real challenge, try this variation on an old classic. Your family, driving down a road in a camper, encounters a low bridge. You stop the camper and discover that the bridge is a fraction of an inch too low for you to drive through. Since you can't go around the bridge, how can you get through? (Answer: let a little bit of air out of the tires.)

Again, make up some puzzlers of your own. The only rule is not to suggest anything you can't solve yourself.

Required:
• Your time only

Breaking out of the Box

C reative thinking means temporarily breaking out of the little boxes that we use to organize the world. Here's an activity that will allow your child's mind to roam unrestricted by convention. It's also a "lifesaver" activity you can do at any time, in any room of the house, with kids (or adults) of any age.

Required:

• Your time only

Point to an object in the room and ask what it's used for. In the kitchen, for instance, point to a spatula. After your child gives the conventional usage, ask what else he or she could do with it. Depending on age, your child might give answers like: "Dig a hole with it." "Scoop sand with it." "Cut snow blocks or shape a snowman." "Use it as a racquet." "Reflect the sun to attract help when you're shipwrecked on an island."

Try this with other kitchen implements—spoons, forks, whisks, plates, and so on. Every room of your house has potential.

By the way, did you ever think of using your mattress to protect your spaceship from meteor damage?

Balloon Volleyball

Safety Reminder

Balloon

A rigorous game of volleyball is probably the last thing you want in your living room . . . unless the "ball" happens to be a balloon.

You can easily turn any room into a safe volleyball court. Clear away a space, then tie a string between the backs of two chairs. You now have a playing field and a net. Blow up a balloon. You're ready for action. For more formal play, decorate the net with streamers, lengths of yarn, etc. While you're at it, spiff up the balloon with markers. Every good volleyball can use a pair of eyes, a nose, and a mouth.

Encourage your kids to develop their own rules; after all, this is no high-pressure tournament. Be inventive. A group of kids might get a special charge out of trying to keep a flotilla of balloons aloft!

This game, which should always be supervised by an adult, is limited only by your imagination—and the size of your living room.

(This game is intended for older children only. Younger children should not play with balloons because of the possibility of suffocation.)

Required:

- Six to ten feet of string
- Two chairs
- Large balloon

Optional:

- Decorating materials

Safety Reminder

Stove

Required:

- Pancake ingredients

Bas-Relief Pancakes

Who says pancakes have to be boring? With this activity you can provide entertainment and good nutrition, too.

Remember that cooking is a grownup activity; keep children away from hot surfaces. Pick a pancake recipe and pour a small amount of batter into the pan in the shape of letters, simple animals (like a dolphin or whale), a face, a car, or anything else you can "draw" before the batter begins to thicken. Once the edges of the "drawing" have firmed up, cover the drawing with a large spoonful of batter on top, enough to make a pancake. Flip it when the pancake begins to get firm, and you'll see whatever you drew on top in relief with a white outline. Alternately, you can make the whole pancake in the shape of the object.

Of course, whatever you draw will be in reverse—very important with letters like "E" and "R." Use the pancakes to spell your child's name; for groups, describe the object you're making—whoever gets it right gets to eat that pancake.

Breakfast may never be the same!

Bean Bag Basics

Do you remember playing "eraser tag" on rainy days back in elementary school? Here's a variation using a bean bag instead of an eraser.

Safety Reminder

Supervise Closely

Required:

- Uncooked beans
- Bags
- Socks
- Twistems

Take a half a cup of uncooked beans and pour them into a small bag. Squeeze the air out of the bag, but leave enough room for the beans to move around when shaken. Seal the bag with a twistem or tie it shut. Then place the bag in the toe of an old sock. Tie the sock with a twistem, then cut off any excess material. You will need to make two bean bags for this game. Arrange an obstacle course with chairs, coffee tables, and other pieces of furniture. Now you're ready to play. Designate one person as "it." Have both players wear the bean bag on top of the head, like a hat. The general object is for "it" to catch up with and tag (touch) the other person—without losing the bean bag. For the person being chased, the goal is to get through the obstacle course without being tagged or losing the bean bag.

There are any number of possible variations for this game—just use your bean.

Bean Bag Olympics

I f you've constructed a bean bag (see activity #19), you've no doubt discovered what wonderfully versatile toys they make. Here are some bean bag games that will test your child's dexterity and aim. You'll need a number of bean bags for these games, depending on how many kids are going to play.

First, toss a bean bag onto the floor. Standing six to eight feet away, each player must toss his or her bean bag and see how close it can land to your bean bag *without* touching it. The winner gets to toss out the next bean bag for the others who are playing.

Alternatively, you can make a line on the floor with masking tape, about six feet away from the players. Whoever throws the bean bag closest to the line without going over it gets to go first the next time.

Then there's bean bag basketball. Use a large pot, placed in the center of your kitchen or living room floor, as the "hoop." Six feet is a good distance for your foul line, but you can start shooting from closer or farther away, depending on your child's abilities.

Required:

- 4 or more bean bags
- Tape
- Large pot

Bedtime for Animals

Do your child's toy animals often complain of backaches in the morning? Are they grouchy when they get up? If so, this activity will help.

First have your child collect his or her favorite toy or stuffed animals. Then find appropriate-sized boxes that can be converted into comfy beds (the boxes in which checks are shipped make excellent beds for small critters). Next, provide some nice soft bedding, like an old towel, shredded newspapers, or, for very small beds, cotton balls from vitamin and medicine bottles.

Have your child rock the animals to sleep, or perhaps sing them a lullaby. Perhaps they'd like a story. Your child can make one up or "read" from a book that he or she likes.

To ensure the most peaceful night's sleep for the animals, place their beds near your child's bed—just in case anyone gets scared in the night and needs a comforting hug.

Required:
- Boxes large enough to hold stuffed animals
- Pillows, towels, newspapers, or cotton

Big Kids' Bingo

This is a game that will delight children who have acquired basic spelling skills.

Each player will need a bingo card, which can be made from pieces of cardboard or heavy paper. (Have safety scissors handy if your child will be doing the cutting.) With lines, divide the cards into four or six squares. Let your child write a letter in each square—make the selection of letters random.

Next, create a stock of letters on small cardboard squares. You can cut up squares and, with your child, write a letter on each one (making sure, as you do so, that all the letters used on the cards are represented). Alternatively, you can cut letters out of magazine ads and articles and affix them to the cardboard backings.

The caller places the letters in a bag, shakes them up, then draws and announces them one by one. Players cover the corresponding squares with a marker. When all the squares on a card are filled, the player announces "BINGO!"—but must also make up a sentence with words that begin with each of the letters in sequence. That can make for some strange sentences: RBAEPC might turn into "Red brontosauruses always eat pink cereal"!

(See also Little Kids' Bingo, #179.)

Required:

- Cardboard or heavy paper
- Crayons or markers
- Safety scissors

The Biggest and the Smallest

Children often pay far closer attention to details than we adults do. So if you're looking for a way to draw on your child's powers of observation, consider this activity.

Instruct your child to conduct a household search for the smallest and largest items in various categories. Books, for example—have your child scour the house and report on the whereabouts and description of the biggest and smallest books in the house. Try the same with pots and pans in the kitchen or house plants, to name just two possibilities.

Groups of kids can be divided into teams — big thing specialists and small thing specialists. The teams can then switch jobs, and when the dust settles, everyone can compare notes.

Keep a record of everyone's findings... and as your household acquires new items, try the activity again to see if your child still has an eagle eye!

Safety Reminder

Small Parts

Required:

• Paper and pencil

Biodegrading Lab

Here's an easy way to show what degrades and what doesn't.

Collect four-inch squares of paper, cardboard, plastic wrap, and polystyrene. Have your child "plant" them outside, partially below the soil (about two inches down). Do not compact the soil. If you don't have any garden or flower bed space, you can plant them in a plastic tub filled with soil from elsewhere in your neighborhood. (Note: Potting soil doesn't work—it's been sterilized, and is therefore free of the bacteria needed to carry out the biodegradation.)

Every few days, check the "lab." Depending on the temperature and rainfall, the microbes in the soil will break down the paper products. But the plastic and polystyrene will remain intact for as long as your child cares to look—in fact, for hundreds of years.

Use the experiment to explain that we have to choose carefully what gets tossed into the trash, and that some things should be reused as much as possible.

Required:

- Paper sheet
- Cardboard sheet
- Plastic wrap
- Piece of polystyrene

Blindfold Guide

Safety Reminder

Supervise Closely

Required:

- Piece of cloth for blindfold

- Household items

This activity is quite popular at creativity boosting seminars—it gets you out of "autopilot" mode. It's fun and will foster an appreciation for the gift of sight. Here's a version that you can do with your child.

It works like this. You wear a blindfold, and your child serves as the "eyes" for both of you. (Make sure that all steps are barricaded or off limits, and that you are conducting the activity in a safe area.)

Your child leads you around the house, advises on eating and drinking (not feeding, mind you, but telling you how to get a spoon into the mouth), helps you sit, play catch, and so on.

The activity can be very amusing as your child tries to describe actions that are normally taken for granted, like using a utensil. You're sure to evoke belly laughs when you sit at the table with a dollop of peanut butter on the tip of your nose.

(See also: Instruction Manual, #154; Lip Reading, #178; Silent Game, #288.)

Body Trace

Have your child lie face-up on a large sheet of paper (unprinted newsprint stock is good; see the Introduction). Trace the outline of your child's body with a crayon or marker. When you're done, cut the image out and glue it onto a large sheet of posterboard.

Now set your kid loose with crayons, markers, colored paper, tape, paint and whatever decorating materials you have on hand. Suggest drawing in facial features or clothes. You might choose to emphasize the ridiculous—suggest a 12-inch bow tie or bowling-ball-sized shoes. (Alternatively, your child can glue on "clothes" fashioned from construction paper.)

You can also use brads (metal fasteners you can buy at a stationery store—not for young children). Put them at the major arm, leg, shoulder, and hip joints. Be sure to paste the tracing on cardboard first before cutting up the individual parts and reassembling them with the brads.

Have your child sign the art and date it – then display the new masterpiece prominently. You may end up with a life-size Louvre.

Required:

- Large sheet of paper
- Scissors
- Crayons and markers
- Sheet of poster board

Optional:

- Brads
- Colored paper
- Paint

Box Car

There's no need to wait until your child is of driving age for this activity.

Find a cardboard box about two and a half feet long and a foot and a half wide and deep. Close and seal the top and bottom of the box with tape. Cut a large hole in one side, about midway along the length, and big enough for your child to fit through—this is now the bottom. Next, cut a door on the other side, hinged toward the front. Fold it forward (see illustrations); this is the dashboard. Tape it to the hood. Finally, cut two hand holes, one on each side of the car, midway down the length of the box and about three inches from the top. The slits should be about two inches long, and an inch high.

Affix four paper plates to the sides for wheels. Now have your child decorate the box. You and your child can either draw gauges and buttons or affix plastic container lids to the dash with brads (tape the pointed ends for safety). Cut an X-shaped hole in the dashboard, then push the knob on a pot lid through the hole—the lid will become a moving steering wheel. Make up a license place, use lids for lights, and a find an old cake rack for a grill.

Have your child step into the box, then grasp the sides by the pairs of hand holes and lift. Start your engine!

Safety Reminder

Small Parts

Required:
- Cardboard box
- Markers, crayons

Optional:
- Lids from plastic containers
- Paper plates
- Pot lid
- Brads
- Cake rack

Brainstorming, Part One

How does your young child go about solving problems? These "brain teasers" are designed to provide fun and help you get a glimpse of how your child thinks.

First, try some "free-form" creative problem solving. Ask your child to imagine that he or she is in a locked room and wants to get out and play. The door-knob is reachable, but the key is on a peg much too high to reach. How can he or she fetch the key and get out? You'll probably hear answers ranging from "Stand on a chair" to "Call Mommy or Daddy."

Now boost the challenge. Tell your child that the room is empty—except for a yardstick, some string, and some paper clips. How can these items be used to fetch the key? (One answer: make a "fishing pole" with the paper clip as a hook and pull the key off the peg.)

Try making up some puzzlers of your own. Just keep them simple, and be prepared for many "right" answers. The idea is to give your child a challenge, not prepare him or her for early college entry.

Required:

• Your time only

out a trembling hand and lightly pressed her fingers against his cheek.

The relief was short-lived. A hand twice the size of her own flew like a rocket from under the sheet and wrapped around hers.

"What are you doing?"

Her heart jumped into her throat, the beats vibrating through her suddenly frozen body.

Nikos raised his head and blinked the sleep from his eyes, trying to clear the thickness from his just-awoken brain, and stared at the motionless form standing beside him.

"Marisa?" His voice sounded thick to his own ears, too.

As his eyes adjusted, he saw the shock in her wide eyes before his gaze drifted down and noticed the buttons of her dress around her bust had popped open in her sleep, showing the swell of her breasts in the black lace bra she wore.

Arousal coiled its seductive way through his bloodstream as he remembered the taste of her skin on his tongue and the heady scent of her musk. He tugged her closer to him, suddenly filled with the need to taste it again, taste her again, to hear the throaty moans of her pleasure and feel the burn of their flesh pressed together. It was a burn he'd never felt with anyone but her.

Her lips parted. Her breath hitched. Her face lowered to his…

His mouth filled with moisture, lips tingling with anticipation. He put his other hand to her neck and his arousal accelerated.

It had been so long…

Then, with her mouth hovering just inches from his, she jerked back and snatched her hand away. It fluttered to her rising chest.

"I'm sorry for waking you," she whispered, backing away some more. "I was just checking I hadn't dreamed you."

Don't miss
The Secret Behind the Greek's Return,
available August 2021 wherever
Harlequin Presents books and ebooks are sold.

Harlequin.com

HPEXP0721

Marisa opened her eyes, going from heavy sleep to full alertness
in an instant.

Nikos.

He was alive.

Or had she dreamed it?

A look at her watch told her it was four in the morning.

She threw the soft blanket off and her stockinged feet sank into
thick carpet.

Rubbing her eyes, she stared at the sofa. At some point while
she'd slept, Nikos had put a pillow under her head, laid her flat on
her side and covered her.

She hadn't dreamed him.

Heart in her throat, she found herself in the adjoining room
before she even knew she'd opened the door and walked into it.

The light in there was incredibly faint, the little illumination
coming from the lamp Nikos had left on for her in the living area.
It was enough for her to see the shape of his body nestled under the
covers, breathing deeply.

She definitely hadn't dreamed him.

Nikos was alive.

The relief was almost as overwhelming as it had been the first
time, and, eyes glued to his shadowed sleeping face, she stretched